Arizona

Lawrence W. Cheek
Revised by Edie Jarolim

Photography by Kerrick James

COMPASS AMERICAN GUIDES
An imprint of Fodor's Travel Publications

Compass American Guides: Arizona

Editor: Sarah Felchlin
Designer: Tina Malaney
Compass Editorial Director: Daniel Mangin
Editorial Production: Stacey Kulig
Photo Editor: Jolie Novak
Archival Research: Melanie Marin
Map Design: Mark Stroud, Moon Street Cartography

Cover photo by Kerrick James, North Rim of the Grand Canyon

Sixth Edition
ISBN 1–4000–1265–1
ISSN 1542–3271

Compass American Guides, 1745 Broadway, New York, NY 10019
PRINTED IN SINGAPORE

10 9 8 7 6 5 4 3 2 1

To Patty, who made my life in the desert complete.

C O N T E N T S

Literary Extracts

Topical Essays and Sidebars

FACTS ABOUT ARIZONA

GRAND CANYON STATE

Capital: Phoenix

State Flower: Flower of saguaro cactus

State Bird: Cactus wren

State Tree: Palo Verde

Entered Union: February 14, 1912 (48th state to do so)

First European Settlement: 1629

■ POPULATION: 5,472,750

TOP CITIES BY POPULATION:

Phoenix	1,365,675
Tucson	507,085
Mesa	427,550
Glendale	227,495
Scottsdale	214,090
Chandler	194,390
Tempe	159,425

Nearly 80 percent of Arizonans live in two counties: Maricopa (Phoenix area, 3,296,250) and Pima (Tucson area, 890,545). (The population totals above are official Arizona state estimates for 2002.)

■ GEOGRAPHY

Size: 113,635 square miles (sixth-largest state)

Highest point: Humphreys Peak, 12,643 feet

Lowest point: Colorado River at Mexican border, 70 feet

■ CLIMATE

Wettest Place: Crown King, Yavapai County, 28.26 inches annually

Driest Place: Yuma Valley, Yuma County, 2.7 inches annually

Lowest Temp: Hawley Lake, January 7, 1971, minus-40 degrees Fahrenheit

Highest Temp: Parker, Yuma County, July 7, 1905, 127 degrees Fahrenheit

■ INTERESTING FACTS

- Arizona's state tie, the bola, was created by Vic Cedarstaff in Wickenburg in 1949 and first called the "piggin' necklet." When that didn't hasten sales, Cedarstaff renamed it after the *boleodora,* a South American rope device used to rein in cattle.

- Arizona's name is derived from a Indian word, *Arizonac,* meaning "little spring," or "young spring."

- Yuma is the country's largest producer of iceberg lettuce.

- Phoenix's original name was Pumpkinville, after the gourds planted along the canals abandoned by the Hohokam. It was renamed by Darrell Dupa, an English settler with a classical education who believed that a town could rise on the ashes of that earlier civilization.

- Thirteen species of hummingbirds are found in southeastern Arizona, a larger variety than anywhere else in the United States.

- Though much of their state is a desert, Arizonans own more boats per capita than residents of any other U.S. state.

- Arizona has the largest continuous ponderosa pine forest in North America, stretching along the Mogollon Rim from near Flagstaff to the White Mountains.

■ FAMOUS ARIZONANS

Cochise ■ Zane Grey ■ Sandra Day O'Connor ■ Percival Lowell ■ Cesar Chavez ■ Charles Mingus ■ Barry Goldwater ■ John McCain ■ Bruce Babbitt ■ Geronimo ■ Erma Bombeck ■ Linda Ronstadt ■ Steven Spielberg

INTRODUCTION

I first stared at Arizona in 1973 through the window of a commercial jet cruising somewhere in the lower stratosphere. I was flying from Des Moines to Tucson for a job interview, and what I still remember with startling clarity, as I pressed my nose to the glass and looked at the Sonoran Desert 7 miles below, was a feeling of hollow, gnawing alienation.

I thought: I won't take the job. I cannot live in this place.

The barren earth appeared the color of sun-bleached cardboard. It was raked and torn and furrowed by corrosive wind and bogus rivers that would flow, with luck, 10 days in a year. The mountains seemed equally desolate and hostile; from this altitude I had no inkling of their heroic natural architecture or the kaleidoscopic changes of the plant and animal environments on their slopes. The entire Arizona landscape appeared to hold no life, no interest, no promise.

My reversal of heart did not come quickly or painlessly. For the first several years after I accepted a job in Tucson, I oscillated between a reporter's fascination with the place and a tentative resident's annoyance with it. I didn't like the bugs, the ferocious cutlery that poses as desert plant life, or the exhausting summer heat. I missed the sensation of four distinct seasons, and remembered in demented wistfulness the soft, cold feel of snow on my neck. I was peeved at the strange forces that seemed to be pulling on Arizona's political compass. I remember my astonishment one day in 1974 when I first saw a billboard demanding "Get US out of the UN!" on the interstate between Tucson and the Mexican border. (It took 20 years for the desert sun to bleach it into illegibility, but then the John Birch Society put up a fresh one north of Tucson.) I detested Phoenix, and over time developed a modest reputation as the Tucson journalist who wrote more vitriolic essays about that other city than anyone in modern history. This mini-specialty peaked with a call from the *Arizona Republic,* Phoenix's morning paper, wanting to interview me about the tradition of hostility between the two cities. I still hadn't come to terms with Arizona, but on certain topics I was at least an authority.

Yet during my 14-year tenure at the *Tucson Citizen,* Tucson's afternoon daily, I slowly and inevitably nurtured an affection for the state.

Arizona contains many water-sculpted "slot canyons," hundreds of feet deep and only a few feet wide.

There were some pivotal moments. One came at a time when I was beginning to indulge seriously in bicycling—this after a couple of years of mostly staying indoors, bitching about the sunshine. On Sunday mornings I began a ritual of pedaling out to Saguaro National Park, a 20-mile round-trip from my house, and riding the hilly 8-mile loop road through the pristine cactus forest in the foothills of the Rincon Mountains. On a spring day I was wobbling up a long and pain-inducing hill when a Buick wearing Minnesota plates swished past. Four uncomprehending faces stared at me through sealed windows; their expressions resembled anthropologists observing some primitive aborigine praying to a pinecone. I realized at that moment that by insulating themselves from the desert—from its physical demands and its miraculous beauty alike—they were failing to understand even the first thing about it.

Another moment of clarity came in 1975, the year after a Phoenix lawyer named Bruce Babbitt was elected state attorney general. He opened his office once a month to any Arizonans who wanted to come in and talk about their problems. I spent one of those days with him, and his connection to the land and culture of Arizona touched me. For the first time I liked an Arizona politician.

More than most other states, Arizona tests its people. Its jagged landscapes and diverse cultures dare us to comprehend them. Its climatic extremes challenge our stamina, will, and common sense. The everyday trials of living in a place that has grown more rapidly than sensibly cause many people either to leave or withdraw into their private worlds, taking no part in the public life of the place. We have a volatile population: for every three souls who arrive, two leave. Yet, it is from this instability that opportunity is given birth. In Arizona, whether you lean to art, politics, land fraud, or journalism, you can invent yourself.

This book is partly about that act of inventing, which forms so much of Arizona's history and contemporary culture. It also is a guide to the state's attractions and eccentricities—there are enough things to experience described in here, from hidden canyons to museums of archaeology, to keep any visitor occupied for years. It does not read very much like a conventional guidebook. It is highly opinionated and occasionally cranky, and when it turns to some of the misuse and abuse my sorry species has visited on this magnificent land it bounces peevishly between anger and sorrow. It does manage to say some fairly nice things about Phoenix. (Either I have matured or that city has.) It says even more about the joy of taking part in the extravagant life of the deserts, the canyons, the mountains, and the forests that make up this amazing land. In the end, this book is about falling in love.

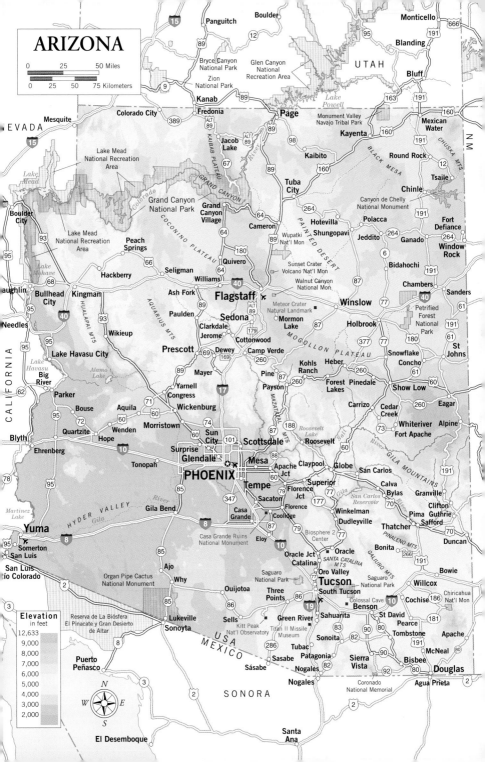

D E S E R T S

A Sonoran Desert story: A crowd of vacationing Israelis piles out of a bus at the Arizona–Sonora Desert Museum, the world-famous desert zoo and arboretum a dozen miles west of Tucson. They buy their tickets, then gather under the ramada that overlooks the museum grounds. Their eyes sweep across a forest of saguaro cacti interspersed with woody sprays of ocotillo wearing their flame-shaped orange flowers of spring. The spindly, green-barked palo verde trees are veiled in yellow blossoms, the velvet mesquite and ironwood trees are in luxuriant leaf, and even the homely prickly pear cacti are erupting with peach- and yellow-colored flowers, some the size of coffee cups.

One of the Israelis asks, not joking: "So where's the desert?"

Another story: It is May 2001, still gentle spring in the pines of northern Arizona, but already a time of soaring, searing temperatures in the Sonoran Desert. The weather does not deter the illegal immigrants from Mexico. Somewhere east of Yuma, men and teenage boys cross the border into Arizona—where they are abandoned by their "coyotes," as the smugglers who deal in human flesh and hopes are known. The coyotes promise to come back with water and instruct the men to walk for "a couple of hours" to a highway. But they never return, and the highway turns out to be more than 50 miles away.

After wandering in the rugged terrain of the Cabeza Prieta National Wildlife Refuge in 115-degree weather for days without water, five men spot members of the Border Patrol, and ask for help. An all-out search for the next five days turns up one additional survivor about 25 miles from the Mexican border—along with 14 corpses. Dr. David Haynes, who treated the survivors, says they had suffered kidney damage and looked shriveled: "Have you ever seen a mummy from ancient Egypt? That gives you an idea."

It is the worst illegal immigrant tragedy in Arizona, breaking the record of July 1980, when 13 Salvadorans died of exposure in the same brutal border region. Unfortunately, similar deaths involving Mexican or Central American refugees occur each year. Arizona became a popular crossing point for illegal immigrants in

A blooming ocotillo cactus in Organ Pipe Cactus National Monument, where the average annual rainfall measures less than 9 inches.

the 1990s, after crackdowns in California and Texas pushed more people to try to enter the country through the state's remote and dangerous areas.

"People are very, very ill-prepared to understand the distances and the dangers and threats to their lives," said the Rev. Robin Hoover, a Tucson pastor who sets up water stations for border crossers. "For many of the people who cross, they have no idea what they are encountering."

The desert gives life abundantly, the desert revokes it disinterestedly. "Here death is like breathing. Here death simply is," wrote Charles Bowden in *Blue Desert*, a provocative collection of essays. The late Edward Abbey, who was Bowden's inspiration, frequently mused about death in the desert—though never the death *of* the desert. In the closing pages of *Desert Solitaire*, his finest book, he wrote:

> Whether we live or die is a matter of absolutely no concern whatsoever to the desert. Let men in their madness blast every city on earth into black rubble and envelop the entire planet in a cloud of lethal gas—the canyons and hills, the springs and rocks will still be here, the sunlight will filter through, water will form and warmth shall be upon the land and after sufficient time, no matter how long, somewhere, living things will emerge and join and stand once again, this time perhaps to take a different and better course.

In the desert, death is exposed, not concealed in the shadows and underbrush of a forest. An hour's walk along any trail in the desert will yield reminders of the fragility of life and the inevitability of its end: a coyote's skull, tufts of coarse, gray-brown fur still clinging to its lower jaw; a century-old saguaro fried by lightning (or perhaps strangled by air pollution), yet still standing, its naked, woody ribs splaying like a fountain spray and bleaching in the relentless sun. A cottontail darts across the trail and freezes in the shadow of a creosote bush, assuming it's thus invisible to predators—which, of course, it isn't; a coyote's eyes lock easily onto that fluffy white ball of a tail. The bunny adapts by breeding prolifically during its short, timorous life. Bad news for the individual, adequate protection for the species. The desert offers no regrets.

The paradox is that this same desert also welcomes life. Because the desert's plants and animals are so keenly adapted (as were its pre-Columbian peoples), they impose themselves on the land with insane determination. A few thimblefuls of sediment wash into a fissure between two boulders, and inevitably a barrel cactus will sprout, seemingly growing out of rock at whatever crazy angle it needs to stake a claim for some sunlight. The cholla, most bloodthirsty of all cacti, will fight off a human armed with pliers and forceps, yet the cactus wren blithely and safely nests in it. The most common misconception about the deserts of the Southwest is that they are desolate, barren, lifeless places. In fact, they teem with life—weird, colorful, perfectly adapted, interdependent, fiercely obstinate life.

Few *Homo sapiens* fall in love with, or understand, this desert life at first encounter. It appears exotic but threatening. Arizona is home to 11 species of rattlesnake, 30 species each of scorpion and tarantula, the black widow and brown recluse spider, the giant (up to eight inches long) desert centipede and the Gila monster—this last species being one of only two venomous lizards on the planet.

People coming to Arizona from moist, green places frequently ask the natives: "How can you live here with all these rattlesnakes, scorpions, and Gila monsters?"

The Arizonan, oddly, responds by *exaggerating* the menace of this terrible triad.

Even among Arizonans, who ought to know better, the Gila monster is credited with an amazing list of frightful features: The monster is poisonous because it has no rectum, so a lifetime's waste is stored in its body. When it bites, it will hold on until it hears thunder. And even its breath is poisonous.

According to an 1890 account in the *Tucson Citizen*, "A woodcutter lay down to sleep . . . they found him stone dead, and near his body a Gila Monster . . . as the body of the man bore no marks of a bite or other wounds, we must suppose that his death was caused by the mere exhalation of the lizard."

All this is fanciful nonsense, as is the belief that these shy, waddling, hardly "monstrous" 12- to 16-inch lizards will spring out of hiding to attack an unwary human. In fact, virtually all *Heloderma suspectum* bites occur because someone is trying to harass or toy with the lizard.

"This is exactly what one will do if you approach it in the wild," says a curator of small animals at the Arizona–Sonora Desert Museum. "First, it will pick up its pace and lumber away with as much dignity as it can manage. If there's any kind of a dark recess nearby, it will crawl inside. If it's cornered it will finally turn around and face the threat and inhale and exhale forcefully. This is its defensive posture. At this point, anything that touches its body or comes within reach of its jaws is going to get bitten."

(following pages) Rainbow over the Mitten and Merrick Buttes in Monument Valley.

Even then—contrary to another cherished belief—the bite is not fatal. The Gila monster's venom is chemically primitive, primarily defensive, and sub-lethal. Nature, as usual, makes perfect sense here. If a coyote were bitten by a Gila monster and died from it, the lizard would still have to fret about the next coyote. But if the predator is bitten and (narrowly) survives, it learns that the Gila monster is not part of *its* food chain. Over time, this "knowledge" becomes encoded in the species' genetic memory, and coyotes and Gila monsters give each other a wide berth, to their mutual advantage.

So even though newspapers continue to cite human death tolls from Gila monsters, the reports simply are not true. The best research has unearthed only one possible fatality in Arizona history: that of a "Col. Yearger" in 1878—who, according to reports, also had been on a month-long drinking binge.

Why all the myths? Because the desert is a strange, and in many ways harsh, environment—and by exaggerating its strangeness and harshness, the people who live in it can convince themselves that they are braver for having conquered it. This mythology is harmless enough to us humans, but not to the rattlesnakes, scorpions, and Gila monsters—which people routinely kill even in the wild for no better reason than that they are venomous animals.

Arizona's lizards, snakes, arachnids, and insects probably get more press than they deserve, proportionately speaking. The state's deserts, especially the Sonoran, support a spectacular variety of wildlife. A complete catalog here is impossible, but consider a few.

"Parody pigs with oversize heads and undersize hams" was Abbey's classic description of the collared peccary, or javelina. He wasn't exaggerating their strangeness. If some political party were to adopt a pig as its symbol, a political cartoonist, wanting to portray it as scrappy and aggressive, would draw something like a javelina: small (about 2 feet high at the shoulder), with short, muscular legs, a big head tapering into a long, probe-like snout, and dagger-like canine teeth. The desert's most social mammal, javelina invariably forage in groups, usually five to 15 individuals strong.

Seldom does any writer type the word "javelina" without the modifier "bad-tempered." It has become a desert cliché. Hogwash, the javelina would reply, if it could. Every desert animal has evolved some defensive strategy; the collared peccary's is to bristle, snort and stand its ground—en masse. No predator in its right mind would risk charging into such a platoon in search of a tasty youngster.

Within the group, javelinas are extremely cordial to each other, the females even nursing each other's offspring—a rare phenomenon in nature. The sociability of these animals makes javelina-watching one of the great pleasures of visiting the desert (when undertaken, as with the Gila monster, from a discreet distance).

Coyotes, even though discouraged from dining on javelina and Gila monsters, arguably are the desert's most intelligent and adaptable creatures. They will eat virtually anything that can't eat them. Because of this, they are the one desert mammal that actually has benefited from the cities now sprawling through their habitat.

"Urban coyotes," as wildlife-management officials term them, are ubiquitous—and urbane. A regional supervisor for the Arizona Game & Fish Department has told of watching a coyote standing at the curb of a busy six-lane thoroughfare in Tucson, carefully monitoring the traffic in both directions, and finally loping across in safety. More often, the animals use their natural freeway system—the normally dry arroyos that cut through the desert cities—to get around and hunt for food. Garbage and household pets are particularly favored. A coyote can easily kill a domestic cat or a dog its own size, and should a bigger dog start running after a coyote, the dog often will find an unpleasant surprise waiting at the end of the chase: more coyotes.

Humans who encounter an abandoned litter of urban coyotes and "adopt" the cute, fuzzy pups also get an unpleasant surprise. At the age of about five months, they begin biting everything in sight, including the hands that feed them. They cannot be domesticated, and it's contrary to state law to try. Coyotes are best enjoyed from a distance. Open the windows on a warm spring night, and eventually, sometimes just before dawn, their uncannily melodic howling and yipping will float on the still desert air into the house. It sounds like a celebration, as well it may be. Nothing in the desert seems to live better than a coyote.

Most species have more to regret from the encroachment of *Homo sapiens*. No one would expect the hermit-like spadefoot toad to be among them, but because of advances in recreational technology, it may be.

Scaphiopus couchii spends nearly all its life alone in a sealed burrow 3 feet underground. No one is quite sure what it does down there except wait for the ground to shake from thunder. When the summer storms come, the spadefoot is thus reminded to burrow to the surface to feed and mate in the shallow ponds that collect on the desert floor after heavy rains. The tadpoles then begin a frantic race to adulthood before the ponds evaporate.

DESERT PHOTOGRAPHY

Arizona's landscapes and various human cultures form a photographer's dream, but there also are a few difficulties.

The light is one. Except on overcast days, the Arizona sky is brighter than in most places in North America. A modern camera's metering program doesn't realize that it's *supposed* to be bright, and often will choose a smaller aperture or higher shutter speed than it should. Then the rest of the picture will be underexposed. The solution is to point the camera a bit downward, at what appears to be an average brightness level in the scene, and use that meter reading. Also, remember that in the deserts, broad daylight is flat light. It bleaches color and nuance out of your pictures. The best landscape photos are shot in the early morning, late evening, or when a storm is threatening.

Another problem is overexposure—not of your film, but of the state itself. Arizona has been photographed so extensively (and so expertly) that it is quite a challenge to come up with a fresh image of a familiar attraction such as Monument Valley. Keep alert for unusual details—say, a rattlesnake on a boulder that could be used for a foreground—and pray for unsettled weather.

Finally, Arizona's natural environment is not particularly gentle with camera equipment. Camera repair shops warn customers not to leave cameras in a car parked in the sun on a hot day; the heat can melt lubricants and allow them to ooze onto components where they don't belong. The heat will not affect unexposed film, but do have it processed promptly after shooting.

John Alcock, a zoologist at Arizona State University and the author of several gracefully written books about life in the Sonoran Desert, described an experiment in which tape recordings of loud motorcycles were played above spadefoots buried in a terrarium. The toads mistook the din for thunder, and burrowed to the surface—a waste of energy that could prove fatal in their marginal existence in the desert. Thus, wrote an angered Alcock, off-roaders enjoying their "trivial human inventions" may endanger one of the least-seen and most elegantly adapted of all the desert's animals.

A saguaro skeleton is indicative of the harsh Lost Dutchman State Park environment.

The desert's plants are no less strange, no less strategically endowed to cope with their environment, and in some sad cases, no less threatened by the humans around them.

Of the four distinct deserts that extend into Arizona, the Sonoran (again) features the most extravagant community of plants. This is a function of climate. The Sonoran is fairly wet, for a desert, with annual rainfall averaging 7.5 inches in Greater Phoenix, 12 inches in Tucson, and 8.82 inches at Organ Pipe National Monument. Fragile plants also are not in much danger of a hard freeze—at least not below elevations of 3,000 feet. Tucson, at 2,630 feet, records an average of 17 freezing lows per year, but it very rarely falls below 25 degrees, and never for more than a few hours. If it did, the city's signature plant, the giant saguaro, would not exist.

The saguaro inhabits a more-or-less horseshoe-shaped chunk of southern Arizona that includes Tucson, Phoenix, and the 4,335-square-mile Tohono O'odham Reservation. The cacti then march south into the Mexican states of Sonora and Baja California. But even though the plant's range is tightly restricted by climate, it has come to serve as a symbol of all Arizona and even the entire frontier West. So essential is its emblematic value that in *Broken Arrow,* the classic 1951 James Stewart western, the film crew scattered plaster-of-Paris saguaro among the red rocks of Sedona. A saguaro would no sooner grow in cool Sedona than in San Francisco.

An average human lifetime, about 75 years, expires before it occurs to a saguaro to perform the act that makes it so impressive to humans, which is to grow its first arm or two. Thus outfitted, the still-adolescent cactus takes on an anthropomorphic character. Some individuals seem to raise their arms in surrender, others in supplication, a few in bewilderment. One monster in the foothills of the Santa Catalina Mountains currently sports 21 arms curling in a swirl around its trunk, like a mutant green Baryshnikov in a pirouette frozen for eternity. The sentient human, wandering about a forest of these 30-foot creatures, feels like an explorer in the midst of a race of strangely still and silent alien beings. This eerie sensation is multiplied 10-fold in the moonlight.

This most prominent living object in the Sonoran Desert is a good citizen, serving the biological community in several remarkable ways. Gila woodpeckers chisel apartments in mature saguaro trunks and nest in them, staying both cool and safe from climbing predators. After the woodpecker moves on, any of several other species will move in—screech and elf owls, purple martins, Wied's crested flycatchers. The saguaro's flower, which grows only at its top on the ends of its arms, provides bats with an energy-rich nectar; the bats reciprocate by pollinating

FEROCIOUS FLORA

Tree, bush, plant and grass—great and small alike—each has its sting for the intruder. You can hardly stoop to pick a desert flower or pull a bunch of small grass without being aware of a prickle on your hand. Nature seems to have provided a whole arsenal of defensive weapons for these poor starved plants of the desert. Not any of the lovely growths of the earth, like the lilies and the daffodils, are so well defended. And she has given them not only armor but a spirit of tenacity and stubbornness wherewith to carry on the struggle. Cut out the purslain and the iron weed from the garden walk, and it springs up again and again, contending for life. Put heat, drought, and animal attack against the desert shrubs and they fight back like the higher forms of organic life. How typical they are of everything in and about the desert. There is but one word to describe it and that word—fierce—I shall have worn threadbare before I have finished these chapters.

—John C. Van Dyke, *The Desert,* 1901

The cereus is just one of the many blooms to be seen at the Desert Botanical Garden.

other saguaro. Spanish and Mexican settlers, Tohono O'odham and Pima Indians, and probably their prehistoric ancestors as well, harvested the fruit to make jelly and wine, and employed ribs from dead saguaros as roofing material.

Yet people also abuse the saguaro. As early as 1854, a pioneer explorer, J. R. Bartlett, found arrows sticking into saguaros in the Yuman Indian lands of far west Arizona. In the early 1980s, a Phoenix man fired a shotgun into a saguaro until it toppled, killing him. Sometimes even *good* intentions doom the plants. Mature saguaros, which landscape architects love to use in their designs, usually die when transplanted. The Arizona–Sonora Desert Museum has seen a 95 percent mortality rate among transplanted saguaros 12 or more feet high, and has quit moving them. Developers haven't, because they don't often connect the transplant with the cactus's demise: A mature saguaro, the perfect symbol of both the desert's perseverance and fragility, takes three to five years to die.

Heat and light also shape the character of Arizona's deserts. Most people naturally think of them as excessive, as a dismaying drawback to year-round residence in at least half of Arizona. A few—the author Edward Abbey was prime among them—welcome the heat because it discourages further arrivals.

Summer comes early to the low desert and holds it in relentless lock for five long months. On average, Greater Phoenix endures 91 days of 100-plus readings per year. Buckeye, Gila Bend, and Casa Grande all have been brutalized by 100-degree marks in March. The first 100 usually strikes Phoenix by mid-April; Tucson by early May. (In Tucson, the first 100-degree day of the year is hailed as the day "the ice breaks on the Santa Cruz." This is doubly dry humor; the Santa Cruz is a dry riverbed.) By June, the desert is under siege. June 26, 1990, was especially memorable, a torrid day that toppled more weather records than any other date in modern history. A sampler:

CITY	ELEVATION (in feet)	TEMP: HIGH (F)	TEMP: LOW (F)
Bisbee	5,490	106°	68°
Phoenix	1,092	122°	91°
Safford	2,920	112°	68°
Sedona	4,240	110°	76°
Tucson	2,630	117°	80°
Yuma	141	122°	85°

Note the predawn "low" of 91 for Phoenix. This was a ghastly demonstration of what meteorologists have begun to call the "heat island" effect: the metropolis's immense size is making its summer climate worse. Heat absorbed by asphalt and concrete and roof tiles during the day is radiated at night and trapped by atmospheric inversions. Lows in the 90s are no longer unusual in Phoenix.

Chambers of commerce struggle to put the best possible spin on these numbers. "But it's a *dry* heat!" is their mantra. True, but it's also a relentless heat. A T-shirt popular around Phoenix depicts a couple of bleached skeletons lounging in patio chairs, taking in the sun. One remarks, cheerfully, to the other: "But it's a *dry* heat."

According to the U.S. Geological Survey, Arizona has more "hell" place names than any other state—a total of 55. (Utah places second with 46.) Hell Hole Valley, Hellgate Mountain, Hell's Neck Ridge, no fewer than four Hell Canyons—it is a creative list, but no one who has endured a few desert summers would call it fanciful.

Outside on a 115-degree midsummer day, it is difficult to be conscious of any sensation but the heat. Its pressure pushes on every square inch of the body. Even in shade, the face reddens, the torso moistens, the will to do anything productive—except lurch toward the nearest air-conditioned building—vanishes. Tempers seem shorter; police answer more domestic-disturbance calls in the summer. It isn't unlike Alaskan cabin fever; the seasons are simply reversed.

With the heat comes a quality of light unique in North America. Observed Reyner Banham in *Scenes in America Deserta,* "The full sun of the desert—the Mojave in particular—gives a spectral, hurtful light that is a close brother to heat, and strikes equally hard." John C. Van Dyke, a much earlier essayist, felt that with the pain came an incomparable reward: "In any land what is there more glorious than sunlight! Even here in the desert, where it falls fierce and hot as a rain of meteors, it is the one supreme beauty to which all things pay allegiance." Both interpretations are most true in June, when none of Arizona's deserts can hope for rain, or clouds, or even enough humidity to soften the light. At midday, the sky is not quite blue; it appears bleached, almost white. Mountain ranges on the horizon lose both dimension and color; they appear as flat, washed-out cardboard cutouts propped against the sky. Even buildings become painful to look at.

But in other months the desert's light is miraculous. In July, August, and early September come the summer storms, romantically if inaccurately termed "monsoons" in Phoenix and Tucson. Even in the mornings, the humidity is higher, diffusing the sun's glaring fury (while rendering evaporative coolers worthless). In the afternoons, platoons of gray, overweight cumulus clouds rumble in from the south. Inside an hour, the sky turns to charcoal and dumps torrents on the desiccated land. Then after maybe 15 minutes, the storm begins to break up and slivers of late-afternoon sunlight scythe through the clouds, selectively highlighting a few acres of mountain, desert, or city with golden fire.

In the winter—what passes for winter in the desert—the light is softer still but no less dramatic. Early morning sun will backlight a forest of saguaros in such a way that the light squeezes through their spines, glinting and diffusing on its way, so that each cactus seems to wear a glowing yellow halo. Afternoon light is penetrating and incisive, and if the air is particularly still and dry, one can see astounding details in the landscape at preposterous distances. I have stood on a peak near Hannagan Meadow at the eastern edge of the state and traced ridgelines in the Santa Catalina Mountains near Tucson, a straight-line distance of 130 miles—with naked eye.

It is the evening light that is the most spectacular, even startling. Arizona's winter sunsets are clichéd ad nauseam in curio and commerce—sweatshirts, bus benches, even automatic teller machines are decked out in painted sunsets—but the real thing, the nightly ballet of light in the western sky, is so unpredictable and varied that nobody grows jaded.

We do sometimes lose perspective, though. Former Gov. Bruce Babbitt has told a story about watching a group of tourists one evening as a world-class sunset unfolded. Someone snapped a Polaroid, and all turned their backs on the real sunset to watch the photo of it develop. The anecdote may illustrate a peculiar truth about Arizona's light and landscapes: sometimes the reality is so overwhelming that image is easier to comprehend.

Four deserts—the Great Basin, the Mojave, the Sonoran, and the Chihuahuan—distinctly different in climate, biology, and scenery, extend into Arizona. Combined, the deserts make up something between one-half and two-thirds (scientists quibble about the definition of a "desert") of the state's 113,635 square miles.

Agatized sections of tree trunks are scattered throughout Petrified Forest National Park; the best specimens of petrified wood can be found in the park's southern section.

■ PAINTED DESERT *map page 31*

The Colorado Plateau, which sprawls north and east of the city of Flagstaff, includes portions of the high Great Basin Desert—its Arizona appendage more commonly called the Painted Desert. It is strange, haunting country, its geology as bizarre as the Sonoran Desert's more abundant biology. The land is scored by jagged canyons and punctuated by heroic sandstone skylines of cliffs, mesas, buttes, and spires up to 1,000 feet high. The visitor experiences a palpable, sometimes uncomfortable sensation of insignificance out here; the scale seems too gigantic to comprehend.

Most people assume that water, over a few hundred million years, carved spectacles such as Canyon de Chelly, while wind-whipped sand abraded the buttes of Monument Valley. The truth is a little more disquieting, particularly if one is standing on the rim of a canyon or at the base of a butte. Rivers started the erosion process, and runoff abetted it, but natural weaknesses in the rock formations also allowed pieces to crumble and fall away. Monument Valley, which used to be a solid plateau of sandstone roughly as high as the tops of the "monuments" today, literally is crumbling away in huge splinters and sheets. The reassuring news is that geologic time, like the monuments themselves, is so vast as to be almost irrelevant to the puny humans standing around, gaping in awe.

For the most part, the Painted Desert curves along the lower reaches of the Navajo Reservation. Its rounded, soft-looking formations are visible from U.S. 89 as you drive south from Lake Powell; and looking north from I-40 as you drive east from Holbrook. Its eroding layers of clay, siltstone, and sandstone are represented in an array of subtle colors, from off-white to russet to several shades of gray.

■ MONUMENT VALLEY NAVAJO TRIBAL PARK

Straddling the Arizona-Utah border near the town of Kayenta, Monument Valley is a dramatic landscape of towering sandstone monoliths and buttes. Over time, each formation has been carved by wind and rain into its own unique shape. Though the dozens of Westerns filmed here since the 1930s give the impression that such formations are ubiquitous throughout the West, that is hardly the case. Monument Valley is a quirk of nature that looks best in the golden light of early morning or late afternoon.

Visitors usually take the 17-mile unpaved loop drive through the park, but some of the valley's most fascinating and eerie sandstone totems lie well away from the

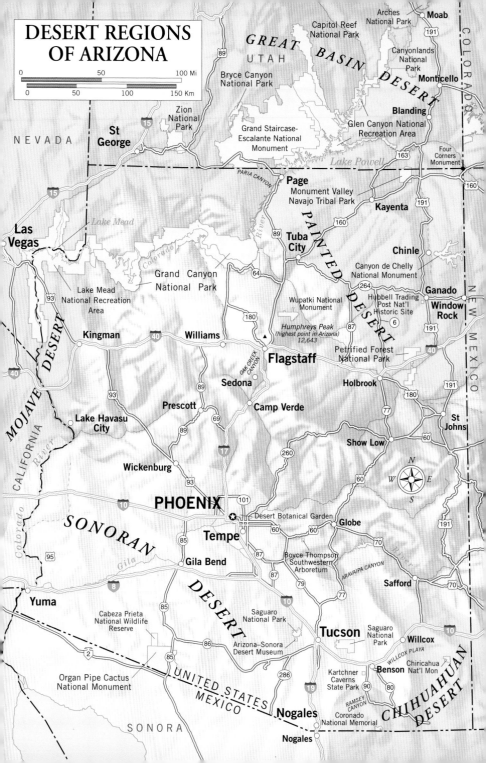

road. The Navajos strictly forbid hiking, rock climbing, and off-road driving, though guided tours with more intimate photo opportunities may be booked at the visitors center. To get a better look, visit Valley of the Gods, a similar cluster of enormous spires and buttes only 30 miles to the north, which can be visited without restrictions. Consult a Utah map for directions. *To reach Monument Valley from Kayenta, take U.S. 163 north for 27 miles and turn right at the junction. Follow signs for 5 miles to the visitors center; 435-727-5870.*

■ PETRIFIED FOREST NATIONAL PARK

Conveniently, the best stopping place to view the Painted Desert is Petrified Forest National Park, a dry, barren landscape strewn with something rare in nature: prehistoric petrified logs. A spectacular 27-mile drive leads through a garden of mineralized logs and petroglyphs left by the ancestral Puebloan people.

A detail of precious petrified wood.

Eight overlooks at the park's northern end offer the best Painted Desert vistas, whereas the most impressive clusters of petrified wood lie in the park's southern section. Backcountry hiking is permitted here, but anyone leaving the road should pack a plentiful supply of water, even in winter. *Painted Desert Visitor Center: take I-40 to Exit 311, 30 miles east of Holbrook. South entrance and Rainbow Forest Museum: take U.S. 180, 19 miles southeast from Holbrook; 928-524-6228.*

■ MOJAVE DESERT *map page 31*

The Mojave, at Arizona's northwestern edge, is the state's driest desert. Only 4.52 inches of rain fall in an average year at Lake Havasu (a man-made lake, of course, traversed by an imported London Bridge; see page 241). The minimal precipitation does not nourish much plant life, but what manages to thrive is fiercely tenacious. The creosote bush, a spindly, scruffy shrub, is believed to live as long as 11,000 years, making it the oldest living thing on earth. Joshua trees, some of which live 500 years, are as distinctive a signature plant to the Mojave as the saguaro to the Sonoran. A member of the yucca genus, they grow as high as 30 feet, sending out a tangle of arms that terminate in fists spiked with green daggers.

From its jagged peaks to its coarse valleys, the Mojave appears to be the harshest of Arizona's deserts. Sculpted daily by the wind and baked hard by the sun, the land's architecture seems to hold itself up as a challenge to human survival. The Mojave is most often seen by travelers on U.S. 93 between Wickenburg and Las Vegas. Along the way are a Joshua tree forest, miles of creosote bushes, and mountains that look as friendly as saw blades.

■ SONORAN DESERT *map page 31*

The Sonoran is the desert of superlatives. It is the most colorful, most varied, most lovely, most crowded, most dangerous, and most threatened of its ecological brethren. More species of birds, about 300, make their homes in the Sonoran Desert than in any other arid region on the continent. More rain falls in the Sonoran Desert than any other in North America; there literally are forests—called *bosques*—of mesquite in this desert. This is a noisy place, and not just because of the intrusions of humans and our mechanized contraptions. Cactus wrens screech at each other in an appalling tenor rasp, cicadas lay down an omnidirectional drone, coyotes yelp, crickets tick, the ubiquitous Western whiptail lizards swish from bush to bush, rattlers helpfully advise stray humans to buzz off. Except in the midday summer sun, when most of these creatures are sensibly taking a snooze, it is hard to feel alone in the Sonoran Desert. And it is becoming harder all the time. In large part because of its beauty and lushness, more Arizonans live in the Sonoran Desert than in any other geographic region of the state: more than three-fourths of the total 5.1 million people. This crush of bodies, with the pressures they impose on the desert's modest resources, is the state's most ominous problem.

The Sonoran is celebrated, studied, and preserved in several parks and museums in central and southern Arizona. In summer, early-morning visits are recommended.

■ DESERT BOTANICAL GARDEN, PHOENIX
This lovely botanical garden features some 20,000 desert plants from the Sonoran and other deserts. Its exhibits explain historic uses of plants in the Sonoran Desert, and a demonstration garden struggles (without apparent success) to convince Phoenicians that water-saving desert landscaping is an idea whose time is here. *1201 North Galvin Parkway; 480-941-1225.*

■ ARIZONA–SONORA DESERT MUSEUM, TUCSON
This museum regularly appears on lists of the world's 10 best zoos. Its world is the animals, plants, and natural history of the Sonoran Desert, but its exhibits also encompass this desert's forested mountains, rivers, and seacoast on the Gulf of California. The full range of Sonoran Desert animals is on display here, from the 0.1-ounce calliope hummingbird to the black bear. Allow three hours for a complete visit. *Take Speedway Boulevard west across Gates Pass to Kinney Road. 2021 North Kinney, Tucson Mountain Park; 520-883-2702.*

■ SAGUARO NATIONAL PARK, TUCSON
The desert's saguaro forests can be explored at close range at Saguaro National Park, which is split into two districts: one is 15 miles west of Tucson, and the other lies on the city's eastern edge in the foothills of the Rincon Mountains. The more interesting western district supports a vastly denser population of saguaros as well as a site where you can view ancient rock art. The eastern district has a 8-mile paved loop road that is popular with runners and cyclists, who also take mountain bikes onto some of this sector's more rugged trails. *Western District: 2700 North Kinney Road; 520-733-5158. Eastern District: Old Spanish Trail; 520-733-5153.*

The Horrible "Escorpion"

Strangest of all was the uncouth, horrible "escorpion," or "Gila monster," which here found its favorite habitat and attained its greatest dimensions. We used to have them not less than 3 feet long, black, venomous, and deadly, if half the stories told were true. The Mexicans time and time again asserted that the escorpion would kill chickens, and that it would eject a poisonous venom upon them, but, in my own experience, I have to say that the old hen which we tied in front of one for a whole day was not molested, and that no harm of any sort came to her beyond being scared out of a year's growth. Scientists were wont to ridicule the idea of the Gila monster being venomous, upon what ground I do not now remember, beyond the fact that it was a lizard, and all lizards were harmless. But I believe it is now well established that the monster is not to be handled with impunity.

—John G. Bourke, *On the Border with Crook,* 1892

The Gila monster is at home in Organ Pipe Cactus National Monument.

■ BOYCE THOMPSON SOUTHWESTERN ARBORETUM,
SOUTHEASTERN ARIZONA

This arboretum at the foot of Picketpost Mountain superficially resembles the Arizona–Sonora Desert Museum, but there is an important difference: grown alongside this 1,000-acre facility's native Sonoran plants are cacti from all around the world. Sixteen inches of rain annually turn this into one of the most extravagantly lush areas of the Sonoran Desert, with an herb garden, a eucalyptus forest, a rose garden, and demonstration garden for homeowners. *37615 East U.S. 60 (55 miles east of Phoenix, 3 miles west of Superior); 520-689-2811.*

■ ORGAN PIPE CACTUS NATIONAL MONUMENT,
SOUTHWESTERN ARIZONA

Though common in northern Mexico, the organ pipe cactus occurs naturally in the United States only on this 516-square-mile (330,689-acre) preserve on the Mexican border. The organ pipe cactus, a cousin of the saguaro cactus, is a spectacle, sprouting a cluster of huge vertical arms (up to 12 feet) that resemble—vaguely, at least—the pipes of an organ. Quitobaquito Spring, a historic natural watering hole, attracts more than 260 species of birds. Scenic trails and drives begin a short distance from the visitors center. *Headquarters: Route 1, just off Route 85, 22 miles south of Why; 520-387-6849.*

■ CABEZA PRIETA NATIONAL WILDLIFE RESERVE,
SOUTHWESTERN ARIZONA

Created in 1939 to protect desert bighorn sheep, Cabeza Prieta's 860,010 desolate acres are perfect for getting intimate with the Sonoran Desert—on *its* terms. There are no tourist facilities and no paved roads, and water is scarce. Besides the usual menu of desert dangers—rattlesnakes, heat exhaustion, and dehydration—the reserve is bordered by a military bombing range, and stumbling, literally, upon live ordinance is an additional hazard. Cantankerous "Cactus" Edward Abbey didn't choose to be buried out here for nothing. The valleys here were created by flows of lava from some of the seven mountain ranges that border the reserve, which is administered by the U.S Fish and Wildlife Service. *Visitors center, 611 North Second Avenue (10 miles east of the preserve), Ajo; 520-387-6483.*

The annual growth of an organ pipe cactus is marked by the constrictions in its stem segments.

■ CHIHUAHUAN DESERT *map page 31*

The Chihuahuan is Arizona's overlooked desert. Many travelers head east out of Tucson on I-10, not even noticing the gradual change that marks the transition from the Sonoran into the Chihuahuan Desert, which will remain their host across the lower edge of New Mexico and on into the high, barren badlands of West Texas. Most of the Chihuahuan Desert lies in the Mexican state of Chihuahua; only its northwestern sliver edges into Arizona.

In the 50 miles east of Tucson, the Interstate traveler climbs some 1,500 feet, probably without realizing it. The saguaro give way to yucca, the shrub cover to rolling hills of straw-colored grass. This edge of the Chihuahuan Desert receives from 8 to 10 inches of rain a year, which is less than Tucson, but the higher, cooler elevation makes the rain more efficient—hence the grass.

Two remarkable features mark the edge of the Chihuahuan Desert: **Texas Canyon,** a mountain range literally made of boulders, and the **Willcox Playa,** visible from I-10 just southwest of Willcox. The playa looks like a vast lake shimmering in the distance, but it is a permanent mirage, a cruel optical joke surrealistically imposed on a 50-square-mile basin that *used* to be a lake. Now it is one of the strangest places in Arizona, a parched, table-flat wasteland where absolutely nothing grows from one horizon to another, as far as the eye can see.

A writer for the *Arizona Daily Star* once described it like this: "To walk on the playa is to travel through another dimension. At times, its vast emptiness seems like a gateway to the Twilight Zone." Yet even this most desolate region of the desert supports life. Eggs of three species of miniature shrimp lie dormant below the lake bed for as long as 30 years; after an extravagant summer rain, when water puddles into a soupy mud on the playa, the crustaceans hatch. If the water holds out they may last two weeks, which is just long enough to mate, deposit more eggs and then die—having miraculously assured, a shrimp's eon later, the eventual appearance of their offspring.

■ CHIRICAHUA NATIONAL MONUMENT

Life-forms indigenous to the Chihuahuan Desert are easier to find here. Though best known for its acres of magnificent column-shaped rock formations, it also is home to many plants and animals uncommon north of the Mexican border. Birders flock to the park to spot rare Mexican chickadees, sulfur-bellied flycatchers, and coppery tailed trogons.

Also from south of the border are mammals such as the Apache fox squirrel, and trees such as the Chihuahua pine and the Apache pine. Come by 8:30 A.M. to catch the shuttle for hikers and get a jump on the 20 miles of trails. *Take Route 186, 37 miles southwest of Willcox (127 miles east of Tucson via I-10); 520-824-3560.*

■ KARTCHNER CAVERNS STATE PARK

One of the Chihuahuan Desert's most fascinating attractions is underground—and for many years, that was metaphorically as well as literally true. Cavers Randy Tufts and Gary Tenen discovered Arizona's largest known cave near Benson in 1974, but didn't tell anyone for more than a decade, fearing that its delicate ecosystem would be ruined if people started tramping through it. In 1988, the Kartchner family, who owned the land where the cave was found, sold it to the State Parks Board, which worked hard to find ways to protect it. A Parks Board spokesman explains why it took so many years to get the caverns ready for tourism: "It's a live cave, and we need to make sure we know exactly what keeps it alive." In late 1999, the caverns were finally opened to the public.

Kartchner Caverns remains a work in progress. Many areas continue to be off limits, pending ongoing ecological studies on visitor impact. But it's possible that the town of Benson, which has gleaned great economic benefit from this new local attraction, might end up killing the goose that laid the golden egg: In 2002, the Benson Planning and Zoning Committee approved a developer's proposal to build a luxury spa on a 180-acre parcel of land on a slope northwest of Kartchner Caverns State Park.

The Arizona State Parks staff asked the Benson committee members for time to study the proposed development and its environmental impact on the cave, but were turned down. According to the Parks Department Web site, "This luxury resort may be built on top of a convoluted matrix of limestone (karst) known as the Kartchner Block. This subterranean block may be connected to the cave through the thousands of faults that are created when limestone is formed." Perhaps Tufts and Tenen were right in trying to keep the cave secret. Despite the best efforts of the well-intended, public exposure may turn out to prove Kartchner Caverns' downfall after all. *Eight miles south of Benson on Route 90; 520-586-4112.*

(following pages) Montezuma Canyon in the Coronado National Memorial overlooks classic Chihuahuan Desert scenery.

M O U N T A I N S

It is the summer of 1927, a decade before even the most rudimentary evaporative air-conditioning will become common in Tucson. Editors of the *Arizona Daily Star* and the rival *Tucson Daily Citizen* simmer in their downtown offices, heckling each other and churning out dueling editorials. The issue: how to move Tucson to the cool top of 9,157-foot Mount Lemmon for the five long months of summer.

The forward-looking *Star* predicts that by the 1940s, highways and automobiles will be obsolete. It proposes creating a municipal "air line" and shaving the mountaintop for an airstrip.

> An air line would bring the cooling breezes and tall pines to within 30 minutes of Congress Street. Summer vacationers could breakfast on top of the range, fly to Tucson for a shopping trip, and be back in the mountains in time for lunch. The poor, tired businessman could live at home beneath the pines and be at his office or store for the full eight- or ten-hour shift.

The *Citizen* ridicules the *Star's* aeronautical reverie and presses for a highway up the mountain. The *Citizen* even recruits the local Roman Catholic bishop for its cause, publishing a pro-highway interview with him under the ominous headline:

TUCSON DOOMED TO BE 8 MONTH TOWN UNLESS MOUNTAIN ROAD BUILT

But cost-conscious voters balk, rebuffing $500,000 bond issues in 1928 and again in 1930. The *Citizen's* publisher, Gen. Frank H. Hitchcock, won't give up. In 1933 he hears that the director of the Federal Bureau of Prisons wants to experiment with employing prisoners on highway construction to help "rehabilitate" them. A flurry of meetings ensues, and work begins on the highway within three months.

The Mount Lemmon Highway turns out to be a more daunting project than anyone imagines. By the time the 25-mile road punches into the cool ponderosa pine country, it has taken 18 years, 8,003 federal prisoners, and—even with all that free labor—nearly $1 million. But the result is a road that, mile for mile, is arguably Arizona's most scenic—and one that remains controversial even today.

The trail from Lockett Meadow is a favorite place to view aspens in the San Francisco Peaks.

■ An Archipelago of Rocks

The popular image of Arizona is that of a parched, wrinkled landscape of hostile desert plants set off by a distant backdrop of cardboard-cutout mountains propped against the sky. The nature of those mountains, in this image, remains something elusive and mysterious. This is as it always has been. In the theology of many of Arizona's Native Americans, the spirits dwell in the mountains.

In less mystical terms, the mountains are the reason for Arizona's great environmental diversity. Biologists call them "sky islands," a fitting metaphor. The environment at the summit of a 10,000-foot Arizona mountain is as radically different from that of the desert floor 8,000 feet below as that of Hawaii from the water around it. Early boosters of the Mount Lemmon Highway liked to tout it as being the equivalent of driving from Mexico to Canada in an hour.

On an average Arizona mountain, the temperature falls three to four degrees Fahrenheit and precipitation increases about 4 to 5 inches for every 1,000-foot gain in elevation. These profound variations create dramatically evolving laminations of biotic communities on the mountains. As many as six of these distinct life zones occupy the sky islands of southern and central Arizona. Biologists sometimes disagree on the names and boundaries of these zones, but here is an attempt to sort them out:

Desert shrub, from 2,000 to 3,500 feet. This is essentially an extension of the plant and animal communities of the desert floor rising into the mountain foothills. Generous rainfall and runoff from higher elevations, however, produce more lush growth than in the flat basins. Forests of saguaro, mesquite, and palo verde dominate, and in years of above-average winter precipitation, these elevations wear spring carpets of wild poppies, mustard flowers, and other colorful blooms.

Chaparral, from 3,500 to 6,000 feet. This is a temperate zone dominated by tall grasses, tough-leafed evergreen shrubs and one remarkably unfriendly succulent: the descriptively named shindagger agave. The manzanita is its signature plant, a shrublike tree that grows only 5 or 6 feet high and sports a distinctive and lovely glossy, cherry-red bark.

Oak woodland, from 4,500 to 6,000 feet. The dominant species is Emory oak, interspersed with some Arizona oak and Mexican oak—and still the occasional yucca and prickly pear cactus. Not yet dense enough to be considered forest, the trees are fairly sparse except in riparian habitats.

Piñon-juniper woodland, from 5,000 to 7,000 feet. Substantial snow falls at these elevations, even in the southernmost ranges. The piñon, or Mexican pine, is

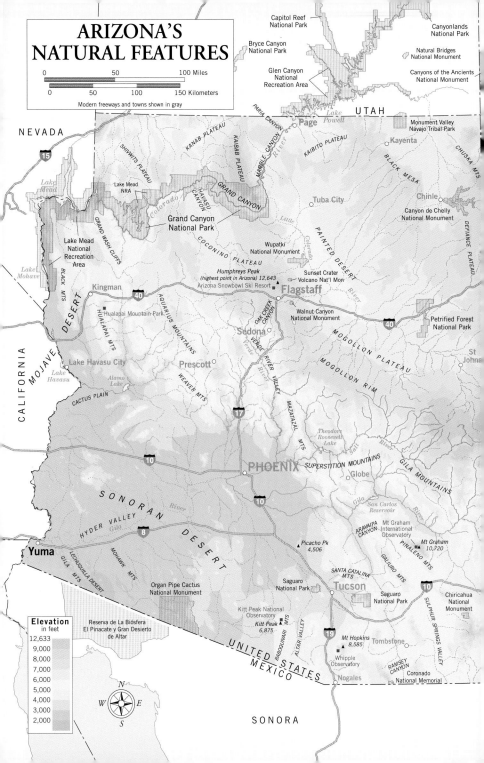

ARIZONA'S NATURAL FEATURES

0   50   100 Miles

0   50   100   150 Kilometers

Modern freeways and towns shown in gray

NEVADA

UTAH

CALIFORNIA

Capitol Reef National Park

Bryce Canyon National Park

Glen Canyon National Recreation Area

Canyonlands National Park

Natural Bridges National Monument

Canyons of the Ancients National Monument

Lake Powell

Page

Monument Valley Navajo Tribal Park

Kayenta

PARIA CANYON

KANAB PLATEAU

SHIVWITS PLATEAU

KAIBAB PLATEAU

MARBLE CANYON

KAIBITO PLATEAU

BLACK MESA

CHUSKA MTS

Lake Mead

Lake Mead NRA

GRAND CANYON

HAVASU CANYON

Tuba City

Chinle

Canyon de Chelly National Monument

DEFIANCE PLATEAU

Grand Canyon National Park

Colorado

Little Colorado

PAINTED DESERT

GRAND WASH CLIFFS

Lake Mead National Recreation Area

COCONINO PLATEAU

Wupatki National Monument

Lake Mohave

Humphreys Peak (highest point in Arizona) 12,643 Arizona Snowbowl Ski Resort

Sunset Crater Volcano Nat'l Mon

St Johns

BLACK MTS

Kingman

Flagstaff

Walnut Canyon National Monument

Petrified Forest National Park

MOJAVE DESERT

HUALAPAI MTS

Hualapai Mountain Park

AQUARIUS MOUNTAINS

OAK CREEK CANYON

Sedona

MOGOLLON PLATEAU

MOGOLLON RIM

Lake Havasu City

Lake Havasu

Alamo Lake

Prescott

VERDE RIVER VALLEY

Verde River

WEAVER MTS

CACTUS PLAIN

MAZATZAL MTS

Theodore Roosevelt Lake

Salt River

GILA MOUNTAINS

PHOENIX

SUPERSTITION MOUNTAINS

Globe

San Carlos Reservoir

Gila

S O N O R A N   D E S E R T

River

Gila

ARAVAIPA CANYON

Mt Graham International Observatory

Mt Graham 10,720

HYDER VALLEY

GILA RIVER

PINALENO MTS

Yuma

LECHUGUILLA DESERT

MOHAWK MTS

Picacho Pk 4,506

SANTA CATALINA MTS

GALIURO MTS

Organ Pipe Cactus National Monument

Saguaro National Park

Tucson

Saguaro National Park

Chiricahua National Monument

Elevation in feet

| 12,633 |
| 9,000 |
| 8,000 |
| 7,000 |
| 6,000 |
| 5,000 |
| 4,000 |
| 3,000 |
| 2,000 |

Reserva de La Biósfera El Pinacate y Gran Desierto de Altar

Kitt Peak National Observatory

Kitt Peak 6,875

BABOQUIVARI MTS

ALTAR VALLEY

Mt Hopkins 8,585

Whipple Observatory

Tombstone

SULPHUR SPRINGS VALLEY

RAMSEY CANYON

Coronado National Memorial

U N I T E D   S T A T E S

M E X I C O

Nogales

N W E S

S O N O R A

a tree too diminutive and gnarled to be of interest to the timber industry, but its abundant nuts provide food for large communities of birds. The Clark's nutcracker, a jay that has evolved a special nut pouch under its tongue, has been found flying with as many as 95 piñon nuts at a time.

Ponderosa pine forest, from 7,000 to 9,000 feet. These are authentic forests dominated by the gigantic ponderosa. Mature trees probe up to 125 feet into the sky, fighting for sunlight, and the winners live 200 to 400 years. The world's largest stand of ponderosas is in northern Arizona, girdling the San Francisco Mountains, but the forests are profuse enough in the desert sky islands to the south that logging operations have been carried out since the 1880s.

Canadian life zone, from 7,500 to 10,000 feet. The common name of this zone is not at all misleading; its dark, mossy forests of Douglas fir, white fir, and quaking aspen—and its abundant black bears—closely mimic the biology of Canada's forests 2,000 miles to the north.

The higher one ascends through these life zones, the more compelling the "island" analogy becomes. A squirrel happily adapted to crunching nuts at 9,000 feet will spend its entire life on that one mountain, as will its extended family. Even if something were to happen on that mountain that threatened its survival (such as a forest fire), it would have no options; it could not survive a 50-mile trek through open desert to another "island."

This is true of most other mountain-dwelling creatures, although bears, provoked by the intervention of *Homo sapiens,* have tried it. Periodically the Arizona Game & Fish Department will try moving a "problem bear" from one mountain to another; in some cases the extradited bear, guided by an amazing homing instinct, may strike out for his old home, crossing deserts, highways, and suburban backyards en route.

For many plants and animals, confinement to one mountain island means species inbreeding. As long as the pool of available mates is large, this by no means spells trouble—though over time, it may well become a unique subspecies, different in important characteristics from its relatives on the next mountain over. If the gene pool is too small, however, the animal will edge toward extinction: the Mexican gray wolf and the grizzly bear both disappeared from Arizona's mountains in the 20th century (although a controversial reintroduction of the gray wolf got under way in eastern Arizona in early 1997). As more and more human beings cluster around and settle in the Arizona mountains, the problem of saving these island environments for their original inhabitants is producing a swarm of controversies.

A Bird in Hand

It's a clear, sunny afternoon in the San Pedro National Conservation Area east of Sierra Vista, weepy cottonwoods barely stirring, just a few wispy clouds in the sky. Gazing treeward and cloudward is generally a major activity at this popular bird-watching spot, but the group gathered around a shaded picnic table is staring raptly downward. "That's a big guy," declares Sheri Williamson, the genial cofounder of the Southeastern Arizona Bird Observatory (SABO). She is sitting next to a miniature set of scales. "We don't see many male Rufouses his size."

"Big," of course, is a relative term: The bird's weight, carefully recorded by volunteer Rachael Brantley, along with characteristics such as beak length and coloration of throat and tailfeathers, is 4.5 grams. A creature about the size of a thumb is being held aloft in a sling no longer than a Band-Aid.

But in the hummingbird world, this fella's a pig.

My friend Bernadette and I are outside the preserve's San Pedro House to take part in SABO's hummingbird band-and-release program. Flitting between their tropical winter retreats in Mexico and Central America and their nesting grounds in the upper United States and Canada—a journey that can span as many as 2,700 miles—almost a dozen different species of hummingbird stop off along the San Pedro River for a rest, a drink, and a nosh. By tracking their annual migration patterns, SABO is trying to determine whether the birds—and by association, their habitats—are being threatened.

I grew up in Brooklyn, where migrating birds meant pigeons visiting from New Jersey. I have no patience for standing around and staring at branches, trying to see something I'm not going to be able to identify—and why would I want to? Birding hasn't exactly been at the top of my try-before-I-die list. But Bernadette, who's done this before, swears it's a lot of fun. I've gone along because hummingbirds are easy to recognize, and anything that can eat twice its body weight in food each day has got my attention.

Getting these itty-bitty critters, which are not only speedy but smarter than your average bird, into a position where tiny bands can be put on their tiny legs is challenging, to say the least. But the three SABO staff members—along with Williamson, her husband, Tom Wood, and naturalist Ron Hunt—have got it sussed. They use sugar water–filled feeders ("Forget the coloring and the pricey commercial stuff," says Williamson, "clear sugar water works just as well") to lure the birds into fine nylon mist nets, which they and the SABO volunteers watch vigilantly. As soon as a bird takes the bait, it's chased to the back of the net, placed into a mesh bag, and carefully carried over to the table, where the weighing and measuring commence.

Hunt, who's on net watch, waxes rhapsodic when asked about Southeastern Arizona and the "sky islands" formed by the many mountain ranges and rivers criss-crossing the region. It seems that features of the lower Rockies and the upper Sierra Madres, as well as of the Mojave, Chihuahuan, and Sonoran Deserts, all converge here. "It's one of the world's great biodiverse regions," he enthuses, "as interesting to many naturalists as the Serengeti Plains or the Galapagos Islands." You won't find huge animals anymore, although mammoths and mastodons used to roam the area, but there are more than 450 different species of birds and almost 300 types of butterflies.

The small group surrounding Williamson is now watching her measure an Anna's hummingbird, slightly larger than the Rufous and green with patches of black and grey. Seeing the bird at close range, I'm amazed at its iridescent throat colors, flaming pink shading into psychedelic red and orange. According to Williamson, these flashy feathers indicate that the bird is an adult male. He uses them not only to attract females but also to frighten off other males—"Kind of like gang colors," she says, adding that the male birds tend to do a lot of mouthing off but little follow-up. "You do see them body-slamming each other on occasion, but most of the time one of them punks out and just flits away."

Although the aluminum band that Williamson twists into place on the Anna's leg is minuscule—about the diameter of an eyeglass screw—she contends that hummingbirds are actually easier to deal with than many larger birds. They're not as dangerous to handle as, say, birds of prey, and not as vulnerable in many ways as shore-birds and songbirds that have

Broad-billed hummingbirds are a common sight in southern Arizona.

long, fragile legs. The hummingbird's intelligence—it's got quite a large brain relative to its body size—and its fearlessness also keep it from getting overly stressed during the banding process.

Still, the poor little things are bound to be traumatized after being manhandled by various featherless giants. As soon as Williamson completes her measurements, each bird is handed over to 8-year-old Erin Hodges, who holds it up to a feeder for a shot of sugar water—a parting energy boost, as well as a reward for being poked and prodded. Then the bird is gently passed along to another volunteer, whose open, outstretched hand serves as a bird launching pad. It usually takes a hummingbird about half a minute to realize it's finally free to flee.

Now it's my turn. Yikes. I've been enjoying myself, but I haven't been channeling Dr. Doolittle. What if my nervousness somehow gives the bird even more agita? But the Anna's doesn't seem to be aware that I'm obsessing. He just settles in on my hand, making a sound that feels like purring (that's his rapid heartbeat, I'm told). Some of the others come over to stroke him, including a small boy who seems a bit aggressive in his poking—OK, so I'm starting to feel protective—but most of the group just looks on, amazed. By the time my cutie finally flies away, it's clocked 10 minutes later. According to Erin, who's been helping out at SABO bandings since she was five years old, I've broken some kind of hummingbird staying record.

"Maybe your hand was sticky," little Poking Boy suggests.

I don't care. I'm thrilled, and I know the truth, although it flies—or, should I say, rests—in the face of my Brooklyn-bred cynicism. That hummingbird liked me. He really liked me.

—Edie Jarolim

The San Pedro House visitors center of the San Pedro Riparian National Conservation Area is 7 miles east of Sierra Vista on Route 90. Banding usually takes place on Saturday afternoons from early April to early June, then again from early July through September; you'll see the greatest numbers and most diverse species from mid-August through September. The sessions are open to the public at no charge, but donations are accepted. The Bisbee-based Southeastern Arizona Bird Observatory (520-432-1388; www.sabo.org) runs for-fee bird-watching tours, walks, and workshops, many involving avians other than hummingbirds.

■ Humans and Mountains

"The spirit of the mountain is a woman, and she is troubled," says Berniece Falling Leaves, a half-Sioux mystic and metaphysicist.

Black Mountain is a strange knob of brown granite and black schist that rises abruptly out of the desert 35 miles northeast of downtown Phoenix. Two small communities, the eccentric Cave Creek and the affluent Carefree, curl around it and press into it. Mansions worth as much as $3 million cling to its sides. According to Falling Leaves, those houses are unwelcome.

To prove her point she tells about a ceremonial dance performed in honor of the mountain's spirit just as development was beginning to accelerate. The day was mild and sunny, but suddenly, as the dance was coming to a close, an enormous shudder of thunder erupted in the blue sky over Black Mountain. "We knew our energy had been transferred to the spirit of the mountain," she recalls.

Many Native American cultures regard mountains as sacred, and for a desert people, mountain spirits are part of an elegantly logical theology. Rainfall was and is their most vital resource, and in the desert, thunderstorms almost always begin over the mountains.

Likewise in modern Anglo culture, mysteries tend to reside in the mountains. By far the most durable is that of the Lost Dutchman mine, in the Superstition Mountains, 40 miles east of Phoenix. The legend dates from the 1870s, when two German-born prospectors named Jacob Waltz and Jacob Weiser supposedly made a sensational strike somewhere deep in the craggy Superstitions. Every time they showed up in Florence, the little desert town to the south, they paid for their supplies from pouches bulging with gold nuggets—or so the story goes.

Weiser met with an untimely demise. One account suggests Waltz did it; another, suspiciously colorful, reports him crawling out of the mountains stuck full of Apache arrows and dying in a doctor's office. Waltz continued mining, and eventually retired to Phoenix. Shortly before he died, he dictated enigmatic directions to the mine to a bakery woman who had become his close friend. That was in 1891, and people have been combing the Superstitions in search of it ever since.

Some of the fortune hunters are kooks, some are casual hobbyists, some are serious and indefatigable. The Superstitions, though, seem determined to preserve their secret. A curiously large number of people—at least three dozen, according to *Arizona Highways*—have died in these mountains since Jacob Waltz departed with his terrible and compelling mystery. Some have been weekend hikers and climbers who fell to their deaths, but many others were on the trail of the mine when they were mysteriously shot or just disappeared. One ghostly corollary to the legend says that Waltz is doing it, but it has been documented that some of the murders were committed by prospectors who feared a rival would find the mine first.

From the 1970s to the present, movements to protect Arizona's mountains have gained considerable public support. Pima County and the city of Scottsdale passed the state's first hillside ordinances to halt the steady creep of subdivisions up the suburban mountain slopes. The late Rep. Morris K. Udall, once the dean of Arizona's congressional delegation, managed to jam 3,750 square miles of pristine Arizona land, much of it mountainous, into a 1990 wilderness bill. Udall, who served 15 terms in Congress, said that wilderness protection for his home state was one of the achievements of which he was most proud.

In 1980, the University of Arizona first approached the U.S. Forest Service about leasing a few acres on top of Mount Graham (near Safford) for a cluster of new observatories. During the ensuing environmental studies, scientists found a unique rodent inhabiting the site—the Mount Graham red squirrel, one of those subspecies that had been evolving in isolation for an estimated 10,000 years. A string of studies ensued, accompanied by lawsuits and demonstrations. By 1993, the university and environmentalists had become bitter enemies, and construction of the observatories had begun. The battle illustrated the depth of the passions that often swirl around Arizona's mountains.

There is another interesting example in *Frog Mountain Blues,* a 1987 book by the environmentalist Charles Bowden, which argues from beginning to end to close that most spectacular of Arizona roads, the Mount Lemmon Highway.

The Bullock Fire in the summer of 2002 and the Aspen Fire in the summer of 2003 closed the road temporarily and forced the evacuation of Mount Lemmon, but it's hard to imagine that the highway could ever be shut down permanently. In winter, Mount Lemmon is popular with émigrés from colder climes who miss the snow. And all it takes is a clear summer day, a good friend, a picnic basket, and a convertible with the top peeled back to convince most of us that the mountain should be asked, gently, to please suffer this one intrusion. However, it is unlikely, were this highway being proposed today, that it would be built. The mountain would remain wild, and would almost surely be the better for it.

(following pages) Amazing cactus and wildflowers abound in the Superstition Mountains.

Star Search, Southern Arizona

With its abundance of clear nights, dry air, mountain ranges, and, in its largest city, Tucson, a major scientific research institution, southern Arizona boasts some of the most astronomy-friendly real estate on this planet.

It's a quick 35 miles southeast from Tucson to the foot of Mount Hopkins and the visitors center of the **Fred Lawrence Whipple Observatory,** established by the Smithsonian Astrophysical Observatory in 1968. The longer leg of the journey, and also the most breathtaking one, is the 10-mile guided van trip to the top of the 8,550-foot peak. As you wind your way through the Coronado National Forest, ascending from the Sonoran Desert to the equivalent of Canadian alpine terrain, you'll see an impressive variety of trees, including alligator juniper, so named for its scaly, shaggy bark. Other shaggy occupants of the mountain tend to make their presence known less directly: The mystery vandal of a mirror positioned at a curve in the narrow road to alert drivers to oncoming traffic turned out to be a black bear.

Among the group of astronomical instruments arrayed on a ridge at 7,600 feet is the infrared Two Micron All Sky Survey (2MASS) telescope, which has a twin at the Cerro Tololo Observatory in Chile. Together, the two are engaged in an ambitious mission: mapping the entire night sky. Less than halfway into their three-year celestial survey, the duo discovered L-dwarfs, a new class of star.

But the real king of the astronomical hill sits atop Mount Hopkins. The Multiple-Mirror Telescope (MMT), built in 1979 with the University of Arizona, was the world's first all-electronic telescope, aimed and tracked entirely by computer. The boxy four-story building that the MMT called home—a compact, economical departure from the usual dome—was literally revolutionary: offices, labs, and public areas all rotated along with the scope. The building is still swiveling, but advances in the technology of large-mirror casting led to the early retirement of its first occupant: In 1999, the MMT's six 1.8-meter mirrors were replaced by a single 6.5-meter reflector. *Full-day tours are offered from mid-March through November, weather—and attendance—permitting; 520-670-5707.*

The original MMT may be just a memory, but you can visit some of its progeny at the **Mount Graham International Observatory,** southern Arizona's newest astronomical facility. From Tucson, it's 130 miles east to Safford and the Gov Aker Observatory, the departure point for a 45-mile guided van trip to the upper reaches of the 10,720-foot Mount Graham. It's worth making the trip: Along with the mountain's natural attractions, including Ladybug Saddle, the springtime stomping ground for millions of the spotted insects for which it's named, this area is rich in history, particularly of the outlaw kind. At the foot of the mountain is the federal lockup that held John Ehrlichman and other Watergate conspirators in the 1970s, and from an overlook about halfway up the peak, you can peer down at Fort Grant and the nearby Bonita store, where Billy the Kid killed his first man in 1877.

The history-makers who spend their time at 10,400 feet are definitely more heaven oriented—especially those affiliated with the primary sponsor of Mount Graham's 1.8-meter Lennon optical telescope, the Vatican Observatory. Several of the scientists are, in fact, Jesuit priests, but you don't have to belong to an order to get religious up here. The astronomers apply for their limited time on the telescopes far in advance, so when they finally arrive on the mountain, they all begin praying for good weather.

But what's good weather for some isn't necessarily ideal for others. For the scientists searching the cosmos with the neighboring Heinrich Hertz Submillimeter Telescope, the most accurate radio telescope ever built, it's dryness rather than clarity that's most crucial. Radio telescopes also differ from optical telescopes in that they don't require darkness to register the very short wavelengths they seek. Thus daytime visitors can watch the German astronomers from the Max Planck Institute for Radio Astronomy at work—or, perhaps, making coffee in the observatory's kitchen. It's a bit like Tucson's Biosphere 2 in the early days, except here you can converse with the scientists—and they can leave the premises. *Tours are offered most Saturdays from mid-March to mid-November. Attendance is restricted to 15 and reservations must be made at least two weeks in advance; 520-428-6260.*

Kitt Peak National Observatory, established in 1958 as this country's first national observatory and managed by a consortium of more than 20 universities, has the world's greatest concentration of optical telescopes—22, to be precise—as well as two radio telescopes. The top of the 6,875-foot mountain, some 56 miles southwest of Tucson, also serves as mission control for the University of Arizona's Spacewatch Project, created to monitor the heavens for straying asteroids and comets. If a huge chunk of space debris is going to crash into Earth, the folks at Kitt Peak will be the first to know.

Although free guided and self-guided daytime tours of Kitt Peak have been popular for years—the world's largest solar telescope is among the three instruments with visitor galleries—the night sky had long been bogarted by the astronomers. In 1996, however, a 16-inch telescope was installed next door to the visitors center and the public was invited up to dine and drink in the stars.

The program, which kicks off 45 minutes before sunset, includes a history of the night sky, exploring the Roman myths that gave the constellations their names as well as several Native American creation legends. The latter are particularly apropos: Kitt Peak is part of the Quinlan range, considered sacred by the Tohono O'odham

Kitt Peak National Observatory has two dozen telescopes watching the worlds go by.

Indians, from whom the observatory's 200 lofty acres are leased. The current occupants of Ioligam, or Kitt Peak, have been incorporated into Tohono O'odham stories: The astronomers have been named Men with the Long Eyes.

You'll also get instruction in using a planisphere, the moveable star chart designed to locate heavenly objects. Pay attention. The person who shines at this exercise gets first shot at controlling the dome driver, the remote device that rotates the circular ceiling of the telescope room, where you'll spend the rest of the evening peering at the universe. It's an awe-inspiring experience—and a unique one on Kitt Peak, as you're the only ones on the mountain with an actual eye to the sky. These days, astronomers work almost exclusively with sheets of numbers or images generated by computers, very rarely looking through a lens. *Guided tours of the facilities are given several times a day. The dinner programs are offered nightly, weather permitting, year-round. They're restricted to 34 people and are very popular; so book as far in advance as possible; 520-318-8726.*

—Edie Jarolim

■ MOUNTAINS OF NORTHERN ARIZONA

■ SAN FRANCISCO PEAKS

Just north of Flagstaff, Arizona's highest mountain range reaches 12,643 feet at the summit of Humphreys Peak. The San Francisco Peaks are "stratovolcanoes," composed of alternating layers of lava and ash. During the summer the lower reaches of these peaks are an Eden of sunny meadows and shady forests of pine and quaking aspen. The challenging summit trail up Humphreys Peak is well maintained and affords tremendous vistas of northern Arizona. You can also ascend via the cable chairs that loft skiers up to the **Arizona Snowbowl Ski Resort,** which has 32 trails slicing down the peaks. *Take U.S. 180 north of Flagstaff to the Snowbowl turnoff on the right. Drive another 7 miles on the paved road to the ski area and the trailhead to Humphreys Peak. Snowbowl; 928-779-4577.*

■ SUNSET CRATER VOLCANO NATIONAL MONUMENT

More than 400 Arizona mountains are the remnants of volcanic activity. The most recent known volcanic eruption in Arizona was in the winter of A.D. 1064–65, when a volcano just north of present-day Flagstaff blanketed 120 square miles of countryside with lava, cinders, and ash. The most prominent memento of that drama is Sunset Crater, a 1,000-foot-high cinder cone. Trails lead among the lava flows, but not up the cone. The rich soil that resulted from the eruption has also given rise to a variety of Native American settlements; see "The First Arizonans" chapter for details on Wupatki National Monument, which is connected to Sunset Crater via a loop road. *Take U.S. 89, 14 miles north of Flagstaff; 928-526-0502.*

■ HUALAPAI MOUNTAIN PARK

Located 14 miles southeast of Kingman, lush Hualapai Mountain Park rises unexpectedly out of northwestern Arizona's desolate Mojave Desert landscape. Most people driving through Kingman en route to Las Vegas or Laughlin, Nevada, can't even imagine that an inviting alpine oasis could exist in such country. It's too bad, because this county park has thick forests, stellar views, hiking trails, picnic areas, rustic cabins—and no crowds. *Take Hualapai Mountain Road southeast out of Kingman until you reach the park. For information call Hualapai Ranger Station at 928-757-3859.*

■ MOUNTAINS OF CENTRAL ARIZONA

■ MOGOLLON RIM

The most sublime natural attraction running northwest of the White Mountains is the Mogollon Rim, a weird and spellbinding escarpment that plunges 2,000 feet in one vertical slash from the undulating mountain country to the Tonto Basin. Spectacular and vertiginous views are best from the Rim Drive (Forest Road 300), a good but lonely gravel road closely paralleling the rim for 43 miles. *From Payson, take Route 260 east for 30 miles to the Woods Canyon Lake turnoff. Turn left and follow paved Lake Road to unpaved Rim Drive. Payson Ranger Station; 928-474-7900.*

■ WHITE MOUNTAINS

The White Mountains, 120 miles northeast of Phoenix, comprise Arizona's best-known and most intensively developed mountain vacationland. Recreation is the strong suit in these mountains, not solitude.

The incorporated community of Pinetop-Lakeside offers a small theater, guided full-moon ski tours, and frequent golf tournaments; the nearby town of Show Low has such recreational oddities as a summer Grand Prix for bathtubs on wheels.

See the "Modern Indians" chapter for a description of the various enterprises of the White Mountain and San Carlos Apaches, whose adjoining reservations are in this area.

■ APACHE-SITGREAVES NATIONAL FOREST

Arizona's least-known high-country scenery lies in the Apache-Sitgreaves Forest, whose peaks range up to 10,995-foot Escudilla Mountain. For an introduction, take U.S. 191 from Clifton to Alpine, a federally designated Scenic Byway. There is not one town along the winding 95-mile route, but wildlife is abundant: deer, elk, wild turkeys, mountain lions, and black bears. *928-333-4301.*

■ SUPERSTITION WILDERNESS

The 235-square-mile Superstition Wilderness is Phoenix's nearest great, wild mountain area. A jagged, forbidding range, the Superstitions can be admired from the base at Lost Dutchman State Park or attacked on trails. The Superstitions are not a remarkably high range; the tallest peak is Mound Mountain at 6,266 feet. This is, however, a truly intimidating range; after scouring it for the Lost Dutchman mine for more than 30 years, Arizona's onetime attorney general, Bob

Sunset Crater is evidence of Arizona's most recent volcanic eruption.

Corbin, confessed to the *Arizona Daily Star* that he had vast canyons left to search. "You'd need ropes to get into some of these areas," Corbin said. "The place we're messing with now, I can't get a horse within half a mile of it." *From Phoenix, take the Superstition Freeway (U.S. 360) east to the Apache Trail (Route 88) in Apache Junction. For a day's adventure looping around the Superstitions, take Route 88, 75 miles from Apache Junction to Globe, and then follow U.S. 60 west back to Phoenix. Lost Dutchman State Park; 480-982-4485.*

■ MOUNTAINS OF SOUTHERN ARIZONA

■ PICACHO PEAK

Picacho Peak, between Phoenix and Tucson, masquerades very effectively as a volcanic cone, but it actually is the eroded remnant of other lava flows. The precipitous climb up Tunter Trail to the summit, a 1,500-foot elevation gain, erodes the remains of many hikers' courage. The view, however, is spectacular. *Off I-10 at Exit 219, 74 miles southeast of Phoenix; 46 miles northwest of Tucson. Picacho Peak State Park; 520-466-3183.*

NATURAL ATTRACTIONS

Monument Valley, straddling the Utah-Arizona border and resplendent with red-gold sandstone towers, has been carved by the forces of nature for millions of years. *(see page 30).*

The **Grand Canyon** is one of the wonders of the natural world—277 miles long, from 4 to 10 miles wide and 5,000 to 6,000 feet deep. Your eyes can get lost in the canyon's rich colors and varied textures. *(see page 64).*

Canyon de Chelly, quieter and more intimate than the Grand Canyon, has a different type of beauty, with its vermilion cliffs, ancestral Puebloan ruins, and small Navajo farms. *(see page 78).*

The **Petrified Forest** is a rarity in nature. Clusters of mineralized wood believed to be more than 220 million years old are scattered in the wild and beautiful landscape of the multi-hued Painted Desert. *(see page 32).*

Oak Creek Canyon, just north of Sedona in central Arizona, is a juxtaposition of intense colors—vibrant reddish-pink rocks, deep green oaks and conifers, and bright blue sky. *(see page 82).*

Chiricahua National Monument in southeastern Arizona is rich in both history and scenery. The hideout of the Chiricahua Apaches, this beautiful park is known for its acres of column-shaped rock formations and its unusual desert plants and animals. *(see pages 38 and 61).*

■ SANTA CATALINA MOUNTAINS

The Santa Catalinas on Tucson's north edge are one of the few major Arizona ranges to be probed by a paved road, the Mount Lemmon Highway, which was upgraded and widened in the late 1990s and early 2000s. Picnic grounds, campgrounds, and awesome geologic spectacles pop up every couple of miles along the road, which climbs 5,293 feet in 25 miles.

In the summer of 2003, the 84,750-acre Aspen Fire wreaked havoc on the two popular sites at the end of the Mount Lemmon Highway, Ski Valley (the southernmost developed ski area in the United States), and Summerhaven, a community with a few unpretentious inns, restaurants, and boutiques. Plans to restore the two areas will unfold over the next few years. (See the "Canyons" chapter for descriptions of the Sabino and Romero Canyons in the Santa Catalinas.) *Palisades Ranger Station, at milepost 19.9; 520-749-8700.*

■ CHIRICAHUA MOUNTAINS

The Chiricahua Mountains were the ancestral homelands of the Chiricahua Apaches, and when their leader, Cochise, negotiated peace with the U.S. Army in 1872, he was promised the mountain range as a reservation. Cochise died two years later, and in 1875 the promise evaporated and the Apaches were herded north to the San Carlos Reservation. In 1924, President Calvin Coolidge designated the most spectacular part of the range as a national monument.

A graded road, Bonita Canyon Drive, crosses over the northern end of the Chiricahuas, but the best way to appreciate them is on foot. There are more than 111 miles of developed trails in the Chiricahua Wilderness, and maps are available in the monument visitors center. The most ambitious can take the Morse Canyon Trail to 9,357-foot Monte Vista Peak and 9,795-foot Chiricahua Peak. One of the most interesting features in the Chiricahuas is erosion-sculpted volcanic rocks bearing names such as "Duck on a Rock." *For hiking information, contact the Douglas Ranger District Office of the Coronado National Forest; 520-364-3468.*

(above) Cochise Stronghold in the Dragoon Mountains.
(following pages) View of Monument Valley from Hunts Mesa.

C A N Y O N S

Canyons enclose and define worlds. They nourish unique biosystems and work unpredictable magic on the pliant human mind. A canyon can fill one with wonder, fright, or both at once.

There are literally thousands of canyons in Arizona, far too many to canvass here. There are V-shaped mountain canyons, formed more by volcanic upheavals than by erosion. There are sandstone "slot canyons" on the Colorado Plateau only a few feet wide and hundreds of feet deep. There are urban canyons that flood with people every weekend, and canyons so remote that only the most determined backpackers ever get into them. Following are the best canyons I know—beginning with, inevitably, the Grand Canyon.

■ GRAND CANYON *map pages 66–67*

Shortly after the end of World War I, Marshal Ferdinand Foch, the supreme commander of the Allies, visited the Grand Canyon as a guest of Jack Greenway, former Rough Rider and Arizona mining magnate. Reporters hovered around, waiting to record Foch's reaction. He stared into the great chasm for a moment, then turned to Greenway and said something in French. Greenway turned to the reporters and translated: "Marshal Foch says that the canyon is the most beautiful manifestation of God's presence on the entire earth." What Foch actually had said was, "Let's have a cup of coffee."

Bruce Babbitt, a former Arizona governor and former U.S. Secretary of the Interior, recounts this story in *Grand Canyon: An Anthology*. As Babbitt interprets it, Foch wasn't being indifferent; he just wasn't comprehending what he was seeing. His brain had no precedent for processing visual information on this scale. John Muir, who had visited the canyon in 1898, articulated the problem perfectly:

> No matter how far you have wandered hitherto, or how many
> famous gorges and valleys you have seen, this one, the Grand
> Canyon of the Colorado, will seem as novel to you, as unearthly in
> the color and grandeur and quantity of its architecture, as if you had
> found it after death, on some other star. . . .

Spectacular hiking on banded sandstone in the Vermillion Wilderness.

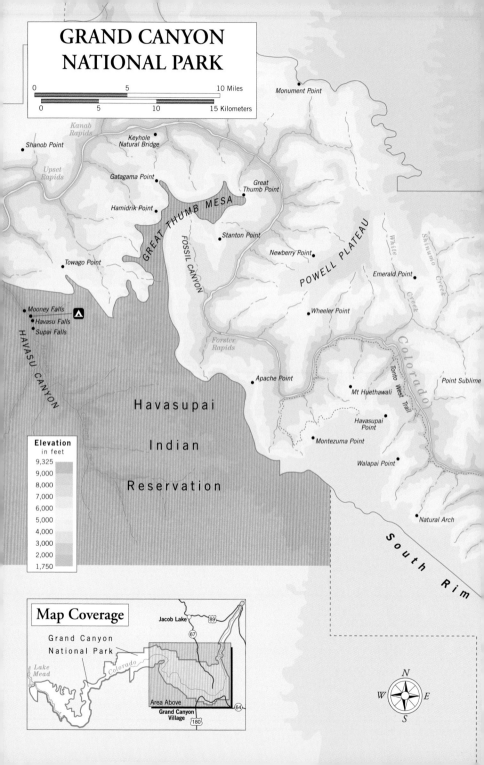

GRAND CANYON NATIONAL PARK

| 0 | 5 | 10 Miles |
| 0 | 5 | 10 | 15 Kilometers |

Monument Point

Kanab
Rapids

Keyhole
Natural Bridge

Shanob Point

Upset
Rapids

Gatagama Point

Great
Thumb Point

Hamidrik Point

GREAT THUMB MESA

FOSSIL CANYON

Stanton Point

Newberry Point

POWELL PLATEAU

White Creek

Shinumo Creek

Emerald Point

Towago Point

Wheeler Point

Mooney Falls
Havasu Falls
Supai Falls

HAVASU CANYON

Forster
Rapids

Apache Point

Colorado

Point Sublime

Mt Huethawali

Tonto West Trail

Havasupai

Indian

Reservation

Havasupai
Point

Montezuma Point

Walapai Point

Natural Arch

South Rim

Elevation
in feet

| 9,325 |
| 9,000 |
| 8,000 |
| 7,000 |
| 6,000 |
| 5,000 |
| 4,000 |
| 3,000 |
| 2,000 |
| 1,750 |

Map Coverage

Jacob Lake   89

Grand Canyon
National Park

Colorado

Lake
Mead

Area Above
**Grand Canyon
Village**   64

180

67

N
W   E
S

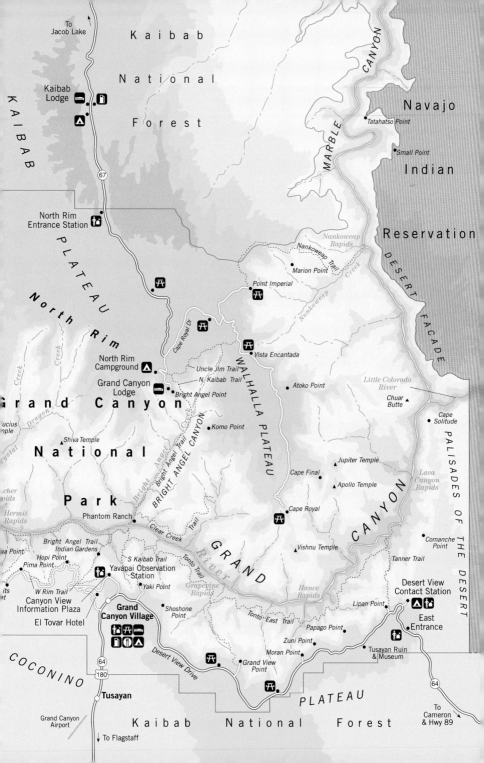

I have been to, and into, the Grand Canyon many times, and my senses, too, keep failing me. My notes, scribbled in a hip pocket notebook, always seem later as limp and banal as a televangelist's sermon. I am irritated with myself, but also consoled by the observation that many other people fail to come to terms with the canyon: in its presence, all human endeavor seems banal.

■ ■ ■

Nature carved the canyon with the Colorado River, then enlarged it over time with relentless whittling winds, geologic uplifts, and erosive rains and runoff. The gorge is young compared with the strata of its rock walls. The youngest layer, the Kaibab limestone at the top, is around 250 million years old. The rock at the bottom may be 2.6 billion years old. Human beings have lived around and inside it for at least 4,000 years. John Wesley Powell, a courageous and fascinating man who had lost his right arm in the Civil War, led the first thorough U.S. expedition through the canyon in 1869. He set out from the Colorado tributary of the Green River in Wyoming on May 24 with 10 men and a flotilla of four 16- and 21-foot rowboats. The tattered remains of the expedition—two boats, seven men—arrived more than three months later at the mouth of the Virgin River (now somewhere under Lake Mead in Nevada's southeastern corner). Powell's dramatic and meticulous chronicle, published by the U.S. Government Printing Office in 1875, ranks among the most compelling and literate explorers' journals ever written.

Three of Powell's companions died on the expedition—the ones, ironically, who had balked at running Separation Rapid (also now inundated by Lake Mead) and tried to walk out of the canyon. Three days later, Shivwits Paiute Indians encountered them on the North Rim and killed them. Powell's reports from this and a subsequent expedition in 1871 introduced the canyon to an astonished country, but tourism took hold slowly. Even to settlers in Utah and Arizona Territory, the canyon had seemed remote and inaccessible. In 1883, however, John Hance, an itinerant miner and raconteur, built a log cabin on the South Rim and began leading paying guests into the canyon on trails. Hance, it could be said, was the father of Grand Canyon marketing. In 1886 he advertised in Flagstaff's newspaper:

> Being thoroughly conversant with all the trails leading to the Grand Canyon of the Colorado, I am prepared to conduct parties thereto at any time. I have a fine spring of water near my house on the rim of the Canyon, and can furnish accommodations for tourists and their animals.

It wasn't until 1901, when the 64-mile railroad punched through from Williams to the South Rim, that tourists began flocking to the canyon in serious numbers. By 1905 the luxurious El Tovar Hotel was complete, and in 1922 Phantom Ranch—then as now the only accommodation on the canyon floor—opened for guests. Today's routine amusement of river running, however, remained an exotic and frequently deadly venture for a long time: Powell's first successful river trip ran through the canyon in 1869, but it was more than 80 years before 100 other people had done the same.

What turned the Colorado into the relatively benign stream it is today was the completion of Glen Canyon dam in 1963. Environmentalists still consider the dam an unspeakable outrage, a crime against nature, and are still fighting for its demolition. Interestingly, Theodore Roosevelt, who visited the Grand Canyon in 1903 and proclaimed it a national monument five years later, would surely have agreed with them. In a speech he made at the South Rim during that 1903 visit, he said:

> In the Grand Canyon, Arizona has a natural wonder which, so far as I know, is in kind absolutely unparalleled throughout the rest of the world. . . . I hope you will not have a building of any kind, not a summer cottage, a hotel or anything else, to mar the wonderful grandeur, the sublimity, the great loveliness and beauty of the Canyon. Leave it as it is. You cannot improve on it. The ages have been at work on it, and man can only mar it. What you can do is keep it for your children, your children's children, and for all who come after you, as the one great sight which every American . . . should see.

■ VISITING THE GRAND CANYON

No single mode of exploring the Grand Canyon is enough to fully appreciate and comprehend it, and standing on the rim and staring in is the most inadequate of all. One needs to engage the canyon with all the senses. Hike its trails, feel its walls, challenge its river. Fly over it—at twilight, if possible, when its vivid afternoon auburns, greens, purples, and browns converge into a mist-like, saturating blue; its sharp edges melt away in the faint light; and the sensation of mystery grows as bottomless as the chasm itself. You can call the park service for a free trip planner; visit the Web site for camping and other information. *928-638-7888; www.nps.gov/grca.*

(following pages) Fresh snow blankets the higher reaches of the Grand Canyon.

From the Diary of John Wesley Powell, Grand Canyon

And now we go on through this solemn, mysterious way. The river is very deep, the canyon very narrow, and still obstructed, so that there is no steady flow of the stream; but the waters wheel, and roll, and boil, and we are scarcely able to determine where we can go. Now, the boat is carried to the right, perhaps close to the wall; again, she is shot into the stream, and perhaps is dragged over to the other side, where, caught in a whirlpool, she spins about. We can neither land nor run as we please. The boats are entirely unmanageable; no order in their running can be preserved; now one, now another, is ahead, each crew laboring for its own preservation. In such a place we come to another rapid. Two of the boats run it perforce. One succeeds in landing, but there is no foothold by which to make a portage, and she is pushed out again into the stream. The next minute a great reflex wave fills the open compartment; she is water-logged, and drifts unmanageable. Breaker after breaker rolls over her, and one capsizes her. The men are thrown out; but they cling to the boat, and she drifts down some distance, alongside of us, and we are able to catch her. She is soon bailed out, and the men are aboard once more; but the oars are lost, so a pair from the *Emma Dean* is spared. Then for two miles we find smooth water.

—John Wesley Powell, 1869

Choosing Which Rim to Visit

The Grand Canyon is a 277-mile furrow cut by the Colorado River into the Kaibab Plateau of northwestern Arizona. While you can see across the canyon, the drive from the South Rim to the North Rim is long—the shortest route being 235 miles via the Navajo Bridge. Most visitors choose one rim from which to see the canyon, and then figure out how to get down into it.

The **South Rim** of the canyon can be reached by driving north from Flagstaff on U.S. 180 to Grand Canyon Village (78 miles), a route lined with pines. Another choice is on U.S. 89 to Cameron and Route 64 west (107 miles), which is more circuitous but affords glimpses of the Painted Desert. Or you can head north off I-40 from Williams on Route 64 (59 miles).

At the South Rim are lodgings, restaurants, thousands of visitors, and few places to park. Yet with a little effort and ingenuity you can get away from the crowds and enjoy the canyon.

The **North Rim,** located south and east of St. George, Utah, off U.S. 89 and Route 67, is more remote, has fewer amenities, and draws fewer visitors. Because its elevation at 8,200 feet is 1,500 feet higher than that of the South Rim, it's also colder and gets more precipitation. Thanks to the abundant snow, it is open to visitors only from mid-May through mid-October.

Driving

Roads follow both the North and South Rims of the canyon for short distances. Overlooks are marked, and, in some sections, it's possible to simply drive along, park your car, get out, and look. On the South Rim, Desert View Drive (Route 64), which follows the rim for 26 miles east of Grand Canyon Village to Desert View, is open to private vehicles throughout the year. Hermit Road, which goes along the rim for 8 miles west from Grand Canyon Village to Hermits Rest, is closed to private vehicles much of the year (winter excepted), but the park runs a free shuttle bus to provide transportation to overlooks. When the North Rim is open, there's access by car to all its overlooks.

At the South Rim, orient yourself at the **Canyon View Information Plaza** (opened in late 2000 and designed to be a terminus for a public transportation system that's been put on hold indefinitely). It's located about 150 feet from Mather Point, the first overlook you come to. If you don't find parking at Mather Point—an iffy proposition in high season—drive farther into the park and take one of the free shuttles back to the information plaza. If you're coming into the South Rim from the east, you can get oriented at the **Desert View Contact Station,** from which you can see all the way to the Painted Desert.

On the North Rim, follow the signs along Cape Royal Scenic Drive to Point Imperial, which at 8,803 feet provides views of the Painted Desert, Vermillion Cliffs, and Navajo Mountain.

Hiking

The best times to hike are morning and evening, when the air is cool and the colors enhanced by angled light. Easy walks and hikes along maintained trails are the best way for most people to get a sense of the canyon's majesty. Hiking to the bottom is memorable, strenuous, and best undertaken by people in excellent physical condition who take the precautions necessary in a desert landscape. The elevation change is dramatic, water stops are few and far between, and midday summer temperatures are often over 100 degrees. Hiking shoes or boots are a must.

Ambitious hikers should consult the hiking guides available in the stores, visitors centers, or the Backcountry Reservations Office (928-638-7875). Talk to rangers and buy maps. Backpackers need permits; day hikers do not.

Many hikers prefer professionally guided overnighters. The **Grand Canyon Field Institute** offers three- and four-day educational programs on a variety of topics, including geology, wildlife, and photography. *928-638-2485.*

South Rim Hikes

An easy walk along the South Rim is via the **West Rim Trail**—a partially paved, fairly level trail that begins at the Yavapai Observation Station (just northeast of Grand Canyon Village) and ends 10 miles later at Hermits Rest. The wonderful overlooks along the way aren't as crowded as those that can be driven to, and from April through October the road adjacent to the trail is closed to all vehicles but shuttle buses. Many people walk to Hermits Rest, get something to eat at the snack bar, and take the shuttle back to the Village.

South Kaibab Trail begins at Yaki Point, 4 miles east of the Village. An excellent day hike is the 3-mile round-trip from Yaki Point to Cedar Ridge, which has magnificent views all along the way. On the journey down, the elevation drops 1,500 feet. Early morning is the best time to go, when the air is still cool and the colors are magnificent. From Cedar Ridge you will get a sense of the depth and majesty of the canyon; the hike to the bottom of the canyon is 7 miles long, descends 4,620 feet, and is exceedingly hot, dry, and grueling.

Bright Angel Trail is the easiest and most overused rim-to-river trail in the canyon, dropping 7.7 miles and 4,460 feet. A strenuous day trip along this trail takes you to the magnificent river views at **Plateau Point.**

North Rim Hikes

Uncle Jim Trail is a fairly easy walk through forest with little elevation gain. It leads to several quiet canyon overlooks. Begin by following the Ken Patrick Trail at the North Kaibab trailhead.

North Kaibab Trail follows an exceedingly beautiful route, beginning in the forest on the North Rim and descending along Bright Angel Creek to the Colorado River, where it meets the South Kaibab Trail. A good day trip on this route, if you're very fit, is to go as far as the Roaring Springs picnic ground—about 4.6 miles each way. The trailhead leaves from a parking lot 2 miles north of Grand Canyon Lodge.

Hikes along the North Rim of the Grand Canyon offer astounding views.

Mule rides along the South Kaibab Trail are a great way to explore the canyon.

Mule Trips

Wrangler-guided trips ranging from seven hours to two days are available on the South Rim; the latter include a stay at Phantom Ranch at the bottom of the canyon. Rides are often booked a year or more in advance, but sometimes riders don't show up, so if you want to go, it's worth stopping at the Bright Angel Transportation desk to get on a waiting list for the next day's ride. Mule rides on the North Rim (offered from May 15 until the North Rim closes), range from one-hour trots around the rim to full-day trips down to Roaring Springs; reservations need only be made a day or two in advance. On both rims, the concessionaire requires that riders weigh less than 200 pounds and be fluent in English. Warns the brochure, "Those who are disturbed by heights or large animals should reconsider." *Reservations: South Rim, 303-397-2757 or 888-297-2757; inquiries about last-minute rides 928-638-2631. North Rim, 435-679-8665, ext. 222 preseason; 928-638-9875 from May 15 until the North Rim closes.*

Rafting

The raft trip down the Grand Canyon is one of the great wilderness adventures in the world, but not for the faint of heart. Rapids such as the 19-foot drop at the Sockdolager are terrifying but definitely unforgettable. Once you've done it, you'll probably spend the rest of your life hoping to run into other people who've done it so you can relive your experience with them.

Rafting from Lee's Ferry 277 miles to Lake Mead is about a 12-day trip. Shorter trips go to Phantom Ranch (three days, 89 miles) and to Bar 10 Ranch (seven to 10 days, 188 miles). Along the way you can swim in turquoise pools, shower under waterfalls, and hike the side canyons. The canyon changes dramatically as you travel forward: cliffs rise thousands of feet overhead and it's possible to see bighorn sheep, beaver, mule deer, and peregrine falcons.

From mid-May to mid-September, a one-day "float trip" (i.e., no rapids) can be taken on Zodiac rafts from Glen Canyon Dam to Lee's Ferry. *For float trips, call Wilderness River Adventure, 928-645-3279 or 800-528-6154. More than a dozen companies are authorized by the National Park Service each year to offer white-water trips that range from one to 19 days. Whether you choose wooden dories, small oar-powered rafts, or large motorized rafts, the average cost of a guided trip is $225 per day per person. To make a reservation, call 800-473-4576.*

Steam Train

Since 1989, South Rim visitors have had the intriguing option of driving to Williams, then riding a vintage steam locomotive to the South Rim. The **Grand Canyon Railway** ceased regular service in 1953, but now, after restoration and a popular revival, it slices through 64 miles of scenic high plateau country and the Kaibab National Forest. Reservations are strongly advised in summer. One big advantage to visitors who arrive by train is that they do not have to search for scarce parking spaces. *800-843-8724.*

Helicopter or Airplane Tours

Grand Canyon Airport is now Arizona's third-busiest airport, and the canyon's airspace can be hazardous, but most tour operators have excellent safety records—and, for many, the views from up high can't be beat. *Small plane tours: Air Grand Canyon, 800-247-4726; Grand Canyon Airlines, 800-528-2413; or Air Star, 800-962-3869. Helicopter tours: Kenai Grand Canyon Helicopters, 800-541-4537; AirStar Helicopters, 800-962-3869; and Papillon Grand Canyon Helicopters, 800-528-2418.*

■ HAVASUPAI INDIAN RESERVATION

The Havasupais, the most isolated of any Arizona tribe, farm a side canyon to the Grand Canyon and operate a store, lodge, and campground available to visitors. Near their village, Supai, you'll find a red-rock canyon, a stream, and a series of magnificent waterfalls. See the "Modern Indians" chapter for more about the Havasupais.

■ PARIA CANYON   *map pages 31 and 45*

Paria Canyon, a water-tortured gash in the Paria Plateau just west of Lake Powell, may offer the most spectacular canyon trek of any in the state—but it's not for the timid, inexperienced, or claustrophobic. Backpackers, who sometimes must wade through waist-deep water, tell many "thrilling" stories of their experiences in the narrow, twisting canyons of the Paria River. In places, Paria is 1,100 feet deep and 10 feet wide. Flash floods roar through on occasion, drowning some and stranding others for days, and hiking is discouraged from July to September.

Paria Canyon is as wildly beautiful and isolated as any spot in the Southwest. If it's blistering hot up on the desert floor, it's cooler in the shade of the vermilion cliffs. The narrow band of sky overhead is a brilliant cerulean blue, and the smallest hint of greenery seems like a miracle. High overhead, the jumbled sticks that look like bird nests are really flash-flood flotsam.

Before setting out on a trek through Paria Canyon, hikers should call the Arizona Strip Interpretive Office in St. George, Utah, 435-688-3246, for information about permits and weather conditions.

The trailhead is reached from U.S. 89 between Kanab and Big Water in southern Utah. Turn in at the ranger station (which doesn't have a phone) to pick up the required, free permit and maps, then follow the dirt access road south to the campground. The trail begins there and follows the canyon for 35 miles until it ends at the Colorado River, adjacent to Lee's Ferry.

■ CANYON DE CHELLY   *map pages 31 and 45*

Canyon de Chelly (pronounced "d'shay") in northeast Arizona earned its pseudo-Spanish name from the inability of early 19th-century Spaniards to pronounce the Navajo word *tsegi*, which means "rock canyon." A more elegant solution might have been for them simply to call it *el cañón exquisitó*, for it is arguably Arizona's most exquisite canyon.

There actually are several adjoining canyons here, with the largest tributary—Canyon del Muerto—stretching nearly as long as Canyon de Chelly's 27 miles. Although the greatest depth is only about 1,000 feet, the walls themselves form an astonishing spectacle. Generally even steeper and sheerer than the Grand Canyon's walls, some appear to have eroded in layers, like a flaking biscuit, while others look as though they were sliced by a 600-foot knife. One remarkable feature is Spider Rock, a needle-like sandstone monolith shooting 800 feet out of the canyon floor. In autumn, particularly, Canyon de Chelly is a festival of color, with the auburn walls playing off the lime-green and golden cottonwoods that snake along the river at the bottom.

Humans have occupied Canyon de Chelly for almost 2,000 years. The ancestral Puebloans (often called the Anasazi) left some 400 ruins, beginning with primitive pit houses and ending with a three-story masonry high-rise built around A.D. 1284. They also left thousands of paintings on the canyon walls, and when their Navajo successors began to move into the canyon in the mid-1700s, they added their own pictorial stories.

One Navajo canyon painting quite literally depicts the tragic story of Antonio Narbona's 1804–05 Spanish military expedition.

On a chilly January morning in 1805, Narbona and his men discovered more than a hundred Navajos hiding in a remote cave 600 feet above the canyon floor. Narbona later claimed that after a battle "with the greatest ardor and effort," his valiant troops killed "90 warriors" along with a few women and children holed up in the cave—but Navajo oral history holds that the victims were *all* women, children, and old men.

The Navajo version has more of the resonance of truth: the first Spaniard to climb to the cave that day was attacked by a female defender armed with a knife. The massacre gave Canyon del Muerto its haunting Spanish name: it means "Canyon of the Dead."

■ ■ ■

Canyon de Chelly became a national monument in 1931, although the Navajos, who still farm the canyon floors, restrict access to most of it. Today about 30 Navajo families still live in the canyon in summer.

(following pages) The Antelope House is one of the 400 ruins in Canyon de Chelly.

You can pick up maps and directions, and sign up for ranger-led tours (summers only) or guided hikes at the visitors center on the mesa rim, near the entrance. *Canyon de Chelly Visitor Center, Indian Route 7 and Route 64 (3 miles east of U.S. 191); 928-674-5500.*

Overlooks on the North and South Rims top thousand-foot red cliffs; from here you can gaze out over Navajo hogans, cottonwood trees, a few farms, and a stream winding in a swath of sand. **South Rim Drive** begins at the visitors center, passes White House Overlook—from which an unrestricted trail (2.5 miles round trip) winds down to the White House Ruin—and continues to Spider Rock Overlook. **North Rim Drive** also begins at the visitors center, then follows Canyon del Muerto, ending at Massacre Cave Overlook, where 115 Navajo were killed by Narbona's party.

Near the entrance to the canyon (follow signs) is the venerable **Thunderbird Lodge,** from which flatbed truck tours are led by knowledgeable Navajo guides. Both half- and full-day tours lead you into Canyon de Chelly and Canyon del Muerto. In the cooler months remember to take a jacket, as the canyon can be bitterly cold, even on a sunny day. *928-674-5841.*

■ OAK CREEK CANYON *map pages 31 and 45*

A juxtaposition of intense colors—vibrant reddish-pink rocks, deep green forests, bright blue sky—makes central Arizona's Oak Creek Canyon one of the prettiest places in the state.

The U.S. Forest Service maintains about 10 hiking trails into Oak Creek's tributary canyons, all of which are spectacular; a Red Rock Pass is required, however, if you're parking your car on forest land. One hike deserves special mention: the West Fork of Oak Creek, poetically and accurately described in an *Arizona Highways* article by William E. Hafford as "the canyon the moon cannot find." Even in the daytime, West Fork can seem dark. Some of its walls are actually concave, sculpted by a creek into forms that look like frozen ocean waves. The trail crosses the creek repeatedly, so expect to get wet.

Oak Creek Canyon, like the Grand Canyon, is to be avoided during peak vacation times. Its top attraction, Slide Rock State Park (so named for a natural sandstone slide leading into a pool on Oak Creek) draws crowds like a southern

Oak Creek and Cathedral Rock, two of Sedona's loveliest attractions.

A daring Grand Canyon visitor in 1914.

California beach on a warm summer afternoon. Fall is the best season in the canyon anyway, because of the color show staged by its forests of oak, mountain mahogany, sycamore, and sumac. From mid-October to early November, Oak Creek Canyon near Sedona is the most colorful place in Arizona.

The entire length of U.S. 89A through Oak Creek Canyon, which takes you from Sedona to Flagstaff, is about 32 miles. For information on permits, campgrounds, and hiking trails, call the Red Rock District Ranger station; 928-282-4119.

■ Canyons in the Santa Catalina Mountains
map page 45

The rugged Santa Catalina Mountains on the north edge of Tucson include seven major canyons—Bear, Sabino, Esperero, Ventana, Finger Rock, Pima, and Romero. **Sabino,** highly accessible by road-going tram, is by far the best known. Most visitors walk or ride along the canyon bottom, although the easy 4.2-mile Phone Line Trail, which is in effect a man-made ledge 400 feet up on the canyon's south wall, is much more engaging. The **Esperero Canyon Trail** leads 5.5 miles to a lovely seasonal waterfall named Bridalveil Falls; the trail rises about 3,500 feet en route, so it's not recommended on a warm day.

Sabino Canyon lies 13 miles northeast of Tucson's downtown. Take Tanque Verde Road to Sabino Canyon Road and turn north 4.5 miles to the canyon. Sabino Canyon Visitor Center and Santa Catalina Ranger District; 520-749-8700; Sabino Canyon tram information; 520-749-2861. A trail through Romero Canyon is accessible from Catalina State Park, 14 miles north of Tucson on U.S. 89.

■ ARAVAIPA CANYON *map page 45*

Aravaipa, in a remote part of southeast Arizona, is a connoisseur's canyon, an enclosed wilderness whose lush riparian habitat harbors seven species of fish, eight amphibians, 46 reptiles, 46 mammals, and more than 200 species of birds. To preserve them, the U.S. Bureau of Land Management strictly limits the number of hikers to 50 per day. For permits—which are available on a first come, first served basis—contact the BLM Safford Field Office during the week at 928-348-4400.

From Tucson, it's 70 miles to West Aravaipa and 155 miles to East Aravaipa; from Phoenix, it's 120 miles to West Aravaipa and 190 miles to East Aravaipa; all routes require driving at least 10 miles on a gravel road. The gravel road on the east side crosses Aravaipa Creek several times and is subject to closure during wet weather.

■ RAMSEY CANYON *map page 45*

In the Huachuca Mountains just south of Sierra Vista near the Mexican border, Ramsey Canyon is a hummingbird haven from spring to early fall. A lush riparian area with a year-round stream, the canyon ranges in elevation from 4,200 to over 6,200 feet. Fourteen species of hummingbirds have been spotted here; the best place to see them (and other wildlife) is the Nature Conservancy's Ramsey Canyon Preserve, which has a bird observation area, a short nature trail, and a longer trail to an overlook in the Coronado National Forest. There's a B&B just outside the preserve entrance. *Ramsey Canyon Preserve; 520-378-2785.*

THE FIRST ARIZONANS

He was a construction worker, short but with a mountain-man build, a sand-colored beard, and a direct, guileless manner of speaking. He seemed mildly intrigued that I had spent two days tracking him down, so he agreed to tell me firsthand what happened to him one night at an 800-year-old Sinagua Indian ruin near Sedona—so long as I would identify him only by his nickname, "Ropes."

He had worked occasionally as a wilderness guide and had poked around this little-known cliffside ruin for 15 years. Twice he had lingered after dark, and had found that the place spooked him. "I got a real uneasy feeling," he said. "Like I was intruding."

Finally, he packed in with a sleeping bag, determined to spend the night. He watched the red mountains turn violet in the twilight, then a smoky purple, then black against an indigo sky. He was about to drift into sleep. And then he began to hear crying.

"At first I tried to tell myself it was bats. Then I thought, well, it's jackrabbits. Finally I realized I was hearing children. Crying, *in this room.* I kind of chilled out, let the hair come back down on my neck, tried to go to sleep again. And every time I was on the verge of sleep, I'd be awakened by these ungodly sounds. Children crying. It felt like tears in there. All night, it felt like tears."

In the next morning's light, Ropes investigated the room. He found tiny fingerprints that had been pressed into wet mortar nearly a millennium ago. He traced the sun's path and realized that this room would have been the first to receive the winter light and the last to relinquish it, so it would have been the warmest room in the village. It had been some kind of a nursery.

I did not scoff at Ropes's story. I had heard too many others. An *Arizona Highways* editor told me about a night near Sycamore Canyon, 20 miles south of Sedona, when a little Indian kid materialized inside his camper and stared at him through the darkness for several minutes. Indians haven't lived in Sycamore Canyon for hundreds of years. A Tucson restaurant owner, also a credible source, was hiking in ancestral Puebloan land when he spotted a crow that seemed to be trying to get his attention. He followed the bird, which eventually fluttered down beside a prehistoric stone ax. The restaurateur took the ax home and began to suffer an inexplicable string of misfortunes. His health unraveled. Business at his little

Female and male petroglyph figures in Petrified Forest National Park.

crêperie, for no apparent reason, fell off 70 percent. Then one night at home he got out of bed in the dark, stumbled over the ax, and it severed a tendon in his foot. There was, he said, *a lot* of blood. Yet the ax had been wrapped securely in plastic and stashed on top of a table. The next week he took it back.

■ PALEO-ARIZONA

Arizona's prehistory lies literally on the surface of the land, exposed to view in the abundant ruins and potsherds and skeletons and ancient trash dumps. It tempts the imagination.

Possibly the spiritual residue of these civilizations still abides. If not, we may be excused for imagining it. We are steeped in prehistoric mystery.

The place we now call Arizona has been populated for about 12,000 years. The first 10,000 did not produce anything we would recognize as civilization. The original Arizonans, whom archaeologists call Paleo-Indians, were nomadic big-game hunters who roamed what were then grasslands, killing mammoths, bison, and other big game with stone-tipped spears. They probably had some form of social organization based on cooperative hunting. A pile of mammoth bones found on a southeastern Arizona ranch in 1955 had more than a dozen chipped flint projectile points in it, confirming what archaeologists had suspected: a lone Paleo-Indian could only have irritated a mammoth by flinging a spear at it. Not much more is known about these people. Living in nomadic bands, they left no art or architecture for our examination—though looking at the monstrous bones of the slain mammoth, we can imagine that they had steely nerves.

By 6000 B.C. the big game had begun to thin out because the climate was drying, and a new culture, the Archaic, either evolved from or replaced the Paleo-Indian culture. These were small-game hunters and foragers, and their middens, or trash dumps, suggest that they were more resourceful than were their predecessors. They made fishhooks and awls from bones and armed their spears with sharp antler tips—an intriguing *offensive* recycling of their own quarry's defensive arsenal.

The turning point in Arizona prehistory was not the employment of increasingly clever tools, however, but agriculture.

The idea of cultivating food arrived in southern Arizona from Mexico around 2000 B.C. A profound departure from hunting and gathering, farming triggered wide-ranging changes in primitive society. Cultivation required that people live communally and stay in one place, which led to the dawn of architecture and villages and, presumably, some system of managing those villages—in other words, government. Coaxing rainfall and productive crops necessitated new, more complex rituals—that is, religion. Farming provided people with more security and leisure time, which allowed art and recreation to flourish; and it yielded foods that could be stored and transported, such as beans and corn, which could also be traded. Ideas traveled with the traders, so the pace of technological development quickened. By A.D. 1000, the archaeological record tells us, prehistoric Arizona was undergoing an information revolution.

By this time several important cultures lived in Arizona: the low-desert Hohokam, the mountain Mogollon, the high-desert ancestors of the Pueblo Indians (often called Anasazi), and the Sinagua of the Verde Valley and southern Colorado Plateau. In every case, their art, architecture, and perseverance astonish us.

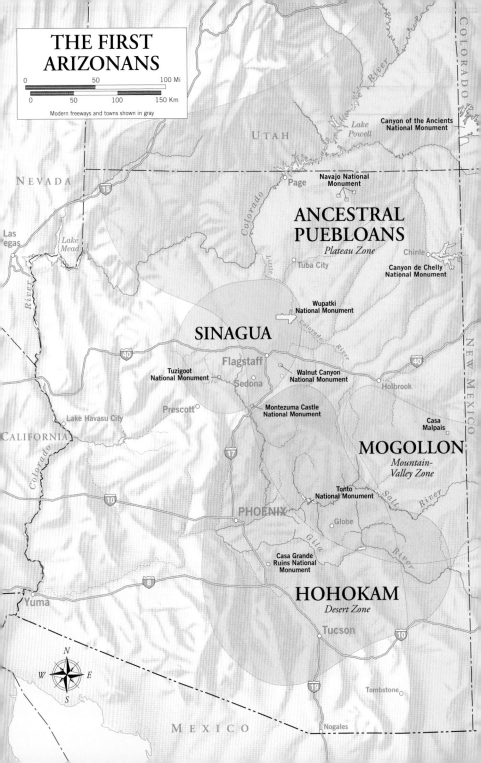

The Big House in Casa Grande Ruins National Monument was built by the Hohokam people.

■ THE CANAL BUILDERS

One November day in 1867, a prospector and speculator named Jack Swilling rode into the Salt River Valley of Arizona and saw something that must have astounded him: the windswept remnants of a vast system of irrigation canals, tendrils probing into the desert as far as 15 miles from the mother river. Swilling couldn't have had any idea how old they were, nor who had dredged them, but he understood their implication: people had successfully farmed this desert before, on an enormous scale, and therefore it could be done again—profitably. He organized the Swilling Irrigation and Canal Company, dredged one of the prehistoric ditches, and began attracting homesteading farmers.

And thus the city of Phoenix was born, inspired by the successes of the Hohokam a thousand years earlier.

The Hohokam world sprawled across a third of Arizona, from the San Pedro River in the southeast to the central Verde Valley. Wherever they settled, they adapted. Around what is now Phoenix, where the Salt River provided a reliable year-round water source, they irrigated their corn, beans, and squash by canals. In the Tucson basin, which probably received more rain but had no major river, they farmed the flood plains of the arroyos and built small check dams on slopes to manage runoff. Everywhere they built pit houses, constructed by digging a hole several feet deep, then raising a wood frame above it and filling in the walls with brush and sticks and a plaster of mud.

Not all their architecture was so modest, however. Around A.D. 1050 they began to build platform mounds; and by A.D. 1350 some were as large as football fields and 10 to 20 feet high, with storage rooms inside and freestanding houses on top. The ruin of just one remains outside the modern town of Coolidge; it is a four-story building made of coursed caliche (a calcium carbonate crust found in desert soils). When the Spaniards discovered it, they called it the *Casa Grande*, or Big House. Its precise purpose is still in dispute, but most archaeologists now believe that it was an ancient astronomical observatory.

The Hohokam arts were, if anything, even more impressive than their architecture and engineering. Their pottery sizzles with life. Scorpions, fish, lizards, turtles, snakes, birds, rabbits, and deer parade in tight formation around ceramic vessels of all forms and sizes. Some are so highly stylized they look like animals molting into geometry, such as a bird in flight that resembles the Greek letter Σ with a bow tie. They made primitive trumpets by cutting off the spires of large conch shells. They turned other shells into jewelry by etching patterns on them, probably by using the mild acid of fermented saguaro cactus fruit. This was centuries before Europeans thought they invented acid etching in the 1400s.

And then something cataclysmic happened in the Hohokam world. The Hohokam vanish. (Around A.D. 1400, the archaeological record begins to evaporate. Datable artifacts, such as pottery, become rare. By A.D. 1450, the line goes flat.) A century later, when the Spanish explorers began to arrive, they found the Pima Indians, a more modest culture of desert farmers, occupying the Hohokam lands.

Why did they leave? All the theories are perforated with holes. And when we consider the contemporaneous neighbors of the Hohokam, the mystery only deepens.

■ "ENEMY ANCESTORS"

The high badlands of northeastern Arizona are gouged by canyons where immense ocher and auburn sandstone cliffs soar hundreds of feet over long, dry riverbeds. Here and there huge alcoves lie at the bases of the cliffs, scooped out by water and wind. In these shelters huddle ancestral Puebloan settlements, the most scalp-tingling prehistoric ruins in North America.

The people long known as the Anasazi first appeared as a coherent culture 2,500 years ago in the Four Corners area, where Arizona, New Mexico, Colorado, and Utah now meet. Today, more than any other prehistoric culture, it is these people who command our fascination. Their large, intricate housing complexes seem like a metaphor for a relationship of perfect harmony between man and nature: they borrow protection from the cliffs but do not deface their dramatic sites. No archi-tecture in modern Arizona evokes the mood and power of the land so thoroughly. The 20th-century architect Mary Colter used the structures they left behind as a model for her Grand Canyon buildings such as Desert View and Hopi House.

Moreover, the spirits of these ancient cliff-dwellers seem restless. It is unlikely that the Navajos, who moved into Arizona later, ever occupied these sites; they had the forbidding air of ghost towns.

Archaeologist Alfred V. Kidder originally picked up the word "Anasazi" from the Navajo language back in 1936, believing it meant "the ancient ones." The more accurate translation, however, is "enemy ancestors." The Hopi, as well as the Zuni and other Pueblo Indians in New Mexico, regard those who occupied these areas as their forebears and consider their pueblos sacred; many of their modern customs and rituals bear this out. However, just as the Spanish name Papago—meaning "bean eaters"—was used for many years in southern Arizona to refer to the Tohono O'odham (as the "desert people" called themselves), so the term Anasazi lingers. It doesn't help that the Hopis favor the term Hisatsinom, ("people of long ago"), whereas the Zunis prefer Enote:que ("our ancient ones"). But both reject the term Anasazi, and it has been replaced by "ancestral Puebloans" or "ancient Puebloans" at such national monuments as Wupatki in Arizona and Mesa Verde in Colorado.

The architect Mary Colter used ancestral Puebloan structures as inspiration for her Desert View Watchtower in Grand Canyon National Park.

Although their culture is easily romanticized, the cold evidence reveals that the lives of the ancestral Puebloans were hard and short. Their physical environment, for all its beauty, was more difficult than anything faced by the Hohokam—hot in summer, dismally cold in winter, with unpredictable rainfall and unreliable running water. Anthropologists have found pitting of some bones, which suggests poor nutrition and anemia. The ancestral Puebloans were short people, the men no taller than about 5 feet 3 inches, and they rarely lived more than 40 years. The cliffside pueblos, hauntingly beautiful in ruin, would have been decidedly less engaging as dwelling places—dark, cold, claustrophobic, and smoky.

But the social and artistic achievements of the ancestral Puebloans are a legitimate source of wonder. The architecture suggests that an entire pueblo of hundreds of people functioned as an extended family. Quite probably they were able to make a primitive form of communism work. Wrote New Mexico anthropologist Linda S. Cordell, "Our notions of personal independence and privacy would be completely foreign to the Anasazi."

The apartment-like pueblos were built to make the most efficient use of space. Most have multiple kivas—large, circular rooms—which implies that a different communal activity took place in each one: religious ritual here, social gatherings there. Or maybe concerts: wood flutes as old as 1,400 years have been found in playing condition in Arizona caves. (Their musical scale was A#, C, C#, D, F, G, A. Improvise on this strange scale and the music seems hauntingly open-ended; it never wants to conclude.)

Like the Hohokam, the ancestral Puebloans cultivated corn and squash, although their arid land may have given the crops reluctant nourishment. To supplement their diet, they devised remarkably inventive hunting techniques. Nets as long as 200 feet were woven from yucca fiber and human hair, then stretched across gulches by a few people while others chased rabbits toward them. If it wasn't the most dignified style of hunting, it must have been effective. The laboriously woven nets attest to that.

But by A.D. 1300, they had abandoned their canyon cities and drifted away, gradually mingling into the Pueblo peoples occupying the high mesas of northern Arizona and the Rio Grande of New Mexico.

The mystery is *why* they left their traditional lands—and why the Sinagua, Mogollon, and Hohokam followed suit a century later.

■ THE ABANDONMENT

Archaeologists term it "the abandonment." Between A.D. 1300 and 1450, several of the dominant cultures of prehistoric Arizona (though not the ancestral Puebloans) either straggled away or reverted to simpler, less urban lives.

The lifeline of any civilization is water. When an arid-land people disappear, archaeologists logically focus their first suspicions on the water supply. And in northern Arizona, these suspicions pay off. Tree-ring studies reveal a devastating drought that lasted from 1276 to 1299.

Tree trunks cut and used for ceiling beams in the houses at Betatakin, one of those ancestral Puebloan cities on today's Navajo Reservation (the Hopis call it Kawistema), form a story line that meshes precisely with the cataclysmic-drought theory. The first three suites at Betatakin were built in 1267. The population expanded to a peak of about 125 in the mid-1280s. The last tree used in construction at Betatakin was cut down in 1286. By 1300, the settlement was abandoned to the spirits.

The Hohokam present a much thornier problem. There is no way to tell whether this drought affected their lands as severely; the desert trees they used in their building provide no reliable ring calendar. In any event, the Hohokam persisted for another 150 years after most ancestral Puebloan cities were deserted. Water, or the lack of it, does not explain their disappearance.

What about an epidemic? One anthropologist has wondered whether some European disease, such as smallpox, leapfrogged up the trade routes from Mexico ahead of the Spaniards' march into Arizona. Not likely, since Hernando Cortes, the original conquistador, was born 35 years after the Arizona abandonment was complete.

Could warfare have been the cause? The anthropological data itself is in conflict. For hundreds of years, the entire Southwest and northern Mexico were a vast melting pot, with the different cultures all trading, learning from each other and even adopting each other's customs. Hohokam ball courts, for example, began turning up in Sinagua settlements around 1100. Some archaeologists have speculated that the ancestral Puebloans intermarried and merged with Mogollon. There is much more evidence suggesting interdependence than large-scale conflict.

By about 1200, though, some kind of unease appeared to be spreading across the land. Ancestral Puebloan and Sinagua settlements from this period onward clearly show a defensive posture. Look at the ruin of Tuzigoot, whose 86 rooms

POTTERY OF ANCIENT ARIZONA

Potters of the Southwest have been experimenting with clays, slips, and forms, both useful and decorative, for 1,500 years. Designs common in the pots shown below are still part of the pottery tradition today.

HOHOKAM POT

This sacaton red-on-buff–style pot was found at Casa Grande National Monument in Arizona. Its sloping shoulders make it typical of this period of pottery-making among the Hohokam people. A.D. 1100.

ANCESTRAL PUEBLOAN POT AND BOWL.

Found at Canyon de Chelly, the cooking pot to the right was made for everyday use. The corrugations are made by pinching coils of clay.

SINAGUA BOWL

This redware bowl was made by the paddle and anvil technique and was found near Flagstaff, Arizona. The Sinagua culture, whose name means "without water," flourished between A.D. 500–1450.

sprawl over a Verde Valley hilltop. The dwellings have no windows or doors; the Sinagua who lived in them would have climbed ladders to drop through the roofs into dismal, pitch-dark rooms. Still, a team of archaeologists who in 1933 and 1934 excavated 411 Tuzigoot burials found little evidence of violent deaths.

Question archaeologists about the abandonment late into the night, and you'll eventually hear an interesting but elusive phrase: "worn cultural patterns." Press for elaboration, and you may hear something like this:

Think about the Hohokam irrigation system, which as time wore on became increasingly extended and complex. A 15-mile-long canal would have served numerous settlements, and that would require some sort of centralized authority to control and maintain it. Over time a network of authorities might have developed special status and knowledge, passing it on from generation to generation, guarding its privilege through mystic ritual, and living apart from the commoners atop mounds or in the big houses. For a suggestive parallel, look on another continent at the same time: at the Roman Catholic priesthood, specifically, during what we think of as the Middle Ages.

There is an engaging sliver of evidence at Casa Grande: a small hole in a wall on the fourth story aligns precisely with the sunset on the summer solstice. Knowledge of the seasons would have been critically important to the Hohokam farmers, yet this information was kept in a special and probably well-guarded place.

There is also evidence that the Hohokam were stretching the land's natural resources alarmingly thin. Archaeologists estimate that by the 13th century there were between 9,000 and 20,000 people living in the valley where Phoenix sprawls today. Over several centuries, this throng probably denuded the valley of trees for building and firewood, and found themselves having to walk farther and farther to harvest mesquite—which in turn would have demanded more human energy—on a diet that was becoming less nourishing. The average adult died in his mid-30s (not so different from life expectancy in Europe at the time).

With fewer natural resources to go around, old trading patterns probably fell apart. Hohokam trade with other tribes, such as the Sinagua and Mogollon, was abandoned. And thus the very complexity and interdependence of these peoples led to their demise. Once they had grown too advanced to be self-sufficient, the unforgiving environment snuffed them out.

Where did the Hohokam go? Some archaeologists speculate that they might have moved to the northern Mexico state of Sonora. Those who survived stepped backward in time, so to speak, and begat the less sophisticated Pima and Tohono

O'odham tribes, which the Spaniards found inhabiting the Sonoran Desert a century later—throwing off those "worn cultural patterns" and retreating into a simpler, more self-sufficient, more marginal lifestyle. The evidence for this continuity is persuasive—for example, some 20th-century Pima houses resemble thousand-year-old Hohokam dwellings excavated on the same sites. As the Hohokam villages shrank, authority disintegrated, the great canals shut down, and the big houses slowly weathered into dust. Life surely became harder: by 1450, these tribes no longer made decorated pottery, which suggests there was no longer the luxury of leisure time. Adaptation to a new way of life may have been the only way a suffering, beleaguered people could manage to survive. Their once complex way of life was considered depleted and therefore expunged from the cultural memory.

The fascinating question: will this same desert land support *our* way of life in modern Arizona for another millennium?

■ ANCIENT INDIAN RUINS

Visiting the places where the first Arizonans lived is not only interesting from an intellectual point of view: the earliest settlers naturally gravitated toward areas that were beautiful and hospitable—and most of them still are.

■ HOHOKAM

Hohokam architecture was mostly mud and sticks, so little remains.

Casa Grande Ruins National Monument, 50 miles southeast of Phoenix, became the nation's first designated prehistoric cultural site in 1892. In addition to a main structure—the purpose of which has not yet been determined—there is also a ball court and the remains of 25 ovens. *1100 Ruins Drive (from I-10, Exit 185, head east on Route 387, which turns into Route 87/287), Coolidge; 520-723-3172.*

■ SINAGUA

The Sinagua, a mysterious culture that borrowed from ancestral Puebloan architecture and traded avidly with the Hohokam, left hundreds of dramatic ruins scattered throughout the Verde Valley and the southern edges of the Colorado Plateau.

Montezuma Castle National Monument, an astonishingly graceful pueblo 87 miles north of Phoenix, has smooth, concave facades that fill in much of a huge cave high in a limestone cliff. A short loop path passes verdant Beaver Creek—which, unlike most Arizona bodies of water, flows year-round. Nearby Montezuma

The Sinagua built Montezuma Castle high in a limestone cliff.

Well, part of the national monument, is a strikingly blue spring-fed pool measuring 368 feet across and 65 feet deep. Neither site, incidentally, has anything to do with Montezuma; 19th-century Verde Valley settlers assumed that the Aztecs had preceded them. *I-17, Exit 289, near Cape Verde; 928-567-3322.*

The 86 rock-walled rooms of the pueblo at **Tuzigoot National Monument,** which flow over the crest of a low hill in the lee of Mingus Mountain, demonstrate Sinagua adaptability. These days, the views of Verde Valley are ruined by the sight of a slag heap (produced in the early 1900s by the mines of nearby Jerome) and a modern cement tower. Regardless, it's still clear why this spot would have appealed to the Sinagua. *Broadway Road (south of Flagstaff off Route 89A, between Old Town Cottonwood and Clarkdale); 928-634-5564.*

Another architectural style of the Sinagua can be seen at **Wupatki National Monument.** The soft, red sandstone houses here bud from outcroppings with such grace and logic that nature and architecture seem to become one. The Sinagua fled

this area when nearby Sunset Crater erupted in A.D. 1064–65 and returned a few decades later to take advantage of the soil's renewed fertility. They shared this territory with the Kayenta and the Cohonina people, who also left behind several structures, making this an especially fascinating archaeological site to visit. This is a combined attraction with Sunset Crater Volcano National Monument (see page 57). *Visitors center: Off Route 89, 34 miles north of Flagstaff; 928-679-2365.*

Only 10 miles southeast of Flagstaff, **Walnut Canyon National Monument,** with its lush stands of ponderosa pine, juniper, and Douglas fir, is worth a visit. Discover the unusual bonus of being able to walk inside most of the site's two dozen Sinagua ruins, which are accessed by the short but somewhat steep Island Trail. Spending a few moments inside one of the cramped, dark dwellings offers memorable insight into the lives of the people who once lived there. *Walnut Canyon Road (3 miles south of I-40, Exit 204); 928-526-3367.*

■ ANCESTRAL PUEBLOANS

Ancestral Puebloan ruins are scattered throughout the deep and forbidding canyons of northern Arizona, particularly on the Navajo Reservation.

Canyon de Chelly National Monument, near Chinle, is the most abundant site both in ruins and astounding scenery. You can hike unescorted to only one of the ruins, the White House, but Navajo guides offer horseback and four-wheel-drive tours to others. See the "Canyons" chapter for more about Canyon de Chelly.

The ancestral Puebloans settled in some of the most gorgeous landscapes in the Southwest. **Navajo National Monument,** near Kayenta, has soaring ochre cliffs dotted with firs and aspens. Between Memorial Day and Labor Day, rangers lead five-hour hikes each morning on a first come, first served basis (limit 25 people) to the huge and graceful 135-room Betatakin. Summer visitors will need to reserve a backcountry permit to visit the 160-room Keet Seel, a 17-mile round-trip hike from park headquarters; permits are given to only 20 people per day. Both sites are off limits for the rest of the year, but you can get a great view of Betatakin from a distance via the scenic mile-long Sandal Trail. Though not the most easily accessible, Betatakin and Keet Seel are the two most spectacular prehistoric ruins in Arizona. *From Kayenta, take U.S. 160 south for 18 miles and Route 564 north for 9 miles; 928-672-2366.*

This red sandstone Wukoki ruin can be seen at Wupatki National Monument.

MUSEUMS OF ANCIENT ARTIFACTS

PHOENIX

The world-class **Heard Museum** houses a staggering collection of more than 35,000 artifacts and artworks that document prehistoric and modern Native American cultures. See page 191 for more information about the museum.

At the **Pueblo Grande Museum** is the best remaining Hohokam mound, along with excavations and interpretive exhibits. See page 196.

TUCSON

The **Arizona State Museum's** enormous holdings of Native Americana and its excellent staff of archaeologists and ethnologists make it one of the state's finest museums. See page 210.

FLAGSTAFF

The **Museum of Northern Arizona** has staked out a special turf interpreting the natural and cultural history of the Colorado Plateau. In addition to its anthropology collection, which includes prehistoric artifacts as well as more contemporary Native American crafts, the museum's holdings range from fossils to fine art. The excellent summer Navajo, Zuni, Hopi, and Pai marketplaces, which also include performing arts events, are a popular tradition. *3101 North Fort Valley Road, (Route 180 leading out of town toward the Grand Canyon), Flagstaff; 928-774-5213.*

SOUTHEAST ARIZONA

The archaeologist William Fulton founded the **Amerind Foundation** museum in 1937 to do research in Southwestern and Mexican archaeology. It has an outstanding collection of Native American artifacts, but it would be worth coming here just for the setting—among the dramatic rock formations of Texas Canyon—and the graceful Spanish Colonial Revival buildings in which the exhibits are housed. *I-10, Exit 318 (60 miles east of Tucson), Dragoon; 520-586-3666.*

Spectacular vintage Navajo rugs are on display at the Heard Museum in Phoenix.

■ MOGOLLON

As would be expected from a group whose remains have been found all the way from Chihuahua (Mexico) to northern Arizona, the Mogollon exhibit many different arts and lifestyles.

The archaeological community was startled in 1991 when word went out that a complex of catacombs existed under the **Casa Malpais** pueblo, on the Mogollon Plateau near the New Mexico border. Nothing of the sort has been found at any other site in the Southwest. The above-ground ruins are open to visitors, but the catacombs are off limits. The ruins may only be visited on 1.5-hour tours—you follow the guide in your car. Tours begin at the Casa Malpais Museum in Springerville, which is on U.S. 60. *Museum: 318 Main Street; 928-333-5375.*

MODERN INDIANS

Twenty-one Native American tribes living on 20 reservations occupy more than a quarter of Arizona's land and represent a variety of languages, traditions, and lifestyles. Museums and shops in Phoenix, Tucson, and Flagstaff display exquisite tribal artwork, jewelry, and crafts, but to understand the people who made these objects, you have to venture away from the cities and onto the reservations.

There is no monolithic "Indian culture" in Arizona. If you've seen one reservation, you have not seen them all. There is no comparing the windswept tablelands of the Navajo sheepherder with the flat desert fields of the Pima farmer, for example. It is also difficult to compare languages: the state's tribes speak a total of 18 distinct tongues, some of which are as unrelated to each other as French is to Russian.

Though many Native Americans wish to live a simpler, more traditional life than that of Arizona's big cities, achieving that goal in the 21st century is not easy. Through television, computers, telephones, and tourism, Arizona's reservations have become increasingly imprinted with the ways of mainstream America. In many respects, the practices of the outside world collide with traditional Native American values and customs. Sometimes the consequences are tragic: alcoholism has bedeviled the reservations for generations; now drugs do, too. At other times the fusion has caused the native culture to do something not necessarily destructive, but antithetical to its nature. Gambling casinos, now operated by 17 Arizona tribes, seem out of place amid the vast expanses of underdeveloped reservation land, yet they have become an economic boon for many tribes. For the Tohono O'odham in southern Arizona, for instance, gambling revenues funded the creation of a fire department, a Head Start program, a community college, a nursing home, and a clinic.

Some tribes seek to benefit in other ways from contact with the outside world. The Navajos, Arizona's largest tribe, have rejected gambling but are trying to increase tourism on their sprawling reservation. The trick for the Navajos, as for other Arizona tribes, is to remain connected with the world beyond the reservation without sacrificing culture and language.

Two decades ago, the older generation of Navajos lamented that their traditional way of life was dying, and feared for the survival of their native tongue. Though

Mary Yazzie, a Navajo weaver, cards wool before the loom.

such concerns still exist, tribe members now have reason to be more optimistic about the future. Nearly three-quarters of Navajos age five and up speak their native language, and the majority are bilingual. Navajo leaders have made a commitment to preserving the Navajo ways—using the schools and media technology to keep both the culture and the language alive. At least 90 minutes of each day in the reservation's primary and secondary schools are devoted to a standardized curriculum focusing on the "Navajo perspective."

"You can't put the native and the Anglo perspectives together because they are too different," says Irvin James, a cultural education specialist for the Navajo Nation. "But the Navajo Nation Tribal Education Policy requires that schools compare the two ways of learning."

On a broader front, Navajo Nation Television 5 broadcasts in the Navajo language to nine communities across the reservation for at least one hour per day from Monday through Thursday. Special events such as the quarterly Navajo Nation Council meetings, the Navajo Nation Fair, high school basketball games, and the Miss Navajo Pageant are broadcast live.

If Western culture has made inroads on the reservations, Arizona's native people have also made their contributions to the life of the state and the nation, influencing art, culture, and attitudes toward the land and animals. In particular, the Navajos take justifiable pride in their unique role in World War II—which began when a California engineer who had grown up in a missionary family on the reservation had the idea of using the Navajo language as a code. He was certain that no Japanese had ever been exposed to enough Navajo to learn it, and equally confident that unlike codes that merely rearranged English, the enemy would have no linguistic foundation for cracking it. To confound the enemy cryptologists still further, the 400 young Navajos who enlisted in the program scrambled words around in their own language, devising a crypto-Navajo that not even their own mothers could understand.

It worked flawlessly. The entire invasion of Iwo Jima, for one, was directed by orders that crackled over shortwave radios in Navajo. More than 800 messages were transmitted and translated for the Marines; not one was in error, and the Japanese never deciphered the code. Years after the war, when the Japanese chief of intelligence finally was told that the code had been based on a Native American language, he reportedly sighed and said, "Thank you. That is a puzzle I thought would never be solved." (In 2002, with the release of the film *Windtalkers,* the story became more widely known, albeit in a Hollywood-influenced version.)

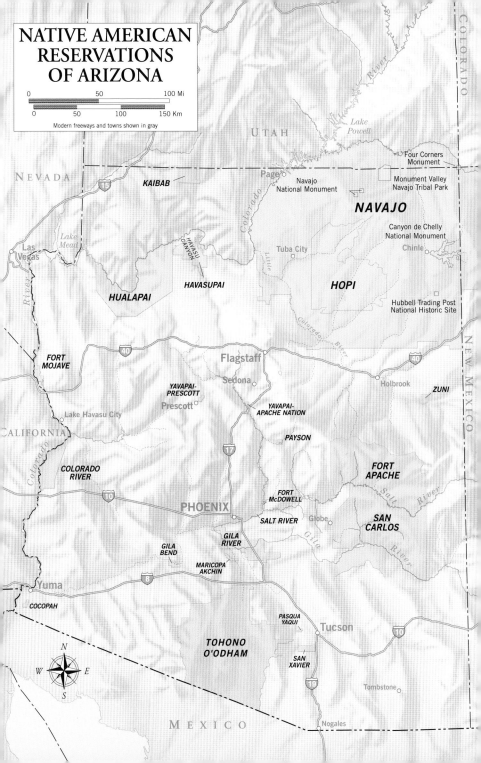

NATIVE AMERICAN
RESERVATIONS
OF ARIZONA

0   50   100 Mi
0   50   100   150 Km

Modern freeways and towns shown in gray

ANOTHER WORLD

For many native people the chasm between their lives and that of urban America has been too deep to be bridged. A letter written by a Tohono O'odham and published in the Tucson Citizen *three decades ago explains this poignantly.*

I am a Papago Indian [Tohono O'odham], very proud to be one, and what I want to say I hope you'll understand for I don't know much about the so-called English grammar.

The main problem I'm concerned with is unemployment for Papago Indians. Some of the problems I have in keeping a job I will discuss. I have worked with white people, but couldn't get along with them or maybe they didn't get along with me.

The people I worked with were all non-Indians. They talked behind my back (luckily I had a nosey friend to tell me all this).

They criticized the way I dressed. A great many Papagos disapprove of the white shirt and necktie bit. This is one reason why the Papago turns away clerical jobs, or vice versa. The Papago tries to be neat in every way—if he can afford it.

They criticized how quiet I was. They wished they hired someone else who'd be a little more lively. Well, this Indian isn't concerned about how much he should open his mouth, but rather how he should get his work done.

They criticized how rude I was not to say: good morning, good afternoon, hi, goodbye, etc., to every one of them. To the Papago it is silly to greet each other with the same word day after day after day, because it will only become meaningless.

The Papago, when greeting on a morning or anytime, will say what he wants to, but it is no greeting like "good morning." At times he will ask "Are you feeling fine," which I think has a little more meaning than the word, "Hi."

They criticized how rude it was not to introduce myself to a new person on the job. If a Papago wants to know who somebody is, he will ask someone else or he'll hear his name mentioned. You know, to the Papago it's quite funny to see people shake hands when introduced. Shaking hands is done only for religious purposes. When meeting a new person a smile shows the person is already accepted as a friend.

They criticized how rude I was not to say thank you when done a favor. To the Papago there is no such word. When a favor is done or a gift is given, he shows appreciation by returning something of equal value to the giver. (Those people never saw the favors I returned which meant thank you.)

These are some of the reasons I was told to quit my job. So now I'm looking for another, knowing I'll face the same problems in the white society.

Native Arizonans still contribute an understanding and respect for the natural world that is as alien to some of us as Navajo speech was to Japanese cryptologists. A newspaper reporter from Tucson learned about it one scorching August day as he walked across the desert with a Tohono O'odham friend.

The Tohono O'odham noticed that the reporter was wheezing from asthma, and he mentioned that his people successfully treated the problem by drinking a hot tea made from the leaves of the creosote bush. But first, he said, you must ask the plant for permission to use its leaves. And then, he said, you must pray to the Great Spirit, and offer appreciation for his kindness in sending such a wonderful plant. And there was one more thing, the Tohono O'odham said:

"It's also better if you find one special tree to use most of the time. In this way you get to know each other and become friends."

■ VISITING RESERVATIONS

Outsiders are welcome on all of Arizona's 20 reservations, although with different degrees of enthusiasm. Sale and sometimes possession of alcohol is prohibited in most places. Hunting, fishing, and camping require permits. In some areas, such as the Navajos' Monument Valley, hiking is outlawed. Where anything is forbidden, signs will be abundant.

Photography and videotaping also are unwelcome in many situations. Hopi villages and ceremonies may not be photographed or sketched, nor their sounds recorded. Visitors to the Yaqui village of Guadalupe will see many signs outside people's homes asking that their outdoor shrines not be photographed. Navajos, however, do a thriving business with photographers, charging a dollar or two for a pose. Even photographing some hogans—Navajos' traditional six- or eight-sided, log, dirt, and cement structures—calls for a "donation."

Since Congress passed the Indian Gaming Regulatory Act in 1988, many reservations have developed a major industry out of parting tourists from their money in gaming halls. Games include poker, keno, bingo, and slots. Some of the reservations have visitors centers and arts and crafts shops. Nearly all the reservations have trading posts in the larger towns. On the Navajo Reservation, hundreds of roadside stands line the highways, selling jewelry and other crafts.

When driving across either the vast Navajo or Tohono O'odham Reservations, bring water and watch your fuel: Filling stations can be as much as 100 miles apart.

NAVAJO RUGS

CHINLE
Named after the town of Chinle in Arizona. These patterns feature designs such as squash blossoms (pictured) within bands of plain color. (Woven by Evelyn Curley)

CRYSTAL
Named after a trading post in New Mexico. Noted for the wavy lines within the bands produced by alternating colors of weft strands. This example features patterned squash blossoms similar to the Chinle. (Woven by Fannie Begay)

TWO GREY HILLS
Named after a village in New Mexico. Usually woven from very fine, natural, handspun wool in white, black, and brown colors with a dark border. (Woven by Maraline John)

GANADO

Named for the town where the Hubbell Trading Post is located. Almost always has a red background and dark border. Considered by many as the classic Navajo rug design because of its long history. (Woven by Evelyn Curley)

BURNTWATER

Named after an area south of Ganado. Features earth tones and a large variety of pastel colors. (Woven by Brenda Spencer)

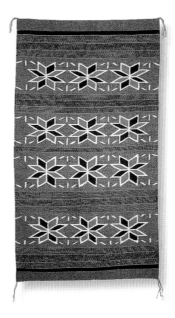

■ THE NAVAJOS

The Navajos are the most populous (180,100) tribal group in the United States, and their huge reservation (25,351 square miles) extends from Arizona into New Mexico and Utah. This high desert land, though hardly suited for supporting a large number of people, includes Arizona's most spectacular prehistoric ruins and many of its most dramatic land forms, including Canyon de Chelly and Monument Valley. Ethnically, the Navajos are related to the Apaches: both came from the same Athabaskan stock, migrating from western Canada and Alaska to the Southwest sometime between A.D. 1400 and 1500.

■ VISITING THE NAVAJO RESERVATION *map page 107*

Covering most of Arizona's northeast quadrant, the Navajo Reservation contains more than 15 national monuments, tribal parks, and historic sites. Like the Hopi Reservation it surrounds, the Navajo Nation occupies American soil but feels like another country. The following are among the places most worth seeing:

Hubbell Trading Post National Historic Site has been dealing in first-rate Navajo weavings since 1878, when it was established by Lorenzo Hubbell. Rugs from this trading post, near the town of Ganado, are known for their striking rich "Ganado red" background. The trading post sells all types of Indian crafts, but the specialty is still Navajo rugs (warning: good ones don't come cheap). Weaving demonstrations, lectures, and tours of the 160-acre grounds are also available. *Route 264, 1 mile west of Ganado; 928-755-3475.*

Four Corners Monument Navajo Tribal Park has little to do with Native American culture of any sort; it just happens that the spot where Arizona, New Mexico, Utah, and Colorado meet is on Navajo land. There's nothing to do here but buy fry bread and corn-on-the-cob, and have your picture taken while you're sprawled on all fours, trying to get a limb in each of the state seals that are arrayed on a concrete slab. *Off U.S. 160, 6 miles north of Route 164 at Teec Nos Pos; 928-871-6647.*

Window Rock, on Route 264 near Arizona's border with New Mexico, is the capital of the Navajo Nation, home not only to tribal government but also to the **Navajo Arts & Crafts Enterprise** (Route 264 and Route 12; 928-871-4090) and the **Navajo Nation Museum** (Route 264 and Post Office Loop Road; 928-871-7941). Both have examples of fine Navajo rugs.

The historic Hubbell Trading Post stocks everything from Doritos to 19th-century Indian pottery to Navajo rugs.

One of the best times to visit Window Rock is in early September, when the five-day **Navajo Nation Fair,** one of the largest Indian fairs held in the United States, takes place. (For more about Navajo Nation Fair, see "Festivals and Events" in the "Practical Information" chapter.)

The three most interesting sights on the Navajo Reservation are covered more extensively in other sections of the book:

Canyon de Chelly is a spectacular series of canyons first settled more than 2,000 years ago. The land here is still farmed by the Navajo Indians. (See the "Canyons" chapter.)

Monument Valley is renowned for its majestic sandstone totems and towers. (See "Mountains.")

Navajo National Monument is home to the ancestral Puebloan ruins of Betatakin and Keet Seel. (See "The First Arizonans.")

■ THE APACHES

The Apaches are divided into a number of subtribal families—San Carlos, White Mountain, Tonto, et cetera—that inhabit several Arizona reservations. Despite their long and very prominent moments in Arizona history, Apaches remain poorly understood by non-Indians; their blood-stained past has encouraged more flights of imagination than it has straightforward scholarship.

Arriving in the Southwest about A.D. 1400, they were hunter-gatherers who acquired horses from the Spanish in the 1700s. During the mid-1800s they launched raiding parties against other tribes as far north as the Hopi mesas and as far south as Sonora, Mexico. Led by great warriors such as Cochise and Geronimo, they did not give up their lands and freedom to whites without fierce fighting, and they were greatly feared by Spanish colonists in the 17th century and American pioneers in the 19th century. From the White Mountains to the Mogollon Rim in eastern and central Arizona to the Chiricahua Mountains in the state's southeast corner, the U.S. Army launched numerous campaigns against the Apaches between 1870 and 1886, when Geronimo finally surrendered.

Apache boys, in a photo likely dating from the 1880s.

RIGHTS AND RIFLES

To Americans generally, the aborigine is a nonentity except when he is on the warpath. The moment he concludes to live at peace with the whites, that moment all his troubles begin. Never was there a truer remark than that made by [Gen. George] Crook [commander of the U.S. Army campaign against the Apaches in 1871–72]: "The American Indian commands respect for his rights only so long as he inspires terror for his rifle."

—John G. Bourke, *On the Border With Crook,* 1892

The complete transformation of Apache society over the last 120 years is a fascinating cultural story, for no other tribe has changed as radically. As an *Arizona Highways* publication noted, the once-nomadic Apaches now "excel as cowboys, ranchers, farmers, lumbermen, artisans, [and] businesspeople."

■ **VISITING THE APACHE RESERVATION** *map page 107*
About 200 miles northeast of Phoenix, the White Mountain Apaches own and operate **Sunrise Ski Resort** (928-735-7639), Arizona's largest ski area, with more than 65 runs on three mountains. But skiing isn't all the White Mountain Apache Reservation has to offer. Twenty-five lakes are scattered around this piney high country, making it a haven for fishing, boating, and camping from spring through fall. Tribal permits are required for most recreational activities. The best place to get them is the **Hon-dah** (928-369-0299), a casino and resort at the intersection of Route 260 and Route 17.

Information about other reservation attractions is available at the **Apache Office of Tourism** (928-338-1230), which occupies General Crook's former cabin (1870) in Fort Apache. It's one of the 20 restored buildings on a 288-acre historic site; another is the **Apache Cultural Center and Museum** (928-338-4625), which contains contemporary art and historical exhibits. *5 miles south of Whiteriver (where Route 17 and Indian Route 46 intersect).*

Adjoining the White Mountain Apache Reservation to the south is the **San Carlos Apache Reservation,** which stretches from alpine meadows at its northern reaches down through grasslands and into the desert at its southern end.

San Carlos Lake, the reservation's most popular spot, was formed by the construction of the 880-foot-high Coolidge Dam in 1930. The lake is 23 miles long, 2 miles wide, and chock full of bass. *Marina: 2 miles north of Coolidge Dam on Indian Route 3; 928-475-2756.*

■ YAVAPAIS

The Yavapais are scattered about three reservations: Fort McDowell, Prescott, and Camp Verde. Originally a Yuman-speaking people culturally related to the Havasupais and Hualapais, the Yavapais' history became entwined with that of the Apaches in the 1860s, when the two groups allied to fight the Anglos in the Verde Valley. In 1870, however, the starving Yavapais surrendered to the U.S. Army and began working as scouts for the victors. This gave the army a decided edge, and by 1873 the defeated Apaches and Yavapais were herded onto reservations together. Today pure Yavapai blood has virtually disappeared, and their culture essentially has merged with Apache culture.

■ HUALAPAIS AND HAVASUPAIS

The Hualapais and Havasupais are the people of the Grand Canyon. The Hualapais, whose name derives from a Yuman word meaning "pine-tree people," live on 1,551 square miles of forest and high plateau land abutting the canyon's south rim. The Havasupais ("People of the blue-green water") number only about 600 and are the most isolated of any Arizona tribe: they rejected a Bureau of Indian Affairs scheme to blast a million-dollar road into the village to funnel in tourists. (The decision prompted Edward Abbey to label the Havasupais an unusually wise people.)

■ VISITING HAVASU CANYON *map page 107*
The one Havasupai village, Supai, is in Havasu Canyon, a tributary of the Grand Canyon where travel is by foot and horseback (you can also visit Havasu Canyon via helicopter from Las Vegas). Supai is the only town in the United States that receives its mail by pack train.

At the bottom of this Edenlike spot are the village and store, and the 24-room **Havasupai Lodge** (928-448-2111), as well as the Havasupai Tribal Arts Museum, which has displays of tribal history and local crafts. A trail leads to a Havasupai campground and magnificent waterfalls that plunge from 75 to almost 200 feet down cliffs of Redwall limestone into the turquoise pools of Havasu Creek. Though tourism is important to the Havasupais, they still farm the canyon floor in summer and hunt game and collect wild plants atop Coconino Plateau in winter.

To reach Supai from Grand Canyon Village, travel south on U.S. 180 for 57 miles to Williams, then take I-40 west 44 miles to Seligman. Continue 34 miles west on Route 66 until you reach Indian Route 18. Finally, head north 60 miles on Route 66 through the Hualapai Reservation, park at Hualapai Hilltop (at 5,200 feet), and either walk or ride a mule 11 miles farther into Havasu Canyon (at 3,200 feet). A limited amount of people are allowed in, so you must contact the tribe in advance, even if you're not planning to stay overnight. *Tribal headquarters, 928-448-2120; campground, 928-448-2121; lodge, 928-448-2111. Papillon Grand Canyon Helicopter Tours to the Grand Canyon West depart from McCarran International Airport, Las Vegas; 888-635-7272.*

■ Hopis

The Hopis, defying meteorological odds and conventional horticultural wisdom, have successfully raised corn, squash, and melons on the arid mesas of northeastern Arizona for at least 800 years. Not surprisingly, many of their sacred ceremonies center around the need for rain. Most astonishing is the snake dance, in which Hopi priests carry live snakes—including rattlesnakes—in their mouths. Since they live underground, the snakes are viewed as the logical intercessors to the gods, which in Hopi theology inhabit the underworld. Hopi arts, along with their rituals, are highly developed: their contemporary pottery and katsina dolls are the most refined of all the Native American arts in Arizona today.

The Hopi villages are fascinating to visit, particularly Walpi, the "sky village" appearing to bud right out of the top of a mesa, and Old Oraibi, the oldest continuously inhabited town in the United States (since A.D. 1150).

The Hopi Reservation is completely surrounded by the Navajo Nation, an uneasy living arrangement born of ancient rivalries and U.S. government interference. The 7,000 people who make up the Hopi nation are culturally related to the Pueblo people of New Mexico and Hopi rituals and art reflect those ties.

Hopi life, religion, and society are organized around an all-encompassing belief system called *Hopivotskwani,* the Hopi Path of Life. According to legend, it began when the first ancestors of the Hopis emerged from the spirit underworld to wander until they arrived at the arid mesas that would become their home. The Bear

ANCIENT AND MODERN TRADITIONS

Not so many years ago, archaeologists excavating a Sinagua burial site near Flagstaff were astonished to discover the remains of an ancient Sinagua shaman interred with a dozen wooden wands carved and painted to resemble hoofs and hands. The find paled, however, in the light of what happened next. A modern Hopi, taken to view the remains, could not only identify the uses of the millennium-old paraphernalia, but also tell from them which clan the magician had belonged to.

For archaeologists, the incident was more proof of the long-suspected linkage of the Sinaguas, ancestral Puebloans, and the Hopis. But it also illuminated something else: the phenomenal endurance of Hopi tradition and culture.

Clan, so called because they found a dead bear during their pilgrimage, settled at Shungopovi, in northeastern Arizona. As other groups arrived, they were given land to farm and became accepted into Hopi society once they could demonstrate their acceptance of Hopivotskwani.

The concept of the Hopi Path is extremely difficult for an outsider to grasp, but it has to do with the presence of the spirit world in virtually everything. Every plant and animal has a spirit; every summer thunderstorm is generated in the spirit universe—those storms being critical to Hopi farming. Every winter solstice marks the beginning of ceremonial katsina (pronounced "kat-SEE-na") dancing, which continues until mid-July. The katsinas, men dressed in elaborate and astounding costumes, are in Hopi belief the spirits of departed ancestors. They sing songs of admonition and perfected life, and they take the Hopis' prayers for rain, health, and fertility back to the spirit world.

Katsina dolls, which represent the living katsinas, traditionally are carved by men from cottonwood roots as gifts for their female children. Many published sources say that the gifts are to educate the children in the Hopi way, but the more important reason is to insure their eventual fertility.

Like so many other Native American art forms, katsina dolls now serve both ceremonial and commercial roles in Hopi life. Some Hopis benefit: a top-drawer doll can sell for several thousand dollars. Others grieve, however, that the most beautiful and intricate dolls no longer go to young Hopi girls, but to tourists and collectors. Because of the dolls' commercial success, however, the art of Hopi

Hopi potter Marilyn Sakewa of Polacca decorates her pots with paint made from wild spinach and applies it with a yucca-spine brush.

katsina carving has grown much more intricate and elegant over the last two or three generations. Nineteenth-century katsina dolls were rudimentary and statically posed, and the arms, legs, and fingers were simply implied by bulges extruded from the torso. Modern katsinas explode with energy and detail; they frequently are frozen in a dance pose, and their very distinct limbs ripple with musculature. On the most intricate dolls, carved lines delineate even individual strands of hair and barbs of feathers.

■ **VISITING THE HOPI RESERVATION** *map page 107*
For hundreds of years the Hopis have lived on three large mesas that rise above a wide valley. A road runs through the valley, where a scattering of schools, churches, and government-issue housing stand. Hopis are at best ambivalent about tourism; some of their villages do not welcome visitors, and those that do generally ask outsiders to register at the local community office.

(following pages) Hopi "Rainbow" dancers engaged in a sacred ceremony.

First Mesa

A narrow, gravel road leads up to First Mesa from the more modern town of Polacca. On top, the view is sweeping. Some sections of the stone and adobe houses may predate the arrival of Columbus by 300 years. Of the three small, interconnected villages on top, the first is **Hano,** a Tewa settlement, formed in 1696 by Tewa Indians from the Rio Grande region who had fled from the Spanish. The Hopis let them live here on the condition they guard access to the mesa top. Amazingly, the Tewas have maintained their own customs and language despite centuries of Hopi influence. The most famous Hopi Reservation pottery family, the Nampeyos, is from the Hano settlement. The first of these potters, known simply as Nampeyo, was born here about 1860. Her designs were influenced by prehistoric pottery found by her husband, Lesou, at a nearby archeological dig in 1895. Their descendants carry on the tradition they began, using clay taken from an ancient and proprietary Hopi source, and painting designs with a yucca-spine brush.

Adjacent to Hano is the village of **Sichomovi,** where visitors will find **First Mesa Visitor Center at Ponsi Hall.** It is necessary to park here and register for a guided walking tour. At tiny **Walpi,** ancient houses and old defenses jut out from the rocky cliffs, forming a dramatic contrast of stone against the surrounding expanse of sky. *Take Route 264 west of U.S. 191 through the Navajo Reservation and past Keams Canyon; 928-737-2262.*

Second Mesa

Of the three mesas, Second Mesa is the most amenable to visitors. Below the mesa on the western edge, a complex of buildings, including a restaurant (the best place to eat on the Hopi mesas) and motel, connect with the **Hopi Cultural Center.** The center's museum has fascinating exhibits of Hopi history and culture. The mesa's three villages are **Shipaulovi, Mishongnovi,** and **Shunopavi.** *Route 264 and Route 87 join below Second Mesa. Cultural Center; 928-734-6650.*

Third Mesa

One mile south of Route 264, at the eastern base of Third Mesa, stands the village **Kykotsmovi,** which means "Mound of Ruined Houses." **The Office of Public Relations** is here, along with the **Kykotsmovi Village Store**—stocked with groceries—and a few arts and crafts stores.

Two miles west of Kykotsmovi, **Old Oraibi** is perched on the edge of Third Mesa. Inhabited since A.D. 1150, this small village is considered by many to be the oldest continually inhabited community in the United States (Ácoma also vies for the title). In 1900, the population neared 800, but six years later many villagers left after a widely publicized "push-of-war" contest staged to settle a dispute between two chiefs, You-ke-oma and Tawa-quap-tewa. (The two village leaders amassed their followers on opposing sides of a line cut into a mesa, and the groups simply pushed each other until one side lost.) You-ke-oma and his faction left to establish **Hotevilla,** about 4 miles away. Both villages welcome visitors and are known for their basketry and other crafts. The residents of **Bacavi,** situated across the highway, are also descendants of Oraibi's former inhabitants. *In Kykotsmovi: Hopi Tribal Council, 928-734-3000; Hopi Cultural Preservation Office, 928-734-2244.*

■ TOHONO O'ODHAM

The Tohono O'odham are the quintessential desert people: they believe, no doubt correctly, that their culture will abide in the arid heart of the Sonoran Desert long after we have squandered what we understand of its usable resources and gone on. Before the encroachment of Anglo culture, the O'odham successfully grew corn, squash, and beans on the dry ground and harvested the native saguaro fruit for dessert.

Until recently, most non-Indians' experience of the Tohono O'odham, whose 2.8-million-acre reservation is second in size only to that of the Navajo, was visiting Mission San Xavier del Bac, just south of Tucson, which was built to serve—and convert—the community in the late 1700s (see the "Hispanic Arizona" chapter). But since 1993, the tribe has opened three casinos (two Desert Diamond casinos near Tucson, and the Golden Ha:sañ Casino near Why, in the southwest). Gaming now generates a large percentage of the tribe's annual revenues.

The best place to buy one of the intricately woven baskets made by the Tohono O'odham is at the visitors center of **Kitt Peak National Observatory** (see the "Mountains" chapter), which sits on 200 lofty acres leased by the tribe to the "men with the long eyes." In October, an all-Indian rodeo and fair is held in the tribal capital, Sells. *88 miles southwest of Tucson; 520-383-2221.*

The Pimas, closely related to the Tohono O'odham, live with the Maricopas on the Gila River Reservation just south of Phoenix. In 2002, the reservation opened **Sheraton Wild Horse Pass Resort and Spa,** a 500-room resort with an equestrian center, golf courses, and an upscale restaurant—the first cooperative enterprise of this type in Arizona. *I-10, Exit 175, 11 miles south of Phoenix; 602-225-0100.*

Classic Southwest Jewelry

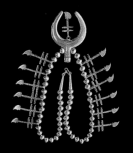

Cochiti Pueblo Silver Squash Blossom Necklace

Traditional squash blossom necklaces have side pendants in the shape of a squash or pumpkin flower. In this necklace, the squash blossoms have been replaced with crosses; this particular design has a double-barred cross with a heartlike bottom, resembling the Catholic sacred heart and the Indian dragonfly that in many Pueblo cultures was the symbol for water.

Zuni Bracelet

The Zunis have two reservations, one in New Mexico and a small one in Arizona. For centuries, Zunis traded turquoise to Plains Indians for buffalo hides and to Mexican tribes for parrot plumes. Over the years the Zunis have become famous for their extraordinary work in turquoise and silver, as exemplified left in this huge, sunburst design cluster bracelet (circa 1930).

Navajo Concha Belts

The idea for concha belts derived from disk-shaped hair ornaments sold to Plains Indians by white traders as early as 1750. Navajos linked hair ornaments to form decorative belts, impressing into the silver Mexican designs (circa 1885).

■ SMALLER TRIBES

The remaining Arizona tribes are much less well-known than those described earlier.

The **Kaibab Paiutes** and **Chemehuevis,** two descendants of the Southern Paiutes of the Great Basin, have very few members today. The Kaibab Paiutes inhabit the 188-square-mile Kaibab reservation on the Utah border. The Chemehuevis, who saw their farmlands become Lake Havasu when Parker Dam backed up the Colorado River in 1938, moved downstream to the Colorado River Reservation.

The **Mojaves,** a tribe of Yuman speakers, straddle the Colorado on the Fort Mojave Reservation, just south of Bullhead City.

Still farther downstream, near the Mexican border, are the related **Cocopahs** and **Quechan** (Yuman) people. Both small tribes depend heavily on agriculture.

The **Pascua Yaquis,** 19th-century refugees from Mexican persecution and considered direct descendents of the Toltecs, inhabit tiny reservations south of Tucson and in the incorporated Phoenix suburb of Guadalupe. The U.S. government officially designated them an American tribe only in 1978; since then they have adopted a tribal constitution and transcribed their language into written form. Though small—about 3,300 members in Arizona—and devoted to operating two casinos south of Tucson, they seem more determined than ever to preserve their heritage. The Pascua Yaqui Easter celebrations, held in Pascua Village in central Tucson, draw many Anglo onlookers.

Few if any **Zuni** Indians reside in Arizona, but the official state map shows a tiny Zuni Reservation a few miles northwest of St. Johns, near the New Mexico border. This 17-square-mile "reservation" is, in Zuni belief, the ceiling of heaven, and it was given to the tribe as part of a complicated land swap in 1985.

Once every four years, immediately after the summer solstice, the Zunis make a 45-mile pilgrimage from their New Mexico reservation to this Arizona annex. They follow the Zuni River to a spring where they bathe, then proceed on to Kolhuwalawa, a dry Arizona lakebed that spreads over their underground spiritual afterworld. There they conduct ceremonies that are believed to date back at least a thousand years.

There are no roads or travelers' facilities on this tiny reservation, but visitors can drive to Zuni Pueblo on the Zuni Reservation in New Mexico. This pueblo was one of Francisco Vásquez de Coronado's fabled Seven Cities of Cibola. *From St. Johns, head northeast on Route 61, continuing 10 miles into New Mexico.*

HISPANIC ARIZONA

One spring morning in 1981 a delegation of Mexican journalists arrived in Tucson bearing a startling gift to commemorate our international friendship: a 14-foot-high bronze equestrian statue of Pancho Villa, guerrilla general of the second Mexican Revolution. A controversial figure even in Mexico, Villa is best remembered north of the border for leading the only invasion of the United States mainland in the 20th century. On March 9, 1916, Villa and his band sacked the small town of Columbus, New Mexico, killing 19 American citizens. President Wilson, probably overreacting, sent 10,000 troops into Mexico to chase him. They never caught him, but the failed manhunt elevated Villa into a hero in the eyes of some Mexicans.

Back in Tucson, City Hall checked the diplomatic wind, concluded it would be bad form to reject the gift, and nervously installed Villa and his mount in a small but prominent downtown park. Tucsonans reacted as if it were the statue from hell. The mayor himself boycotted the dedication ceremony. Historians growled that Villa was hardly a revolutionary Robin Hood, but a bandit and terrorist who also massacred his own people on whim. One midnight commentator slipped into the park with a can of paint and left a yellow stripe cleaving Villa's back.

The statue stayed, and eventually the uproar subsided. Four years later, the *Tucson Citizen,* the evening newspaper, polled its readers on the best public sculpture in Tucson. The winner: Pancho Villa. Following that, however, a local anthropologist began an annual one-man protest, pounding 19 white crosses into the grass beside the statue on every anniversary of the Columbus raid. Several Tucsonans of Mexican ancestry now regularly turn out to protest his protest. A story in the *Arizona Daily Star* quoted one of them as saying it was proper to honor Villa in Tucson, because Tucson ought still to be a part of Mexico.

"This was all our land," she told a reporter. "Your people stole it."

■ SPANISH ROOTS

The first Spaniards entered Arizona around 1540, lured by fables of the Seven Cities of Cibola, legends redolent of riches. Francisco Vásquez de Coronado, the most persistent of the early explorers, probably led his party north along the San Pedro River and around the Mogollon Rim to the Hopi villages of the Colorado Plateau. There they learned that the rumored cities were made of sun-dried mud

Pancho Villa.

and not gold. Worse still, two Franciscan missionaries who stayed behind among the natives were murdered, beginning a pattern that would endure for more than a century between the persistent Franciscans and recalcitrant Hopis.

More than 300 miles to the south, Jesuit missionaries led by the tireless Italian-born Father Eusebio Kino temporarily found a warmer reception among the Pimas and Papagos (now called the Tohono O'odham). In the early 1690s Kino established missions at Guevavi, near modern Nogales, and at Bac, 8 miles south of today's downtown Tucson. These were the northernmost outposts in a chain of 22 missions he stretched across the deserts and grasslands of the Pimería Alta of New Spain, the Land of the Upper Pimans. Kino had no further successes in Arizona, but some 80 years after his death in 1711 the great church of San Xavier del Bac would be completed, and to Kino would go the credit of introducing both Christianity and European civilization to Arizona.

Kino is venerated today in Arizona and in the Mexican state of Sonora. Many Catholics on both sides of the border are campaigning for his canonization. He appears to have been a man of boundless endurance, great charisma, and principle. His contemporary, Capt. Juan Mateo Manje, left a profile of him that in the 20th century could as easily describe Gandhi:

> When [Kino] publicly reprimanded a sinner, he was choleric. But if anyone showed him personal disrespect, he controlled his temper to such an extent that he made it a habit to exalt whosoever maltreated him. . . . He was so austere that he never took wine except to celebrate Mass, nor had any other bed than the sweat blankets of his horse. . . . He never had more than two coarse shirts, because he gave everything as alms to the Indians.

There is a statue of Kino in modern Tucson, as well as a Kino Boulevard, Kino Hospital, Kino Learning Center, and Kino Termite & Pest Control. There is no controversy around him today—but possibly there should be. In the Pimería Alta of the 18th century, the growing Spanish presence was a dubious blessing. The Spaniards introduced cattle ranching and improved agriculture, but also exotic European diseases such as measles and smallpox.

And the more Spaniards that trickled in, the more the natives seemed to grasp the implications. In 1751 the normally peaceful Pimans rebelled, killing more than 100 Spanish ranchers, miners, and priests in an astonishing uprising that ranged from Caborca, near the Sonoran coast, to Bac, near present-day Tucson. The Spanish government responded with a show of force, beginning by building a presidio (fort) at Tubac, a few miles north of Guavavi. What followed was grimly

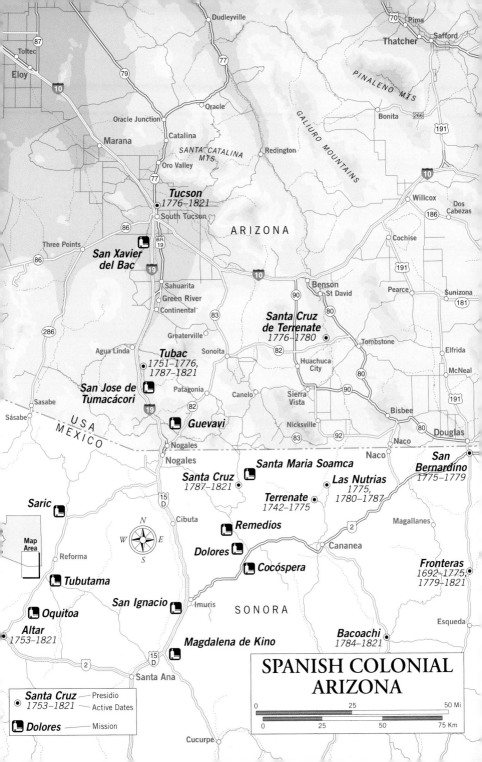

SPANISH COLONIAL ARIZONA

precursive of the U.S. Cavalry campaigns that would follow a century later. As Juan Bautista de Anza, the captain of Tubac, reported in 1767:

> When I took over my present command in 1760, my section of the frontier was faced with an uprising of over a thousand Papagos [Pimans]. After launching various campaigns to subjugate them, I attacked them personally . . . and took the lives of Ciprian, their captain, and nine others. All the rest then capitulated and renounced the inconstancy that has been plaguing the Piman nation.

The Apaches were still more "inconstant," staging hit-and-run raids and ambushes on Spaniards and Pimans alike. They never did come fully under Spanish control, despite long and bloody warfare. In another eerie foreshadowing of the American struggles, the Spaniards resorted to trickery. In 1776, Spain's new Minister of the Indies, José de Galvéz, ordered that Apaches who agreed to make peace were to be rewarded with "defective firearms, strong liquor, and other such commodities as would render them militarily and economically dependent."

In the Southwest, the Spanish Colonial era is sometimes romanticized as a time when simple Indians learned civilized ways under the tutelage of kindly priests, and manly dons ruled over their vast *rancheros* from tiled and arcaded haciendas that recalled the great mansions of baroque Iberia. This is such nonsense that it qualifies as hallucination. For all the respect showered on Kino, and the rich cultural heritage left in Arizona by its Hispanic past, the raw truth is that the 17th and 18th centuries were ugly times in what is now Arizona. The Spaniards, even those marching in alleged humility under the cross, were not welcomed guests, but invaders.

■ That "Mostly Mexican" Town

Sam Hughes, a Welsh immigrant who had been working as a baker in gold-rush California, clattered into the southern Arizona desert aboard a stage one spring day in 1856. Hughes had tuberculosis and was desperately trying to make it to Texas, where he hoped the warm, dry air might prolong his life. The driver, afraid that Hughes would cause him the annoyance of dying en route, kicked him out in Tucson. Hughes must have felt like he was being abandoned in Neverland: of the 500 or so people living in this isolated desert town, the driver assured him, five spoke English.

Tucson, along with the rest of Arizona, had flown the Mexican flag since 1810, the year Mexico began its violent break from Spain. Then in a dozen bloody years, from 1836 to 1848, the Texas Revolution and Mexican War severed Texas, California, Nevada, Utah, and most of Arizona and New Mexico from Mexico's upper body. In 1853, the United States, strong-arming its hemorrhaged rival, bought the southern third of Arizona and the last sliver of New Mexico for a fire-sale price of $10 million and incorporated them into a U.S. territory the following year. Despite all this, the heart and soul of Tucson—the largest and most important town in the transaction, called the Gadsden Purchase—would remain essentially Mexican until the first trains rumbled into town in 1880. Until then, nearly all of Tucson's cultural ties, communication, and trade clung to Mexico.

Gringos who stumbled through Tucson in those days were not enchanted. The most frequently quoted description of Tucson, which dogs the Chamber of Commerce even today, is that of journalist J. Ross Browne in 1864. Modern travel writing is pallid fluff compared with this:

> . . . [The traveler] emerges to find himself on the verge of the most wonderful scatteration of human habitations his eye ever beheld—a city of mud-boxes, dingy and dilapidated, cracked and baked into a composite of dust and filth; littered about with broken corrals, sheds, bake-ovens, carcasses of dead animals, and broken pottery; barren of verdure, parched, naked, and grimly desolate in the glare of a southern sun. Adobe walls without whitewash, inside or out, baked and dried Mexicans, sore-backed burros, coyote dogs, and terra-cotta children. . . .

It's easy to dismiss Browne's raving as gringo bigotry. Yet other early descriptions are not very different. The Tucson of the 1860s, though the largest settlement in Arizona, was severely isolated and still under periodic assault by Apaches; simple survival, not civic beautification, headed the priorities. It was not a charming place.

Things began to change with the arrival of entrepreneurial Anglos, such as Hughes, and professional-class Mexicans fleeing the political tumult to the south, such as Federico Ronstadt. We can sketch the cultural history of pre-1880 Tucson through these two men.

Hughes had no formal education but a deep reservoir of determination. In photos from throughout his long life—he recovered from tuberculosis and eventually

died in 1917, at the age of 88—his eyes, shadowed by bushy, steel-wool brows, glow with confidence and intensity. Such a man could improvise without a blueprint in Tucson; his career eventually comprised ranching, real estate, banking, and politics.

There was one problem for men such as Hughes: women. Four years after he was dumped in Tucson, Hughes married a Mexican girl named Atanacia Santa Cruz. Eyebrows surely arched skyward all over town: Sam was 32 years old, Atanacia 12.

But while the bride's age was unusual, the union across the ethnic line wasn't. Until the railroad came, there was a chronic dearth of Anglo females—in 1860, for instance, there were 132 Anglo males between the age of 15 and 39, but only six Anglo women. The list of Anglo men who took Mexican brides reads like a who's who of territorial Tucson and includes most of the successful merchants, ranchers, and politicians. Hiram Stevens, who became the territorial delegate to Congress, married Atanacia's sister, Petra. It is unimaginable that the local Mexican men weren't angered, yet oddly there is no record, not even an oral history, of trouble. One reason, suggested by the University of Arizona anthropologist James E. Officer, is that the spurned Mexican men of Tucson simply brought in a fresh supply of young women from Sonora. However, none of the pre-1880 Spanish-language newspapers of Tucson survive—and if there had been resentment against the gringos, that was one outlet where it might have been vented.

In fact, Anglos and Mexicans lived in remarkable harmony in territorial Tucson. They went into business together, fought Apaches together and partied together—more so than in any other old town in the Southwest. One reason was that the Hispanic *Tucsonenses* were not mainly peasants and laborers, as they were in early Los Angeles and Phoenix. Many came from ambitious, upper-class families in Sonora.

Ronstadt, an engineer's son, was one of them. He arrived in Tucson in 1882, when he was only 14, signed on as an apprentice wainwright with the firm of Dalton and Vásquez, and eventually built up a coachworks of his own that employed 65 people. The business enjoyed a fine regional reputation; Ronstadt supplied wagons and carriages to ranchers from Colorado to the Sonoran capital of Hermosillo. While Sam Hughes endowed schools, Ronstadt generated culture. He founded the *Club Filarmónico,* one of Tucson's earliest orchestras, and launched a family musical dynasty. His daughter, Luisa Ronstadt Espinel, went on to an

(from left) Hiram and Petra Stevens, Samuel and Atanacia Hughes.

Luisa Ronstadt Espinel, the great-aunt of Linda Ronstadt.

international career singing both opera and Spanish folk music. His great-great-granddaughter, who started her career singing in Tucson coffeehouses in the 1960s, is Linda Ronstadt. Her 1988 CD, *Canciones de Mi Padre,* helped create a new audience for mariachi music among non-Hispanics, and she often performs at the Tucson International Mariachi Conference.

The dominance of Mexican culture in Tucson began to shrivel the day the first train wheezed into town. We can still read the story today in the architecture of the two oldest neighborhoods, El Presidio and Barrio Histórico, which huddle immediately north and south, respectively, of downtown Tucson's modern high-rises.

The oldest houses, dating from the 1860s and 1870s, are pure Sonoran: simple, boxlike shapes with plastered adobe walls 2 feet thick, a wide entry hall called a *zaguán,* and ceilings fashioned of saguaro or ocotillo ribs. By 1880, some of these adobes began to sport porches and peaked roofs of corrugated steel—Anglo newcomers' stopgap efforts to make traditional Mexican architecture into something that felt more like home to them.

By the late 1880s, all but the poorest Anglos had abandoned the adobe neighborhoods and were building modest Victorian houses with yards and fences on tree-lined streets. In Florence, another essentially Sonoran town 70 miles north of Tucson, a newspaper editor in 1887 seemed to sum up Anglo attitudes—and not only about architecture—in an editorial: "The adobe does not make an attractive or a clean building, and Eastern people (that is, eastern U.S.) find it somewhat repulsive in appearance. . . . It is hoped that all new building of any pretensions will be built of brick and the unsightly adobe discarded."

With the discarding came discrimination. The University of Arizona ethnohistorian Thomas E. Sheridan studied courthouse records in Tucson from 1882 to 1889 and found that convicted murderers with Spanish surnames drew average sentences of 3.58 years; Anglos, one year. Mexicans convicted of grand larceny served 3.9 years; Anglos, 1.88. (The fact that stealing was punished more severely than killing, whatever one's ethnic persuasion, says something else about life in frontier Arizona.) As late as the 1950s, speaking Spanish in some Tucson schools was punished with a soapy rinse of the offender's mouth—a sad irony in a town that owed its founding and first hundred years to Spanish-speaking people.

Yet after the railroad and even to the present, prominent Hispanic businesspeople, journalists, and artists retained their status; Anglos and Hispanics continued to marry each other; and Tucson avoided the worst of the ethnic segregation that plagued so many other cities.

Those early days had set the stage. As James Officer once put it, "How were you going to tell a Ronstadt that his kid can't go to your school?"

■ HISPANIC ARIZONA TODAY

Every year on September 16, a crowd gathers at sunset on the still-hot concrete of the Phoenix Civic Plaza. *Ballet folklórico* dancers swirl across a stage; the aroma of *carne asada,* flame-broiled beef, drifts through the air; and here and there Mexican flags flutter in celebration. The party continues well into the night, until all at once the merriment abates and a speaker takes the stage. In Spanish, he recites the *Grito de Dolores,* that spine-prickling call to arms from a parish priest on September 16, 1810, that launched the Mexican Revolution: "My children, a new dispensation comes to us this day. Are you ready to receive it? Will you be free?" As he finishes, fireworks streak through the Phoenix sky, the national anthems of Mexico and the United States swell, and the revelers shout *¡Viva México!* The celebration of *el dieciseis de septiembre,* Mexico's independence day, is as colorful, noisy, and passionate in Arizona as anywhere in Mexico.

Hispanics make up about 20 percent of Arizona's population, and their heritage is celebrated with pride. Not everyone embraces the troubling Pancho Villa, but certain traditions, such as the *quinceañera,* seem to be observed more faithfully now than ever. The *quinceañera* is a special Mass to bless a girl turning 15, followed by an elaborate coming-out party. In Phoenix, some priests have started to complain that their churches' schedules are being overrun with *quinceañeras.*

Some of the more internal aspects of Hispanic culture also remain firmly rooted—for one, the tradition of closely entwined, extended families. There is no shortage of Hispanic yuppies in Phoenix and Tucson, but it is still a little unusual even for well-educated, professional young Hispanics to bounce from city to city to pump up their careers. In Tucson, a city where Anglos joke that anyone who's been around at least 10 years qualifies as a native, fifth- and sixth-generation Hispanic natives are not uncommon.

Anglos like to immerse themselves in the more colorful, accessible aspects of Hispanic culture; it is a way of loosening the jacket of a stiffer Puritan heritage. Mexican food is a virtual Arizona religion. Once a year, when the Phoenix weekly *New Times* and the *Tucson Weekly* poll their readers, they don't even bother to ask which is the best local Mexican restaurant—the question seems too epic to face. Instead they survey the best fajitas, best salsa, best enchilada, even the best beans.

Tucson's former mayor, Lewis C. Murphy, officially trumpeted the city as the "Mexican Food Capital of the World," apparently not pausing to consider how such a proclamation might play to the south. For years, Phoenix, Tucson, El Paso, and Santa Fe sent their top chefs to battle in an intercity Mexican Food Cookoff. One year, when Santa Fe won, irritated Arizonans wrote letters to their editors complaining, in all seriousness, that the godless New Mexicans had used revisionist ingredients such as crab meat in their chiles rellenos.

But when Arizona joined the Official English movement in 1988, with a majority of voters approving a law that required all government and legal business to be conducted in English, Hispanics generally saw it as an effort to keep their culture in its place—that is, under the Anglo heel. If Arizona is good because it is multicultural, they wondered, why isn't it good that it is multilingual?

In practice, the law had hardly any effect, and two years later it was found unconstitutional and thrown out by the courts—only to be resurrected in 2000 as Proposition 203, which eliminated most bilingual classes. The touted educational benefits remain to be proven. Meanwhile, a little more acrimony is left hanging in the air, and a few more Arizonans of Spanish lineage seem willing to say out loud what had been held locked in their hearts before: this, after all, had been their land.

Exploring Hispanic Culture *map page 129*

Most of the "Spanish" architecture the visitor sees in Arizona is the product of Anglo architects unearthing and romanticizing the state's past. The presidio of Tubac can still be visited, however (see "Arizona Towns" chapter), and two Spanish missions survive south of Tucson.

San Xavier del Bac

One of the most beautiful examples of Spanish Moorish architecture in the New World, the graceful San Xavier del Bac mission church, still serves the community for which it was built: the Tohono O'odham Indians. Come to see the restored folk art murals and the prone wooden figure of St. Francis, whose robes have been pinned with *milagros* (literally, "miracles") by those who pray to him for cures. *From Tucson, follow I-10 east to I-19 south, and then take Exit 92 to the Mission; 520-294-2624.*

Experts began restoring the interior of San Xavier del Bac south of Tucson in 1990—a project that consumed several years and a million dollars.

MISSION SAN CAYETANO DE TUMACÁCORI

Mission San Cayetano de Tumacácori, now part of San José de Tumacácori National Historical Park, was founded by Father Kino on the site of a Tohono O'odham village on the Santa Cruz River at the end of the 17th century. But the ruined, red-hued church you see today was built by Franciscan priests from 1800 to 1822 and abandoned in 1848. It's not as grand as San Xavier, but it has a brooding beauty, partly created by its isolated setting. The visitors center has an excellent collection of Spanish Colonial artifacts, and the gardens include a descendent of one of the fig trees transported to Tumacácori by Father Kino. *I-19, Exit 29, 45 miles south of Tucson; 520-398-2341.*

BARRIO HISTÓRICO

Although some gentrification has occurred in Tucson's Barrio Histórico, a stroll along Meyer or Convent Street will offer a remarkably intact impression of pre-1880 Hispanic Tucson; just mentally blot out the power lines and parked cars.

Every Arizona town and city that has a substantial Mexican-American population also has public fiestas on both September 16 and *cinco de mayo* (May 5), the latter celebrating Mexico's rout of the French occupation force at Puebla in 1862. These festivals are wonderful introductions both to Hispanic culture and Mexican history.

The precise origin of mariachi music is still disputed. The modern form, which draws on African, European, and indigenous Mexican traditions, dates from the 19th century and the Mexican state of Jalisco (which also gave the world tequila). Today the mariachi band is a virtual national emblem of Mexico, and the music has incorporated influences from European classicism to American pop and country. A good mariachi band knows a thousand songs, and can stamp its personal imprint on anything from one of Brahms' Hungarian Dances to that famous love anthem to Guadalajara, "*Ay, Jalisco no te rajes.*" The best mariachi bands in the Americas can be heard annually at the Tucson International Mariachi Conference, held each April.

VEINTE DE AGOSTO PARK

Finally, to contemplate the checkered history of Mexican–U.S. relations, park at the fringe of downtown Tucson and walk to Veinte de Agosto Park at Church and Broadway: there, atop a prancing horse, is that concomitant hero and villain, Francisco "Pancho" Villa.

The dome crowning San Xavier's east tower was never completed; the best theory is that the builders simply ran out of money.

MAKING ARIZONA

Charles Debrille Poston liked to call himself the "Father of Arizona." Spiritually, if not literally, he appears to have been exactly that. Were he alive today, however, he would find that the grown-up state little resembles the strange community he created at the old Spanish presidio of Tubac.

Poston was toiling as an obscure law clerk in gold-rush California when he read about the Gadsden Purchase in 1853. He must have sniffed opportunity, because he quickly organized a party of fellow adventurers and set out for the silver-veined hills of southern Arizona. His company moved into the ghost fort of Tubac, began rebuilding it, and commenced lucrative mining operations in the Santa Rita Mountains nearby. Before long, Mexican miners and unmarried women drifted up from Mexico, and Poston installed himself as the town's *alcalde*. The Spanish word literally translates as "mayor," but Poston was more like a potentate. He ran the mines, performed marriages and granted divorces, baptized children, and dispensed justice. Still, he appears to have been no dictator, but a Utopian and a precursor of modern libertarians.

"We had no law but love and no occupation but labor," Poston wrote, "no government, no taxes, no public debt, no politics. It was a community in a perfect state of nature."

This was true in still other ways, in Poston's mind. All the women in Tubac had come from Sonora, which, Poston wrote, "has always been famous for the beauty and gracefulness of its señoritas . . . . They are exceedingly dainty in their under-clothing, wear the finest linen when they can afford it, and spend half their lives over the washing machine."

If the barest tint of condescension seems to color Poston's admiration, well, he was not to be the last Anglo pioneer who held such contradictions. In any event, his utopia was short-lived. In 1861 Apaches reduced Tubac to rubble, and Poston fled for his life, later observing bitterly that the "Government of the United States abandoned the first settlers of Arizona to the merciless Apaches."

Still, Poston never ceased to dream—another quirk of character that would appear in so many pioneers and developers that followed him. He successfully lobbied Washington in 1863 to have Arizona separated from the Territory of New Mexico. He founded serious historical societies in Tucson and Phoenix. He proposed irrigation projects. Then he made a pilgrimage to Asia and became a Zoroastrian, returned to Arizona, and tried in vain to establish a sun-worshiping sect in the land he loved. He died impoverished in Phoenix in 1902.

Not long after Poston's experiment at Tubac, larger waves of Anglo settlers came rolling in. They were mostly of three types: cattle ranchers, agrarian Mormons spilling down from Utah, and miners. Although few of these had such exotic ideas as Poston's, they were, like him, following their dreams and questing in some form for personal freedom. They all faced the same headaches: a shortage of water, and a surplus of Apaches.

■ THE APACHE WARS, 1871–86

No ethnic tribe on the planet has bounced so far and so often between utter vilification and romantic glorification as the Apaches. According to the 1950s novels of James Warner Bellah, they were "blood-drunk and beast-hot . . . fetid-breathed and shrieking . . . lecherous and without honor or mercy . . . the Apaches hate life and they are the enemy of all mankind." A character in Elliott Arnold's 1979 novel, *Blood Brother,* waxes nostalgic about the Apaches, saying that "there is no private

Geronimo (right) and his warriors, depicted in this 1886 photograph, were as well armed as the U.S. Army, and they knew the land much better.

ARIZONA HISTORY TIME LINE

300 B.C. Hohokam begin irrigating land to grow corn in the Gila River Valley.

200 B.C. The Mogollon become the first Southwestern culture to make pottery.

A.D. 200 After hunting and gathering on the Colorado Plateau for several centuries, the ancestral Puebloans begin farming.

1094 Last volcanic eruption in Arizona, at Sunset Crater.

1539 Friar Marcos de Niza and freed African slave Estevanico cross southeastern Arizona, where they note "stone cities" (pueblos) and claim territory for Spain.

1540 Drawn by fables of the Seven Cities of Cibola, Spanish adventurers arrive in Arizona under the leadership of Francisco Vásquez de Coronado.

1604 Juan de Oñate travels west from the Rio Grande across Arizona with Capt. Marcos Farfan, and later lays claim to parts of Arizona, Colorado, Nevada, New Mexico, Texas, Oklahoma, and Kansas for the Spanish crown—and for himself.

1629 Franciscans begin establishing missions among Hopi villages in northeastern Arizona, but their conversions anger many Hopi shamans.

1680 The Pueblo Revolt wipes out many Franciscan missions in Arizona, New Mexico, and western Texas, discouraging Spanish settlement in the region.

1687 Eusebio Francisco Kino, an Italian Jesuit educated in Austria, arrives in what is today the Southwest and northern Mexico. During the next 24 years the priest establishes 22 missions, travels 75,000 miles within Arizona, and teaches farming and ranching techniques to Native Americans.

1751 Rivalry between priests and Indian leaders and anger at the Spanish for taking their most fertile land prompt Pima and Papago (Tohono O'odham) Indians to revolt. Europeans are completely driven out of Arizona for a year.

1752 After blaming Jesuit missionaries for Indian conflicts, Spanish return to Arizona and establish a presidio at Tubac.

1767 Spain's King Charles III expels the powerful Society of Jesus from the Americas. All over Arizona Territory, Jesuits are arrested and expelled.

1774 Franciscan missionary Francisco Tomas Garces embarks on a series of westward journeys from mission at Tubac. He names the Colorado River, becomes the first white man to enter the Grand Canyon from the west, and on July 4, 1776, notes in his journal several meetings with Hopi Indians.

1821 Mexico throws off Spanish rule, takes control of Arizona and other southwestern territories.

1836–48 Following the Texas Revolution and the Mexican War, most of Arizona becomes part of the United States.

1853 James Gadsden, the U.S. ambassador to Mexico, facilitates his country's purchase of the southern third of Arizona.

1857 Jack Snively finds gold in the Gila River and a three-year gold rush ensues.

1869 John Wesley Powell leads first American expedition through Grand Canyon.

1871 Camp Grant Massacre: A posse of Anglos, Mexicans, and Papagos kills between 85 and 100 Apaches, mostly women and children.

1877 Ed Schieffelin finds silver in hostile Apache land and wryly names his stake "Tombstone" after the U.S. Cavalry predicts the Indians will kill him.

1878 The great "pathfinder" John C. Frémont is appointed territorial governor.

1880 First issue of popular newspaper the *Tombstone Epitaph* is printed—in a tent.

1880 Large-scale copper mining begins in Bisbee. It continues until 1975.

1881 Gunfight at O.K. Corral in Tombstone between the Hollidays, Earps, Clantons, and McLowrys. Three people die in 30 seconds of gunfire.

1889 Fred Harvey secures the right to operate all restaurants and hotels on the Atchison, Topeka, and Santa Fe railroad line west of the Missouri River. His upgraded facilities and advertising campaigns generate new tourist interest in Arizona.

1901 Rail link to the Grand Canyon established.

1906–11 Apache Trail created to haul construction materials to the Salt River's Theodore Roosevelt Dam—the first major desert irrigation project in modern times.

1912 Arizona, the last of the 48 contiguous states, is admitted to the Union on February 14—prompting the occasional reference to the Valentine's Day State.

1924 First Arizona Indian votes under provision of Congressional act granting citizenship to non-reservation Indians.

1930 President Coolidge dedicates the Coolidge Dam, the highest multiple-dome dam.

1930 Flagstaff's Lowell Observatory announces discovery of the planet Pluto.

Percival Lowell in 1905.

1948 Arizona Supreme Court allows reservation Indians to vote in primaries—after 20 years of being disqualified from voting as "wards of the state."

1964 Arizona's longtime Republican politician Barry Goldwater is defeated by Lyndon Baines Johnson in presidential election.

1981 Sandra Day O'Connor, an Arizona judge, becomes the first woman selected to serve on the U.S. Supreme Court.

1989 Rail link to the Grand Canyon reestablished.

1992 After a threatened tourist boycott, voters make Arizona the second-to-last state to adopt Martin Luther King Day as a state holiday (the federal holiday was established in 1986).

1997 Fife Symington is convicted of pension fund fraud and resigns as governor.

2000–01 President Bill Clinton establishes four national monuments in Arizona.

2002 Arizonans pass Proposition 202, which requires the governor to enter into gaming contracts with 17 of the 21 Arizona tribes.

hoarding, no cheating. Whatever they have is divided equally. . . . There's no caste system, and no aristocrats and no commoners. . . . I wonder by what standards we have arrogated to ourselves the right to call Indians savages?"

Sentiments about the tribe may vary, but there is universal agreement about the 19th-century Apaches: they were incredible individual fighters. "There were 23 different Apache groups in Arizona, and there was no communication among them," says historian David T. Faust, curator of the Fort Lowell Park Museum in Tucson. "Everybody was fighting his own war, essentially. If they had waged a coordinated war, they probably would have been able to hold out into the 20th century."

In purely objective terms, the Apaches were undeniably aggressors. When they emigrated to the Southwest, probably in the 16th century, they found much of the territory already occupied by agrarian tribes, such as the Hopis and Pimas. The Apaches raided their neighbors when necessary for survival, but their bloody, vengeance-driven war came only after the Spaniards and Anglos arrived.

The Camp Grant Massacre set the savage tone for the war with Anglo Arizona. In April of 1871, a motley posse of Anglos, Mexican-Americans, and Papagos organized in Tucson and rode the 60 miles northeast to Camp Grant, where a cluster of Aravaipa Apaches were living under an informal treaty with the U.S. Army. The Tucsonans, led by former mayor William S. Oury, suspected the Aravaipas of the incessant hit-and-run raids plaguing southern Arizona ranchers and supply wagons—which may indeed have been an accurate suspicion. But when the posse attacked at dawn on April 30, they found hardly any Apache men in the camp; most were out hunting. No matter: the raiders had come to exterminate Apaches. They killed between 85 and 100 people, most of them women and children.

"The attack was so swift and fierce," Oury later boasted, "that within half an hour the whole work was ended and not an adult Indian left to tell the tale."

The massacre focused national attention on the "Indian problem" in Arizona, although the consequences hardly did the Apaches any good. The raiders were tried for murder in Tucson and acquitted. Then President Ulysses S. Grant launched a carrot-and-bayonet effort to coax the Apaches into peace treaties and reservations—or to wage full-scale war against them if they refused. Gen. George Crook, a brilliant military strategist who thoroughly understood his enemy, directed the campaign of 1872–73 and came close to quelling the "problem" in those two years.

A network of 16 army forts, laced through Arizona, provided a base for Crook's troops. The Apaches never attacked the forts directly—that would have been suicidal—but ambushed the troops in small scouting parties well away from the forts. The army employed friendly or "tame" Apaches as scouts to lead them through unfamiliar terrain in pursuit of the enemy. Neither side practiced much charity. If the Apaches captured a soldier alive, they would execute him either by lashing him to a convenient tree or cactus and perforating his torso with arrows, or by suspending him head down over a slow fire. Crook ordered his troops to make "every effort to avoid the killing of women and children," but women and children sometimes accompanied the warriors into the caves or canyons from which the Apaches would stage a last-ditch defense—and then the army bullets were hardly selective.

Nor did the atrocities end with surrender. In 1873, the Verde Valley Apaches and Yavapais surrendered to Crook at Fort Verde. The U.S. government promised them an 800-square-mile reservation stretching 10 miles on either side of the river for a distance of 40 miles. This land would be theirs, they were promised, "for as long as the rivers run, the grass grows, and the hills endure." But this temperate, fertile valley was worth more to territorial settlers than the honor of keeping the promise. After only two years, 1,476 Indians were literally herded 180 miles southeast to the arid San Carlos Reservation. As described by Yavapai scout Rim-Ma-Ke-Na, in an unpublished history of the Yavapai-Apache tribes:

> They drive them like cattles [sic], they have no pity. Some have to be
> left and die. Those that can't go any farther. Even when it's rainy day
> and floody they have to drive them in the flood. And many are
> drowned. And that was one of the saddest thing that I ever saw.

Even with most of the Apaches installed on reservations, sporadic fighting and raiding erupted. The Chiricahua Apaches, led by Geronimo, held out in the mountains of southeastern Arizona until they also surrendered to Crook in 1886. They were then shipped by train to a prison camp in Florida.

Geronimo himself provided a pathetic epilogue to the Apache wars in the years following his detention. He reinvented himself as an exotic celebrity, making the rounds of fairs and conventions, selling autographs, buttons off his clothes, and other trinkets to amuse white Americans. A photo taken at the St. Louis World's Fair in 1904 shows him wearing an ill-fitting wool coat and short hair, gazing stoically yet vacantly. He is selling bows and arrows—a caricature Indian now, lurching gracelessly between two worlds. In that picture he appears as a prescient metaphor for much that would happen to Native Americans in the 20th century.

In the 1980s an Apache man set up shop in a tipi on the western outskirts of Tucson, charging people a dollar each to take his picture. He claimed to be Geronimo's grandson.

■ Grazing, Farming, and Mining

The cattlemen who established their herds in the high desert grasslands of the southeast and the temperate meadows of north-central Arizona contributed an enduring romance to the frontier. They also created its first modern environmental disaster: not many of those grasslands survived. In 1870, an estimated 5,000 cattle grazed Arizona; by 1891 there were 1.5 million. The fragile land could not support them. In 1892 and 1893 a devastating drought occurred. The range was already overgrazed and overtrampled, and between 50 and 75 percent of the animals died. When the rains finally returned, thousands of square miles, gnawed bare by the starving cows, were exposed to erosion. Raw desert replaced many of the grasslands, and ranching diminished.

The Mormons proved to be better custodians of the land, but they weren't unanimously welcomed. Expeditions into Arizona had begun as early as 1846, when the Mormon Battalion, a force of 500 pseudo-military volunteers under the command of Capt. Philip St. George Cooke, punched a wagon trail through the uncharted land to California. This was no missionary or colonialist adventure; Cooke saw no good use for Arizona. It was, he wrote, ". . . a wilderness where nothing but savages and wild beasts are found, or deserts where, for lack of water, there is no living creature."

This wilderness proved compelling to later Mormons, who in the 1870s began spilling down from Utah. They came for three reasons: to colonize new farmlands, to try to convert Indians—specifically the Hopis—and to find refuges isolated enough to discourage the U.S. government from harassing the polygamists among them. They founded settlements along the Little Colorado River in east-central Arizona, where they were harassed instead by floods, and established several more communities in the desert farther south, including Lehi (now the Phoenix suburb of Mesa), Thatcher, and St. David.

Despite unforgiving and unfamiliar environmental conditions, the Mormons became successful farmers. A correspondent of the *Prescott Miner,* writing in 1878, commented that "The work done by these people is simply astounding," and noted

RANCH CHILD

Sandra Day O'Connor, the first female justice of the U.S. Supreme Court, grew up on the Lazy B Ranch, established by her grandfather in the late 1800s along the Arizona–New Mexico border. In Lazy B, *which she wrote with her brother, H. Alan Day, she reflects on life at the ranch.*

A milestone for a ranch child is the first time the child can get a foot in the stirrup without help. Another is being old enough to ride alone beyond the familiar places around the headquarters and then find your way back home again. And still another is driving a motor vehicle. The biggest milestone is being able to provide useful help on a cattle drive or a roundup—solving problems rather than causing them.

As soon as we were old enough to ride, we would ask to go out with the cowboys to the different areas of the ranch, through the cactus and mesquite and over the rocky hills, to gather the cattle in a particular area for sorting, branding, cutting out those to be sold, and then herding them to a holding pasture to await shipment. In time each of us learned enough to become useful. . . . On days when we rode on roundups we were happy if we could stop for three drinks of water during the long day, and ecstatic if we could also have lunch somewhere along the way. Sometimes there was no time for either a drink of water or lunch. The job had to be done while there was daylight to see what we were doing.

—Sandra Day O'Connor and H. Alan Day, *Lazy B,* 2002

that the "alacrity and vim with which they go at it is decidedly in favor of co-operation or communism." Still, polygamy was as unwelcome in Arizona as it was elsewhere. The Territorial Legislature of 1885 disenfranchised polygamists, and Mormon skirmishes with gentile neighbors—ranchers, mainly—were not uncommon. The church ended sanctioned polygamy in 1890, although a handful of wild-cat fundamentalists continue the practice in deepest northern Arizona even today. The more significant Mormon legacy in Arizona, however, is this: the public schools in virtually every community they established remain among the state's best.

Mining powered a third boom, reshaping the state's physical and political landscape far more profoundly than had anything else. Offering the lure of quick and dramatic wealth, the treasure buried in Arizona's mountains attracted a different breed of dreamer than did the range or farmlands.

Arizona's gold rush, a short-lived phenomenon, began in 1857, when an itinerant Texan named Jack Snively swished a pan through the Gila River and saw some residue glinting in the desert sun. Gila City, the town hastily assembled on the site, was a metaphor for the rush itself. After a year it had a teeming population of 1,200 prospectors, gamblers, prostitutes, and assorted other merchants. In another two years the gold began to dwindle. In 1862 the Gila River, as if in moral outrage, went on a rampage and wiped out what was left of the town. When the journalist J. Ross Browne passed through in 1864, he noted with finely tuned sarcasm that "the promising Metropolis of Arizona consisted of three chimneys and a coyote." Much the same fate befell other mining camps.

The silver boom followed gold, and it was not much more durable. The most famous lode was discovered in 1877 by a wandering miner named Ed Schieffelin, who had traveled with a U.S. Cavalry troop from California to establish Arizona's new Fort Huachuca. This was hostile land, controlled by the Chiricahua Apaches. At first, Schieffelin tried to do his prospecting in the company of scouting parties

The town of Bisbee as it looks today.

dispatched from the fort, but he soon realized he would have to follow his own instincts in search of ore. As he left the safety of the fort alone, someone warned him, "All you'll ever find out there will be your tombstone."

Schieffelin lived to have the last laugh, and it was one energized by considerable wealth. He indeed found silver ore, and wryly named his first stake "Tombstone." In 10 years, the hills around the boomtown that adopted that name yielded $19 million worth of silver. But in 1886, the mines flooded and even Tombstone—the largest town in the territory and truly a metropolis—collapsed into the role of a historical artifact.

It was copper that finally etched Arizona onto the global mineralogical map. The copper boom also forged a permanent change in Arizona's character, one that persists today: copper transformed the territory from a frontier into an economic colony, a place largely owned and controlled by outsiders.

Copper mining had little in common with the small-scale, nickel-and-dime operations of men like Poston and Schieffelin. Between 20 and 100 pounds of ore have to be processed to yield a pound of copper, and a mine has to produce hundreds of tons of copper a day to pay off. This requires gigantic investments in land, equipment, personnel, and science. Because no individual in Arizona Territory had such deep pockets, the boom was financed by corporations from back East. And while they brought considerable prosperity to Arizona, they also extracted a painful social price.

Jerome, Clifton, Globe, Bisbee—these copper-mining hubs of late-19th-century Arizona appear quaint today, with their neighborhoods of pint-size Victorian homes snaking up and down precipitous hillsides and gulches. In the middle of a Bisbee intersection stands a socialist realist–style copper statue of a miner stripped to the waist, bristling with muscle and wearing an expression of world-dominating confidence. The inscription reads: "Dedicated to those virile men—the copper miners." Viewing artifacts such as these from the safe distance of the early 21st century, it is easy to romanticize the copper boom. In truth, mining was an ugly business.

The miners worked in stopes, or pits, hundreds of feet underground, drilling holes for dynamite and blasting the ore into rubble to be carted to the surface.

Copper miners below Bisbee, ca. 1910.

There might be water up to their ankles, the temperature would be well over 100 degrees Fahrenheit, and the humid air would be fouled by the stench of carbon dioxide and human excrement. Until well into the 20th century, safety records were not encouraging; in 1913, according to Phelps Dodge records, a laborer in the Copper Queen operation at Bisbee could expect to have a "lost-time" accident once every 474 shifts. There were essentially two ways to die: quickly, in fires or cave-ins or untimely explosions; or slowly, from silicosis caused by breathing the fine quartz dust produced by the drilling. An article in the *Tombstone Epitaph,* written in the florid style of the era, describes in graphic terms the death of one Copper Queen smelter worker:

> Joe Bailey of Bisbee is dead. . . . While pursuing his daily vocation, unmindful that death lurked nigh, a pot containing one ton of molten slag came detached from the crane that was conveying it, and fell to the ground below, a distance of 12 or 15 feet, lighting squarely upon the man. There were no cries of pain, no shrieks of anguish, no pleading for mercy or assistance. The spirit of Joe Bailey had taken its flight.

Aboveground, the miners and their families (in the unusual event that a miner had one) lived in company towns built and owned by the mine operators. On the surface the companies seemed benevolently paternalistic; they provided baseball fields, hospitals, schools, housing at below-market rent, and plenty of credit. A retired Phelps Dodge geologist in Bisbee recalled that the company even gave $50 "Christmas bonuses" to all the ministers in town. But all of this kindness was calculated to ensure obedience to the company. "They used the carrot more than the stick," said mining historian James W. Byrkit, "but the fear of losing these things was always present in the background."

The event that illustrates the political muscle that the mine companies came to have was the bizarre Bisbee Deportation of 1917. To this day it remains controversial in Bisbee; some longtime residents don't even like outsiders asking questions about it. On June 27, 1917, a radical labor union—the Industrial Workers of the World (IWW), or "Wobblies"—called a strike. Although fewer than 400 miners were card-carrying Wobblies, about half of Bisbee's 4,700 workers walked out. The mine's management responded with a public relations blitz painting the IWW as German sympathizers sabotaging the Allies' wartime copper supplies.

The Copper Queen store and staff in Bisbee, ca. 1890.

At 6:30 on July 17, Cochise County Sheriff Harry Wheeler and a colossal posse of 2,000 "loyal Americans" fanned through Bisbee and arrested an equal number of strikers in their homes. The vigilantes marched the captives under armed guard 2 miles to the suburb of Warren. Those who agreed to return to work were freed; the other 1,186 were crammed into 23 boxcars and railroaded to a camp at Columbus, New Mexico. Few ever returned to Bisbee, and union power in Arizona was crushed.

Thus the script for offstage control of Arizona was forged in copper. As a territory and then an adolescent state after 1912, Arizona never found the means to sort out its own destiny. This remains the story today. Most of Arizona's banks are owned out of state. Many of its most ambitious development projects are planned and financed out of state. This is the result of unchained growth: there is money waiting to be made here. The story of Phoenix explains how.

MINING ARIZONA'S MINERAL PAST

The price of precious metals may have bottomed out, but interest in their byproducts, along with other subterranean treasures such as fossils, has only increased over the years. Arizona is a mother lode for everyone from rockhounds, jewelers, and meteorite dealers to New Agers seeking good crystal vibes and folks who just like pretty glittery stuff. The Arizona Mining and Mineral Museum (see below) is a good central resource; those keen on shifting dirt around can contact the Phoenix office of the Bureau of Land Management (602-417-9200) for its brochure, *Rockhounding in Arizona.*

MINE TOURS

In addition to those listed here, several defunct mines such as the Vulture Mine, near Wickenburg, can be explored via a self-guided tour. The Wickenburg Chamber of Commerce (928-684-5479) has maps. It is dangerous to poke around the many abandoned mines that haven't been safety-prepped for visitors.

On-hour tours of the still-operational Mission copper mine, conducted by the **Asarco Mineral Discovery Center,** provide a glimpse into the strip-mining process. The multilevel tailings look like the ruins of an ancient Mayan city, and some of the tires on the modern dirt-movers measure as high as 13 feet—taller than an SUV. *1421 West Pima Mine Road, 15 miles south of Tucson (I-19, Exit 80); 520-625-7513.*

On the **Copper Queen** tour, which is led by former miners, visitors don yellow slickers and hard hats to ride into a mineshaft. The claustrophobic might consider instead the guided tour around the perimeter of the Lavender Pit, a gaping open-pit mine (you can also view it for free from an overlook at the intersection of U.S. 80 and Route 92). *478 North Dart Road, Bisbee; 520-432-2071.*

Gold Road is way off the beaten path, but if you're visiting the nearby ghost town of Oatman, this gives you something else to do besides feeding semi-wild burros. Explorations of the mine, which operated from 1900 to 1998 (when the price of gold dropped too low to make it profitable), range from the one-hour standard tour to the four-hour extreme tour, which goes below ground in a mining car. *Route 66, 2 miles east of Oatman, western Arizona; 928-768-1600.*

MINERAL AND MINING MUSEUMS

Several other museums besides those listed here, especially the Museum of Northern Arizona in Flagstaff (see page 234) and the Stephen House Congdon Earth Sciences Center at the Arizona–Sonora Desert Museum in Tucson (see page 212), have excellent mineral-related exhibits.

Gem, mineral, bead, treasure-hunting, and prospecting geeks in Phoenix gather at the **Arizona Mining and Mineral Museum,** which exhibits more than 3,000 minerals. Highlights include fluorescent stones, lapidary art displays, and samples such as malachite and chrysocolla, from copper mines. It's worth a visit just to see the rocks that look like food. *1502 West Washington Street, Phoenix; 602-255-3795.*

The focus at the **Robert S. Dietz Museum of Geology** is more on fossils (a nest of dinosaur eggs, a Triceratops skull) than on minerals, but a 6-foot-high geode and some petrified wood flank the entryway of this small Arizona State University museum. Also here are a Foucault pendulum and a working seismograph. *Physical Sciences Complex, F Wing (off University Drive, near Palm Walk), Tempe; 480-965-7065.*

Among the interesting displays at the rather disheveled **Superstition Mountain–Lost Dutchman Museum,** in the Superstition Mountains, are 23 maps of the Lost Dutchman mine (drawn, of course, by people who never found it). Mining artifacts from the town of Goldfield are also exhibited. *Goldfield Ghost Town, 4 miles northeast of Apache Junction on the Apache Trail (Route 88); 480-983-4888.*

The **University of Arizona Mineral Museum,** part of the popular Flandrau Science Center, has a superb collection of gems and minerals, including 15,000 cataloged specimens and 6,000 mounted displays. An exhibition of meteorites from far-flung locales is especially popular, and many people come to the museum bearing rocks from their backyards, hoping the fragments will be identified as space debris. *University Boulevard and Cherry Avenue, Tucson; 520-621-4227.*

The small **Mining & Historical Museum,** a Smithsonian Institution affiliate housed in the century-old former headquarters of the Copper Queen Consolidated Mining Company, devotes space to copper mining's gem and mineral byproducts and its impact on Bisbee. *5 Copper Queen Plaza, Bisbee; 520-432-7071.*

GEM AND MINERAL SHOWS

Hardly a month goes by when a gem and mineral show isn't held somewhere in the state—the Web site of the Arizona Department of Mines and Mineral Resources, www.admmr.state.az.us, lists them all—but two stand out for their size and success.

In January and February, nearly a million people converge on the high-desert town of Quartzite for the **Pow-Wow Rock, Gem & Mineral Show,** eight sprawling expositions, one of the largest of which is the Tyson Wells Sell-A-Rama. In addition to hobbyists, these informal tents and storefronts attract jet-setting gem and fossil dealers, who nab bargains and then move on to the mineral feeding frenzy in Tucson. *Quartzite Chamber of Commerce, 495 Main Event Lane; 928-927-5600.*

Tucson's reputation as a major rock mecca began in 1954, when the Tucson Gem & Mineral Society put on a show in a grade school auditorium. The **Tucson Gem & Mineral Society Show,** which has developed into the city's largest annual event, is held these days at the Tucson Convention Center for four days in mid-February and always features a glitzy centerpiece: perhaps rare minerals from South America or Fabergé eggs from Russia.

But much of the megabucks action—in which everything from moon rocks to emeralds changes hands—takes place at the informal shows that have cropped up over the years. There are now several dozen of them, held in hotel rooms, board-rooms, and tents, mostly in the downtown area. During the first two weeks in February, it's tough to get lodgings (or restaurant tables) anywhere in Tucson. *Tucson Gem & Mineral Society Show, 520-322-5773 (for information about other Tucson-area shows call 520-624-1817).*

—Edie Jarolim

The shacks of mineworkers form a mountainside terrace above the United Verde Mine in Jerome.

■ ARIZONA POLITICS

Many an outsider who ventures to write about Arizona politics is visited by a ghostly spasm that causes the fingers to type the words ". . . frontier mentality . . ." Normally they appear not far from the beginning of the commentary, and if the writer is in good form, the reader will be treated to supporting anecdotage: Free-for-all gun laws that have allowed 50,000 Arizonans (so far) to sign up for permits to carry concealed weapons; a state legislature that became notorious for rejecting the Martin Luther King holiday (finally established by popular vote in 1992); and two governors—a car dealer and a developer—forced from office for their misdeeds in the 1980s and 1990s.

Part of the explanation is simply that knaves and crackpots sometimes stumble into public service here, as they do in every other state. But there's also something deeper. Arizonans are fundamentally ornery, willing to defy conventional wisdom and spurn political correctness, and have a tenacious distrust of governing bodies and a ready resolve to take matters into their own hands.

More recent events, however, have flown in the face of Arizona's reputation for being "un-P.C." In 1998, Arizonans elected women to the state's five top offices—Gov. Jane Hull, Secretary of State Betsey Bayless, Attorney General Janet Napolitano, Treasurer Carol Springer, and Superintendent of Public Instruction Lis Graham Keegan—and in 2002 they put Janet Napolitano (who's not only a woman, but a Democrat) into the governor's office. It just goes to show that while the political wind generally blows hard from the right in Arizona, it can be rowdy and unpredictable.

President William Howard Taft was among the first to notice this. Troubled by the populist tilt of Arizona's proposed constitution, with its provisions for voter initiative, referendum, and recall, he refused to approve statehood until recall for judges was removed. (Taft, incidentally, had been a judge.) When Arizona had been inducted into the Union, the first legislature of the new state immediately placed judicial recall on the ballot, and voters restored the privilege.

From 1912 to the early 1950s, Arizona was essentially a one-party state, and that party was Democratic. The party's inclinations were more populist than liberal, however, as most citizens seemed to distrust big government as well as big business. The dramatic shift toward a two-party state, and the later dominance of the Republican party, began in 1950 with the election of a Republican governor,

---

A Slogan for Arizona

The last time I was in Phoenix, the Arizona State Tourist Office was running a statewide contest for a new slogan, to replace the rather lame existing one: "If you knew it, you'd do it." The office's director explained that he was looking for something "people will really latch onto and that will be picked up all over the world," like "I love New York" or "Land of Enchantment" (the title of a book by Lilian Whiting, it replaced the Sunshine State as New Mexico's slogan in 1934).

Maybe Arizona's slogan should be "We don't stymie individualism here." That was uttered by Republican senator Jan Brewer on the occasion of the arrest of Charles H. Keating Jr., an upstanding Phoenician and the principal architect of the savings-and-loan collapse, which ended up costing taxpayers $2.5 billion. . . . After tourism, land fraud is the number two industry in the state.

—Alex Shoumatoff, *Legends of the American Desert*, 1997

Howard Pyle. By the end of that decade, registered Democrats still outnumbered Republicans by 68 to 32 percent, but Republicans were sweeping Democrats out of offices at every level. One explanation, among many advanced by historians, was that conservatives were registering as Democrats in order to have a voice in the dominant party's primaries, then voting for Republicans in the general elections.

Air-conditioning was the prime reason for the rightward swing of Arizona. With the Valley of the Sun newly rendered fit for human habitation, metropolitan Phoenix rapidly attracted major industries and swarms of retirees. Between 1950 and 1960, Phoenix's population ballooned from 106,818 to 439,170, and more were streaming in from the Republican Midwest than from the then-Democratic South. The Phoenix newspapers, *The Arizona Republic* and the *Phoenix Gazette*, became relentless boosters of economic growth and conservative causes. As the state's most influential news media, they certainly enhanced Republican power.

Tucson, which since 1950 has languished in Phoenix's economic shadow, has remained the state's Democratic stronghold. But even Tucson is slowly turning more conservative. Phoenix today has emerged as Republican and progressive; Tucson remains Democratic but more wary of taxing and spending than Phoenix. And an interesting new shift is occurring: the entire state is receiving an influx of liberals as more and more Californians, weary of high real-estate costs and taxes, move to Arizona.

Confused? So is the political theater of Arizona today. Or perhaps "contentious" is the better description.

We are at least true to our conflicted history. Through voter initiative, liberal Arizonans enacted women's suffrage in 1912; conservatives inflicted Prohibition two years later. We gave ourselves the death penalty in 1914 and revoked it in 1916 and revived it in 1918. Today most of the issues at stake are less profound than these, but the list seems endless. Arizonans fight over everything. A county board of supervisors rezones a square mile of desert for a housing development, and opponents fan out through the shopping malls waving petitions to force a referendum.

Most remarkable of all is that Arizonans emerge from this turbulent atmosphere to achieve national political prominence that is out of proportion to the state's population. Since the 1960s, four Arizonans have made a serious run at the presidency: Sen. Barry Goldwater (1964), Rep. Morris Udall (1976), Gov. Bruce Babbitt (1988), and Sen. John McCain (2000). Two Arizonans now sit on the U.S. Supreme Court: William Rehnquist and Sandra Day O'Connor. Ex-governor Bruce Babbitt served as secretary of the interior under Bill Clinton, a job previously held by another native son, Stewart Udall. There are numerous theories to explain all this, but the most logical is that of a former congressman from Tucson, James F. McNulty: "I suppose any 'frontier' state probably encourages the more ambitious," he says. "New growth is where things happen."

In other words, it's the frontier mentality.

■ ARIZONA DREAMS

It is a warm winter day, and I am walking in a park in downtown Mesa listening to a developer talk penguins.

"You know how hot it is here in the summer," he says, unnecessarily. "So imagine the effect of watching 19 penguins frolicking in a fountain around an igloo. It would be absolute dynamite!"

He's serious, he swears; his plan is just on the back burner at the moment because the projected cost of the desert penguin habitat has bloated to about 10 times the original projection. I soberly record all this in my notebook, and a few weeks later report it as part of a special newspaper project commemorating the 75th anniversary of Arizona statehood.

The reason I didn't simply laugh and dismiss him as a crackpot is that his scheme nestled seamlessly into the continuum of Arizona's story.

South Clifton, Arizona, in 1909.

From the Gadsden Purchase of 1853 to today, Arizona has always been a land for dreamers, "a blank slate on which they could etch their visions of the future," in the words of the Arizona State Museum ethnohistorian Thomas E. Sheridan. If penguins and igloos in downtown Mesa seem preposterous, they are hardly more so than the necklace of lakes that now drapes through the heart of the Mojave Desert (complete with London Bridge), or the Victorian hotels in the mining towns, clasped desperately to the sides of mountains and gulches. We have remodeled the land to meet our needs and dreams, rather than accepting it on its own terms. Often we have done no good. Wrote Charles Bowden in *Blue Desert*, "Here the land always makes promises of aching beauty and the people always fail the land." A harsh judgment, but not one without the resonance of much truth in it.

The first miracle of technology that reconstructed the face of Arizona was the railroad. Until this, virtually all the architecture had been native—that is, built with the materials at hand. In the desert towns, that meant dirt, primarily—dirt mixed with water, poured into a form, and dried in the abundant sun to make adobe. The word descends from the Arabic *al-tub*, "the brick," which suggests its fundamental importance in arid lands everywhere. Adobe made perfect sense in the Arizona deserts. Its great thermal mass helped keep interiors cool through the torrid summer. Houses were built close together, which helped shade the spaces between them. Instead of front and backyards patterned after the rural English model, they incorporated shady, enclosed Mediterranean courtyards. But once the railroads came, bringing building materials from back East, pioneer Arizonans

couldn't wait to discard adobe in favor of Victorian architecture. Mud was symbolic of the Mexican past; gables and balustrades represented an affluent, expanding America—even though this architecture made little sense, environmentally or aesthetically, in the desert.

The hunger of the pioneers to make Arizona look like someplace else meant that it would no longer have unique and environmentally sensible architecture. When mirrored glass towers burst into vogue nationally in the 1970s, architects dutifully reproduced them in Phoenix. No one asked the obvious question: why bounce more sunlight around in a place that already has quite enough of it?

Water projects were the next phase in the makeover of Arizona. Mining and farming both require generous and reliable water supplies, which never existed naturally here. Arizona's rivers are trickles one season, torrents the next. It took a network of dams to control them: Roosevelt in 1911, Coolidge in 1929, Hoover in 1935. All were federal projects, as their names imply. Arizona didn't have the money to tame its own rivers, and at that time it didn't have the political influence to wrestle Washington into paying, either. These dams exist because there was money to be made in Arizona, and the people flocking here to make it needed the water.

Thus tricked into unnatural behavior, these rivers made Phoenix green and created the spectacle of vast recreational lakes—Powell, Mead, Havasu, Roosevelt—in treeless landscapes that enjoy from 3 to 10 inches of rain in a year. Other water projects have changed the landscape in ways less obvious to the casual visitor. Driving south toward Tucson along I-10, one views tens of thousands of acres of farmland now lying fallow, choked with tumbleweeds. Thirsty Tucson has bought this farmland for the rights to slurp the aquifer underneath.

But the most important effect of all the water projects has been that they have made big cities possible. This has been both boon and curse. Without the cities, Arizona would have had little to contribute to the arts and sciences, it would hardly seem cosmopolitan, and it wouldn't offer either its residents or visitors the diversity it now does. At the same time, these cities are draining the water, fouling the air, and gnawing away the desert and mountains around them. This cannot go on forever.

A perceptive visitor to Arizona may discern a messy contradiction in what we say about the land and what we do to it. For example, we rhapsodize endlessly over the sunsets and mountain views, but we don't prohibit billboards. Several other scenic states do, notably Vermont, Maine, Alaska, and Hawaii. In Sedona, arguably the town with the loveliest natural assets in all of Arizona, there is little

The architecture of the futuristic Burton Barr Central Library in downtown Phoenix was inspired by Monument Valley.

public access to its sparkling little river—it's mostly private property marked by "No Trespassing" signs. (Slide State Park is 7 miles north of town.)

The contradiction can be explained, even if not easily forgiven. Arizona has grown up too fast for its own good. Our population was 750,000 in 1950; it was 5.3 million in 2001. Most Arizonans are newcomers; too few of us have roots deep enough to provide a better understanding and stewardship of the land. Too many of us moved here pursuing private dreams, and with the notable exception of the pioneer Mormons, we have always been busier developing personal resources than communal ones. City councils find themselves under constant pressure to allow new housing developments and shopping centers (and widen the streets on the way), but there is not enough competing clamor for more parks and greenbelts. Development is enormously controversial in Arizona today, but for 50 years it has been happening so fast that proponents and opponents only lurch from one battle to the next, never finding the time to take a long, careful look at what we really want to do with the land.

There are some positive signs. In 1980 the legislature finally enacted a statewide groundwater code, which mandates that by the year 2025, Arizona wells may draw no more water out of their aquifers than is being replenished by nature. There is a growing positive environmental activism. The Nature Conservancy's Arizona chapter, for example, is buying up endangered land at an astounding rate. In recent years, the Conservancy has fielded multimillion-dollar fund drives to protect 14 threatened riparian corridors along rivers and arroyos. It comes almost too late, however. According to the Conservancy, 90 percent of Arizona's prime riparian woodlands are already gone.

In his bicentennial history of Arizona, Lawrence Clark Powell articulated our difficulties in a few perfectly chosen words. The state's most serious problem, he wrote, is "peculiarly Arizonan, that of a rising flood of people into a land naturally unsuited to large numbers of people." Yet this land's promises of aching beauty have always drawn people with their dreams, and in successive laminations of civilizations they always will. Ours will not be the last.

ART & ARCHITECTURE

Television and marketing, claims conventional wisdom, have almost finished transforming the United States into one homogenized, continental village. From Seattle to Miami, our skylines cut similar profiles, our symphony orchestras play the same music and shudder through identical financial crises, and artists everywhere pursue the same bankable trends.

This book dissents. The arts in Arizona are and always will be unique because they are driven by engines that are distinctly Arizonan: Our history, which still lies close to the surface. Our simmering stew of three distinct human cultures. Our landscapes. Our light. These are cultural and environmental imperatives that always will influence art—for the better, usually.

The sculpture of Prescott artists Rebecca Davis and Roger Asay is one example. They make intellectually challenging art out of the everyday stuff of the Arizona environment: pebbles, boulders, saplings, trees. It isn't just avant-garde kitsch. On the south shore of the little lake in Tucson's Reid Park, Davis and Asay have "planted" five pecan trees—trees stripped of all leaves, bark, and small branches, sanded smooth, painted five different tones of red and, finally, turned upside down. They are as sensuous, in their own curious way, as Renoir's sun-dappled nudes. "We inverted them," Asay explained, "to take them out of context so people don't just dismiss them as bare trees. What we hope is that people will begin to see the trees differently, and more intently." People do.

Another example, on a grand scale, is the artist James Turrell's Roden Crater, a work in progress since 1974. Perhaps it will be completed by 2010, when the artist will be 67. Turrell bought an extinct volcano near Flagstaff—part of the San Francisco Volcanic Field, which also includes Sunset Crater National Monument—and created nine underground chambers in it; he had the crater's bowl hollowed out to serve as an outdoor space. One room, called the Sun and Moon Space, is centered by a 17-foot-tall stone monolith, where the light of the moon at its apogee filters into a southwest-facing tunnel. Another room called the East Portal is dedicated to starlight. In the project's eventual Phase II (Phase I hasn't been completed yet), a northeast-facing tunnel designed to catch the sunrise will be constructed.

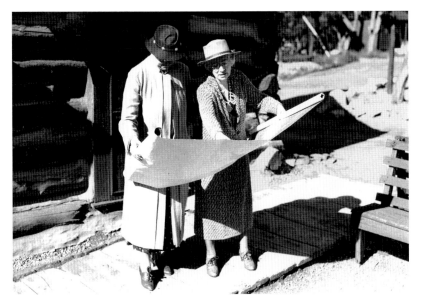

Mary Colter (right) shows Bright Angel Lodge plans to Mrs. Harold L. Ickes, wife of the Secretary of the Interior, ca. 1935.

Or so we are told. Only a privileged few—such as Calvin Tompkins, the interviewer from *The New Yorker* who reported on Roden Crater in early 2003—have actually seen this earthwork-cum-observatory.

Turrell's art has always been devoted to exploring how viewers perceive light. An exhibit in 2002 at the Scottsdale Museum of Contemporary Art, for example, included what initially seemed to be a completely dark room. Those who entered were forced to attend to how a variety of shapes began to materialize—slowly, as one's eyes adjusted to the dimness. So it comes as no surprise that the perception of light is the subject to which Turrell devoted Roden Crater. Perhaps one of the most amazing things about the project, aside from its scope, is how the artist engaged the local community in his work. Turrell managed to get permission from the local planning board, which originally opposed it, to construct an inordinately steep flight of stairs leading to the open air crater bowl by pointing out that, in the kivas on the nearby Hopi Reservation, elders still walk up and down ladders that are practically vertical, carrying snakes in both hands.

■ ARCHITECTURE

In Arizona, the oldest functioning architecture—**San Xavier del Bac**—is also the best. This mission was built 200 years ago, probably by itinerant Spanish craftsmen and bewildered native laborers, in an Apache-besieged outpost a thousand miles from any building of comparable ambition. And yet architects even today seem helpless to do much except sigh in envy, bow in humility, and muddle on making lesser buildings.

San Xavier was intended "to attract by its loveliness the unconverted [Indians] beyond the frontier," wrote the captain of the Spanish presidio at Tucson in 1804. This strategy demonstrates both the naïveté and the arrogance of the Spanish: the Tohono O'odham people's concept of God was and still is rooted in nature, not at the altar of a baroque church.

But the builders spared no expense on their magic show. The church, which is off I-19 just south of Tucson, is built in the traditional cruciform plan, crowned with two belfries and a bravura dome, and decorated with a portal of such architectural sizzle that the eye hardly knows where to alight. This portal has everything—spires, scrolls, seashell motifs, eggs, arches, saints, even a cartoon: a cat and a rodent crouch on opposing scrolls just below the parapet, glaring at each other in eternal standoff. And after this the interior is no letdown, strutting a cavalcade of statuary, murals, and a stunning altar screen that echoes the organization of the portal. In his three-volume survey of American buildings, the architectural historian G. E. Kidder Smith called the

Detail of the interior of the Mission San Xavier del Bac.

interior "hair-raising." His late colleague Reyner Banham went even further: San Xavier del Bac, he flatly proclaimed, "is the most beautiful man-made object in America Deserta."

From the coming of the railroad in 1880 until the dawn of the 20th century, Arizonans were infatuated with Victorian architecture; it was a symbolic way of proclaiming the frontier civilized (and Americanized). In a quick 20 years it seemed to the residents that they were civilized enough, and the time arrived to declare cultural independence from those effete Eastern shores. The result was the Mission Revival architecture of 1900–1915, and the still more romantic Spanish Colonial Revival era, 1915–1930. San Xavier, though, was not the inspiration for these movements; California was. These "Spanish" styles were encouraged by West Coast promoters eager to capitalize on the romantic mythology of the conquistadors. Like Californians, Arizona newcomers were not particularly interested in participating in Hispanic culture, but they loved wrapping themselves in its imagery.

In the 1930s came another reversal. Phoenix and Tucson, finally edging toward the country's economic mainstream, felt they had to begin looking like real cities instead of Iberian fantasylands. Color, ornament, and romance became high crimes, and from then until the 1970s most architecture in Arizona echoed the modernist credo of "less is more." Modernism left Arizona with many of its least ingratiating buildings. Following this came yet another reassessment—and yet another Hispanic revival. This one, still in progress, has no formal name, though one hostile critic has proposed "Taco Deco." It is simpler and cheaper than its predecessors, and repetitive to the point of cliché, but it also is an effort—if not quite a noble one—to perpetuate an architecture with a sense of place.

Since 1970, a growing minority of Arizona architects has tried to establish a different tradition: buildings that reside in harmony with the land. Their inspiration, if not their style, stems from the ideas of Frank Lloyd Wright. These buildings may take their colors, their forms, even their moods from the land. In 1989, New Mexico architect Antoine Predock attempted an astoundingly deep and thorny abstraction of both Arizona's culture and landscape in his design for the **Nelson Fine Arts Center,** (see page 202) in Tempe. Its complex profile, a ramble of colliding boxes, triangles, terraces, and plazas, resembles at once a Hopi pueblo and a desert mountain range. Its color, a washed out gray-purple stucco, was inspired by a rock the architect found on a nearby hill. The building's story line, as Predock has explained it to baffled visitors, is a cultural cross-section of the site: the gurgling pools in the lobby recall the canals of the vanished Hohokam, and a flat panel jutting into the sky suggests an endangered artifact of the modern West, the drive-in movie theater. It is a mystical and magnificent building.

Connoisseurs of architecture will want to view numerous other Arizona buildings, most of them around the two metropolitan areas. Some are discussed in greater detail in the city or regional chapters.

■ GREATER PHOENIX

Brophy Prep (4701 North Central Avenue, Phoenix), erected in 1928, is the state's most lyrical Spanish Colonial Revival building. The 1929 **Arizona Biltmore** (24th Street and Missouri Avenue, Phoenix), though often credited to Frank Lloyd Wright, was designed by Albert Chase McArthur; Wright's contribution as "consultant" was smaller than is popularly believed. With **Luhrs Tower** (45 West Jefferson Street, Phoenix), also from 1929, the El Paso architectural firm of Trost & Trost successfully married the art deco and Spanish Colonial Revival styles; the building remains the best of Phoenix's several dozen high-rises.

Marking a break from borrowed styles, Frank Lloyd Wright designed his Arizona masterpiece, **Taliesin West** (12621 Frank Lloyd Wright Boulevard, Scottsdale), his winter home and school of architecture (see Wright sidebar, page 170), completed in 1938.

The one work of Paolo Soleri worth visiting is **Cosanti** (6433 Doubletree Road, Paradise Valley)—an intimate village, begun in the late 1950s, of earth-cast organic forms. Soleri's much better-known **Arcosanti,** 70 miles north of Phoenix, is uninteresting as architecture; as a social experiment (which began in the early 1970s) it has more to do with totalitarianism than harmonious living with the Earth. Essentially, Soleri would have us all live in concrete beehives. Perhaps he is a better teacher than architectural theoretician. Phoenix's 1995 **Burton Barr Central Library** (1221 North Central Avenue)—whose principal architect, Will Bruder, was one of Soleri's students—is one of the most user-friendly buildings in the Valley.

Many people condemn the 1971 **Tempe City Hall** (31 East Fifth Street) as architectural conceit, but it works. An inverted pyramid of glass and steel bursts up from street level, shading a lovely subterranean courtyard.

■ TUCSON

Two must-see structures in Tucson are the 1927 **Pima County Courthouse** (Church and Congress Streets), done in the Spanish Colonial Revival style by Roy Place; and the 1984 **Loews Ventana Canyon Resort** (7000 North Resort Drive), created by the architectural firm of Frizzell, Hill, and Moorehouse, which drew considerable inspiration from Wright's never-built San Marcos-in-the-Desert hotel of 1928. The West University Historic District, roughly bounded by Speedway Boulevard, Sixth Street, and Park and Stone Avenues, contains several excellent Craftsman Bungalow dwellings.

■ **ELSEWHERE IN THE STATE**

Four miles south of Tubac, see the mission of **San José de Tumacácori,** built by the Franciscans in the early 1800s. The buildings at the **Grand Canyon** by Mary Colter (among them Desert View and the Bright Angel Lodge) and Charles Whittlesey (El Tovar Hotel) are amazing accomplishments. Designed by the sculptor Marguerite Brunswig Staude, the 1956 **Chapel of the Holy Cross,** wedged between a pair of ruddy buttes near Sedona, is a provocative retort to Wright's notion of organic architecture. The concrete and glass creation appears more powerful than the mountains around it. Take Route 179 for 3 miles south of Sedona to Chapel Road, turn left and proceed a mile.

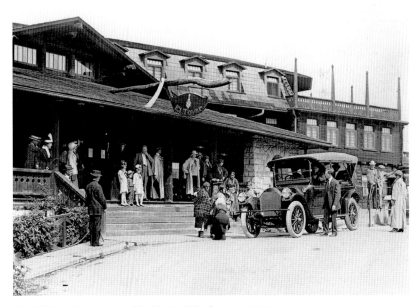

The El Tovar Hotel, designed by Charles Whittlesey, ca. 1922.

FRANK LLOYD WRIGHT

Frank Lloyd Wright died in Phoenix in 1959, a few miles away from his beloved Taliesin West. His had been the longest, most creative and most controversial career of any architect in modern American history. Even today, Wright lives on among his former associates and apprentices as the guiding spirit, the one fountain of Truth in architecture. The commune-like Taliesin fellowship continues as ever, spending its summers in Wisconsin and winters in Scottsdale. The Frank Lloyd Wright School of Architecture still instructs its students in a curriculum more like a medieval apprenticeship than a modern university education. Most oddly of all, the design vocabulary of the Taliesin architects has not changed since Wright's death. They talk of preserving only the spirit of Wright's philosophy of organic architecture, but in practice they also perpetuate his exuberant geometry, his contrapuntal massing, his repetitive ornamentation—all the elements that together make up the thing Wright claimed to despise so virulently: style.

The Frank Lloyd Wright–designed Gammage Center on the Arizona State University campus in Tempe.

Wright designed roughly 50 buildings for Arizona, about one-third of which were built. (Some, like Phoenix's First Christian Church, were finished posthumously by Taliesin Associated Architects.) Among them are both masterpieces and flights of silly fantasy. They have not had widespread influence on architecture in Arizona (except that practiced at Taliesin), which is unfortunate. Early in his career, Wright developed a philosophy of desert architecture that took its inspiration from the spare, angular landscape; at its best, it was and is beautifully harmonious.

"I suggest that the dotted line is the line for the desert; not the hard line nor the knife edge," he wrote in 1940. He had studied the desert's thorn forest—cholla, saguaro, ocotillo—and noticed how the needles of these plants broke up and filtered the harsh sunlight spraying through them. Obviously, a building couldn't literally wear a skin of needles, but an architect could articulate and shade and texture wall surfaces for the same effect. A high, straight, flat wall surface would reflect light and appear as a foreign presence imposed on the landscape, but a broken one—a "dotted line"—would settle gracefully into it. In this respect Taliesin West is the masterpiece; perhaps no other Wright building, architect Pietro Belluschi once said, so perfectly gathers in "the mood of the land."

Wright, however, blithely violated his own philosophy whenever he felt like it. There is little "mood of the land" in Gammage Center, his 1959 auditorium at Arizona State University. Originally designed as an opera house for Baghdad, it looks like a great pink wedding cake festooned with hoops and baubles that appear to have been inspired by the tales of Scheherezade—or that may simply have floated down from Mars. Its acoustics, however, are stunning.

Wright was a genius and a hypocrite, a visionary and a gadfly. In deifying him, the disciples at Taliesin have done him no favor. His buildings speak better for him.

Taliesin West (480-860-8810) offers tours daily. From Scottsdale Road, take Shea Boulevard east for 4.6 miles to Frank Lloyd Wright Boulevard. Turn left and follow the signs. **Gammage Center** (Mill Avenue and Apache Boulevard, Tempe) hosts many concerts, shows, and lectures. You can tour the building, free of charge, between 1 and 3:30 weekday afternoons (480-965-4050). **First Christian Church** (6500 North Seventh Avenue, Phoenix), welcomes visitors from 8:30 to 5 on weekdays. Stop by the church office. The rest of Wright's Arizona buildings are private homes, and are not open to the public.

—Lawrence W. Cheek

Arizona's Architect

Mary Colter created some of the most interesting buildings at one of the most visited national parks in America, in the employ of a company that introduced generations of travelers to the Southwest. Her structures are used and appreciated by millions every year, yet only recently has her name become widely recognized.

A contemporary of Frank Lloyd Wright who became immersed in the Arts and Crafts movement at San Francisco's School of Art and Design in the late 1880s, Colter was hired in 1902 to work for the Fred Harvey Company, which operated all the restaurants, hotels, and on-board food service on the Santa Fe Railway line west of the Missouri. The Harvey Company and the Santa Fe had made travel to the Southwest at the end of the 19th century literally palatable (the food on the rail line had been awful before the Harvey House restaurants introduced high-quality products) and provided safe, aesthetically appealing lodgings along the route.

For many years, the Santa Fe's chief architect was Charles Whittlesey. In 1905, when Whittlesey was commissioned to build the El Tovar Hotel at the Grand Canyon, Colter was assigned the Hopi House gift shop as its accompaniment. Colter's first Grand Canyon project established her architectural and intellectual modus operandi: Whereas Whittlesey built a ski lodge on steroids in high Germanic mode, Colter devised a modest structure of local stone and wood that resembled the dwellings she had seen in Oraibi, on the Hopi Reservation. Hopi House was the first of her series of site-related buildings that eventually inspired the style dubbed National Park Rustic, adapted by the Civilian Conservation Corps during the Depression.

Colter's other Grand Canyon commissions included Hermits Rest (1912), a rest house that looks, at first glance, like a pile of rocks and wood ready to tumble into the abyss; Lookout Studio (1914), an observatory of rough-cut Kaibab limestone that seems to grow out of the canyon's edge; and Bright Angel Lodge (1935), with its vast geological fireplace built of layers of stone that re-create the Grand Canyon's strata. Natural rock strata were also key to the Colter's most acclaimed project at the park, the Indian Watchtower at Desert View (1933), a monolith inspired most directly by the Round Tower ruin at Mesa Verde. Its kiva-like top room, decorated by Hopi artist Fred Kabotie, affords some of the most dramatic views of the canyon, and reminds you that you're viewing a landscape held sacred by much earlier cultures.

Several of the Harvey House hotels that Colter worked on outside the Grand Canyon have been destroyed, but one notable exception is La Posada in Winslow, Arizona, built in 1930 and restored in the 1990s. A departure from her rustic and Native American buildings, the hotel was designed in the Spanish Colonial Revival style to resemble a modest family hacienda. Like all of Colter's work, it was not so much themed as imaginatively re-created—practically channeled—through meticulous research.

Most of Colter's research was done in Arizona and New Mexico, and her milieu was public places rather than private homes. The reopening of La Posada, and the publication in 2002 of Arnold Berke's beautifully illustrated *Mary Colter: Architect of the Southwest* have helped bring Colter to public prominence in the last decade. It's about time. Colter's contribution to the Southwest's architectural history—and to Arizona's premier attraction—cannot be overemphasized.

—Edie Jarolim

Mary Colter's Desert View Watchtower.

■ THE VISUAL ARTS

Virtually all artists who come to Arizona from somewhere else are changed by the environment here. It is not only that new subjects materialize on their canvases; that would be expected. But a fresh temperament, a different attitude, perhaps even a new spirit may also pervade their work. Sometimes it is subtle; more often it is a dramatic change.

Howard Conant, a painter who for 10 years also headed the University of Arizona Department of Art, moved to Arizona from New York City in 1976. He was a geometric abstractionist, and his New York paintings often seemed to express tension and energy and violence; even when the subject had nothing at all to do with the city, the works were jagged and searing. After five years of work in a quiet desert studio, his paintings were still as crisp as ever, but the fury had all evaporated. Gentle, rolling lines had replaced processions of severe, knifelike triangles. He even gave in and painted a sunset, albeit an abstract one.

"A sunset is just about the lowest thing a professional artist can do," he said. "Postcard artists do sunsets. Cowboy artists do sunsets. But I'd fallen so in love with the desert that I finally just decided, what the hell—I've got to do it. I succumbed."

Artists have been interpreting the Arizona environment since some anonymous Hohokam first scratched the likeness of a scorpion onto a boulder. Possibly he was expressing a vivid encounter with that environment—a nasty sting. In 1873, the famous painter Thomas Moran accompanied John Wesley Powell on the latter's third expedition into the Grand Canyon, and the following year completed what is still one of the grandest and most evocative paintings ever made of Arizona: *The Chasm of the Colorado*. On a single gigantic canvas (7 by 12 feet), Moran portrayed the canyon splashed with golden sunlight, splattered by a furious thunderstorm, and haunted by clouds of mist lurking in shadowy abysses—all at once. Moran wrote that the canyon was "by far the most awfully grand and impressive scene I have yet ever seen."

The painting was hung in the U.S. Senate lobby, and viewers were electrified. From there it played a role in the transformation of Arizona. Inspired by the tremendous public reaction, the promotion-minded Santa Fe Railway, in collaboration with the Fred Harvey Company, soon began commissioning artists to come out and paint Southwestern subjects, particularly Arizona and New Mexico. Their work helped create the tourism boom and promote the settlement of these scenic and exotic lands.

Arizona's visual art separates into several basic categories. Landscapes are the most obvious, and among the most abundant, as a day's gallery browsing will show. Western art, less respectfully called "cowboy art," is another.

Western art is controversial in Arizona. The intelligentsia scorn it. Collectors are enchanted by it. The average person cannot afford it—not the capably executed works, at least. Paintings by Howard Terpning, among the most highly regarded of Arizona's living Western artists, have sold for more than $300,000.

Yet art critics turn apoplectic virtually in unison when the subject of Western art arises. In Tucson's *City Magazine,* writer Karin Demorest concluded:

> [The Western artist] is on a treadmill, telling the same story over and over again, stubbornly refusing to stray from the stock images of the genre—the cowboy, the Indian, the horse, the desert land-scape, the mountains, the sunset. Furthermore, his preoccupation with authenticity and technique deprives him of real expressiveness and individuality. . . . Subject matter, authenticity and technical skill are the standards by which Western art is both made and judged, with little if any attention paid to composition, spatial qual-ity or drawing. A piece is considered good, even great, if the subject looks utterly real: the number of feathers in the Indian's headdress correct, the spots on the Appaloosa just the right color, the stirrups flawlessly rendered. . . .

So why the popularity? The answer is as obvious a cliché as the classic cowboy-in-the-sunset painting: the themes in these scenes from a romanticized past are those cherished by the collectors themselves (who, according to Demorest, are almost exclusively white males over 45): independence, heroism, nature in its raw form—and so awaiting a man's challenge—and nostalgia for a bygone era free of cynicism and ambiguity. Interestingly, women seldom appear on Western artists' canvases, except as idealized and therefore untouchable Indian maidens.

Native American art and art portraying Native Americans are two other promi-nent categories. Among the former are some well-known tribal specialties: Tohono O'odham baskets, Apache *ga'an* masks, Navajo sand paintings and rugs, and Hopi katsina dolls. It can be argued that many of these Native American arts have bene-fited from being coveted by tourists. (For more about Native American arts, see the "Modern Indians" chapter.)

Art portraying Native Americans, however, deserves the most respect when it is least commercial. Mass-marketed images of Indians, which have made more than a few Arizona artists wealthy, invariably reduce their subject to cliché: the noble savage, the stoic wife, the innocent, saucer-faced infant. Some artists have been more honest. Among them is Barry Goldwater, later elected to the U.S. Senate, who took a celebrated series of photos of the Navajo people in the 1930s. Even today, the best art portraying Native Americans remains photographic: it is easier to tell the truth through a lens.

■ Viewing Art

Arizona's principal art museums are discussed in the "Phoenix," "Tucson," and "Arizona Towns" chapters. One generalization that can be made about museums in the state is that the ones at universities stay closer to the cutting edge and take more risks than the municipal facilities.

■ Buying Art

Scottsdale's Fifth Avenue galleries are the best-known in the state, and they serve the well-heeled traditionalist best. Prices at Tucson's downtown galleries are often a fraction of those in Scottsdale, and the art tends to be more adventurous, though the quality varies wildly. Sedona has many excellent galleries but little provocative art; Tubac's shops also tend toward conservatism but are lower-priced. Bisbee is a good place to purchase the work of emerging artists at an affordable price. Jerome defies categorization—good news for adventurous buyers. October brings the Phoenix Art Museum's Cowboy Artists of America sale, a social event that grosses more than $2 million in sales.

■ The Performing Arts

Another cliché: Because Arizona is a young state, and because it has relatively little in the way of old wealth, its performing arts organizations are still struggling through their adolescence. As with many clichés, there is some truth to the notion. But this is not the full story.

The oldest arts organization still performing is the **Tucson Symphony Orchestra,** which was founded in 1928. The **Phoenix Symphony** debuted later, but it was the first arts organization in the state to take the plunge into "major" status by offering full-time employment for its musicians. That decision was made in

Sedona's Jazz on the Rocks festival is held each September.

1981, and the years since have, in truth, been difficult: colossal deficits have plagued the orchestra, and emergency fundraising drives and staff layoffs have been necessary to keep it afloat. One of its peculiar curses is, strangely, Phoenix's attractive winter climate. Wealthy and cultured people are drawn to retire in Phoenix (or commute to winter homes here), but although they often attend the Phoenix Symphony, some of them bestow their donations on the orchestras in their snowbound hometowns—Minneapolis, Cleveland, Boston.

The highly acclaimed **Arizona Theatre Company** was founded in Tucson in 1967. It too has faced tough financial times and emerged intact. Now functioning as a statewide organization, though still headquartered in Tucson, it stages several plays each season in Tucson and Phoenix. The **Arizona Opera Company,** likewise based in Tucson but serving both cities, produces four or five operas per season. It lives scrupulously within its budget, a considerable achievement for any opera company, but one reason it does so is its conservative "Top 40" repertoire—Mozart, Rossini, Puccini & Co. In fairness, the Arizona Opera probably can't afford many artistic risks at this awkward point in its life. It is too mature and established to take a wild, youthful plunge into the avant-garde, and yet not financially secure enough to take a planned loss on a production of, say, Krzysztof Penderecki's *Black Mask.* Call it, if you must, adolescence.

Risks are being taken in abundance, however, by smaller groups and determined individuals. The performances put on by Tempe's multicultural **Essential Theater Company** involve improvisation and audience participation. In Tucson, the **Borderlands Theater** stages contemporary works that often incorporate the theme of borders, both in a literal and metaphorical sense; and the all-women **Bloodhut Productions** troupe combines storytelling, movement, and comedy in thought-provoking ways.

■ FOLK ART

Thanks once again to its profusion of cultures, Arizona also is spectacularly rich in folk art—from cowboy poetry to Mexican murals to Tohono O'odham "chicken scratch," a musical style apparently transmitted to the tribe, at least in part, by the

A street mural in Tucson's Barrio Histórico is a good example of Arizona's folk art.

Jesuit and Franciscan missionaries long before Anglo settlement. (Certainly no other tribe plays a repertoire of polkas and two-steps on accordion, saxophone, drums, and electric guitar.)

No broad survey of folk art is possible in this short treatment, but one curiosity unique to Arizona seems especially worth describing: the century-old tradition of Arizonans wryly poking fun at their own habitat in verse, gag, and cartoon image. Most of this folk art, predictably, plays on the heat or the desert's general inhospitality.

In poetry, the tradition dates back at least to 1879, when a ballad attributed to a pioneer Tucson bartender first circulated. A remarkably clever and well-paced tale, it begins with the Devil being given permission (presumably by God, though this detail is left unstated) to select a land as a special annex for Hell. It is, of course, Arizona—and Satan undertakes to improve on it:

> . . . He filled the river with sand till it was almost dry,
> And poisoned the land with alkali
> And promised himself on its slimy brink
> The control of all who from it should drink.
> He saw there was one more improvement to make,
> He imported the scorpion, tarantula and rattlesnake,
> That all who might come to its country to dwell
> Would be sure to think it was almost hell.
> He fixed the heat at one hundred and seven
> And banished forever the moisture from heaven. . . .

The punch line, of course, is inevitable: when the Devil at last completes his "improvements":

> . . . For his own realm compares so well
> He feels sure it surpasses Hell.

None of this is serious put-down. In truth, it is a form of braggadocio. As James S. Griffith, Arizona's preeminent cultural anthropologist of folk art, wrote, "One of the points of the genre is that it takes a real tough character to put up with whatever country is being described." This seems to be no less true today, even given the palliative of air conditioning, than it was in 1879. Wimps dwell not in this land.

■ KITSCH

Arizona may well lead the nation in the production of kitsch, a distinction that need not cause us embarrassment. Kitsch is the natural consequence of having rich landscapes and cultures that invite reduction into sentimental or cartoonish images, along with a vibrant tourist industry that supplies customers with cash in hand. *Objets de kitsch* generate jobs and revenue today, and over two or three generations they undergo a quiet metamorphosis into important cultural artifacts—i.e., antiques. The only immediate problem is telling folk art and kitsch apart. The line is blurry.

Architectural kitsch abounds in Arizona. A fine example is the giant stucco tipi in the old mining town of Globe; it currently houses a bar. A better-known institution is Bedrock City, a Fred Flintstone theme park of free-form boulder-like buildings strategically placed at the intersection of U.S. 180 and Route 64, the two main routes to the Grand Canyon's South Rim. And there is a peculiar building in Amado whose very entrance is a gigantic cow skull and horn.

Of course, most Arizonans still get their kitsch on Route 66. The examples are too numerous to cite, but a few that stand out include the Museum Club in Flagstaff, a rough-hewn log building that you enter through a giant wishbone (actually a split ponderosa pine tree); Rod's Steak House in Williams, where a large neon steer announces the meaty offerings inside (the menu is shaped like a steer, too); and, at the entryway to an unnamed souvenir shop a few miles west of Winslow, a giant plaster jackrabbit, heralded for miles with "Here It Is" signs. For the highest concentration of kitsch in an Arizona Route 66 town, however, top honors go to Holbrook, home to both Wigwam Village, which is just what its name says, and the Rainbow Rock Shop, fronted by several dinosaurs in assorted colors.

Arizona's animals and plants lead to endless production of kitsch. The scorpion and the saguaro seem especially inspirational. In 1971 the legislature proclaimed the bola the state tie of Arizona, and the quintessential bola (for tourists, that is) must have an authentic Arizona scorpion encased in a transparent plastic clasp.

The saguaro, perhaps because of its anthropomorphic friendliness, pops up in boutiques everywhere. There are saguaros made of green-painted stovepipe, stuffed felt, soldered copper, blown glass, and glowing neon. The Arizona State Museum even has a miniature saguaro that was made by a Tohono O'odham artist out of scrap telephone wire. None of Arizona's cultures seems able to resist the siren of

Cigar store cowboys and Indians have always been icons of southwestern kitsch.

kitsch. A recent development is chile kitsch: red peppers are turning up in stained glass windows, dangling from people's ears, and glowing on Christmas trees.

Any image, if replicated over and over, eventually ceases to be usable in fine art or even folk art. It parks in the province of kitsch and from there it will not budge. This is the one thing to regret about kitsch. It is all but impossible today for anyone to paint a saguaro in a sunset, a noble and honest Arizona image, and have it be taken seriously. Literal paintings of Indians have long been snubbed by everyone outside the Western art establishment; recently even highly stylized renderings have become suspect—those images of Navajo women in immense, flowing robes have badly overpopulated the galleries.

Arizona, however, seems inexhaustibly rich in subject matter. If the saguaro is for now too hazardous for the serious artist to approach, there are a few dozen neglected species of cacti still out there, waiting.

P H O E N I X
V A L L E Y   O F   T H E   S U N

Phoenix has been a city that typically defies the desert rather than allowing itself to be defined by it, but weather determines the pace of life here. The sun shines an average of 300 days per year, and for year-round residents this is a mixed blessing. From November through April, the Valley of the Sun (a nickname for Phoenix and its satellite cities) enjoys some of the best weather in the country. Residents, seldom clad in more than a light jacket, drive convertibles with the tops down, eat outside at lunchtime, and devote most of their free time to outdoor pursuits—from golf to hiking the rugged desert mountains and canyons nearby.

From May through October, however, it is a different story. With daily temperatures in the 100-degrees-Fahrenheit range, people stick to their air-conditioned homes, cars, and offices. Foot traffic is light except in cooled shopping malls, and standard attire is a light T-shirt, shorts, sandals, and sunglasses. By mid-summer, those who have adapted to the heat may linger under a shade tree or possibly drink iced tea at an outdoor café that has a "misting system"—water mist that wafts down upon grateful patrons from overhead pipes. But most people would rather be neck deep in a swimming pool.

Phoenicians used to joke and complain about two things: the summer heat and the city's dud of a downtown. As recently as 1990, on weekday evenings and most weekends, you could shoot a cannon down its empty streets. Though Phoenix was on its way to becoming America's seventh-largest city, art and theatrical venues were mostly small and mediocre, and except for a struggling symphony orchestra and a few hotel bars and restaurants near the convention center, there was no nightlife to speak of. Downtown shopping was nonexistent.

All of that has changed. Thanks to a $1 billion "quality of life" bond issue voters passed in 1988—the largest publicly funded culture and recreation effort ever undertaken by an American city—downtown Phoenix has been reborn. In Copper Square, as the freshly banner-decked heart of town has been dubbed, there are a half-dozen new or refurbished museums and theaters, two new stadiums that are home to three sports teams, and many inviting shops and restaurants. The area reverts to its formerly deserted state on the weekends and on weeknights when there are no concerts or sports events, so to longtime locals, the new downtown seems like a mirage.

Flourishing downtown Phoenix.

■ FLOURISHING OASIS

In a way, what has happened to downtown is a realization of the big dreams of the community's founders, who envisioned Phoenix not as a dusty town that would fit into the desert, but rather as a flourishing oasis that might be wrought from it. Early on, agriculture was its raison d'être, and when in 1911 Roosevelt Dam walled off the Salt River, 60 miles to the east, the combined watersheds of the Salt and Verde Rivers became a 13,000-square-mile catchment—an area larger than Belgium—to make Phoenix verdant.

A network of irrigation canals expanded across the valley, serving not only cash crops but also a lush urban landscape. Praising a new housing development in 1920, the *Arizona Republic* noted that the "umbrella of elm and ash trees are set so close together along these drives that the sun's rays barely penetrate the dense forest." Such developments forged the pattern for the next 70 years. Golf courses are now the Valley's most ubiquitous landscape. Suburban Fountain Hills has one of the world's highest fountains, a man-made geyser shooting water 560 feet high. (This is more than three times the height of Yellowstone's Old Faithful.) So many modern subdivisions were being built around man-made lakes that the state legislature finally outlawed the practice in the 1980s. In such a setting the desert seems as distant as another planet. But Phoenix's attitude toward the desert has its roots deep in its history. Bradford Luckingham, the author of *Phoenix: The History of a Southwestern Metropolis,* wrote that the American East, not the emerging West, was the early settlement's model. Pilgrims to territorial Phoenix found beauty in the desert not as it was, but in its potential to be an idealized version of the lands they had left behind: no snow, no industrial grime.

Once Roosevelt Dam guaranteed Phoenix a reliable flow of water, idealism and optimism seemed as pervasive as the year-round sunshine. Something first had to be done about Phoenix summers, however. Evaporative air-conditioning (known as "swamp cooling" to Arizonans today) had been invented in 1908 by one Oscar Palmer at his father's Phoenix sheet metal shop, but amazingly, it was more than two decades before it became commercially available. Into the 1930s, Phoenicians routinely slept outdoors during the summer, on roofs and porches or in screened backyard bedrooms. (Clever residents planted the legs of their outdoor cots in pails of water to dissuade scorpions from crawling into bed with them.) Even after the

Scottsdale's Gray Hawk Country Club has one of Arizona's more than 200 golf courses.

widespread adoption of evaporative cooling, however, the July-August "monsoon" season remained nearly unbearable: during these humid days and nights swamp cooling is about as refreshing as the breath of a panting dog. It was the 1950s invention of refrigerated air-conditioning that finally primed Phoenix for its greatest boom. Without it, the Valley of the Sun would still be an agricultural center and winter resort.

Between 1945 and 1960, more than 300 new industries moved to the Valley, most notable among them Motorola. Phoenix successfully pitched its then-clean air, a climate that would never disrupt a manufacturer's operations or transportation, its leisurely lifestyle, and probably most significant of all, Arizona's right-to-work law passed over the bitter objections of the labor unions in 1946.

During these great boom years, though, Phoenix's character was frequently called into question—a process that continued even into the 1980s. Down in intellectually priggish and older Tucson, people groused that there was nothing going on in Phoenix except the making of money and the playing of golf. The bigger city seemed like a gawky adolescent whose growth hormones had gone berserk, but whose cultural development was stalled at potty training. Except for the Heard Museum, Phoenix had no nationally recognized cultural resources, no pro sports until the 1970s, and no tangible urban atmosphere.

■ TROUBLE IN PARADISE

The engine that drives the Phoenix boom today is the city's raw youth. For practical purposes, Phoenix as an urban entity is little more than 50 years old, which means that only energy and determination matter, not bloodlines or connections.

"There's a competitive spirit here that is almost Darwinian," says Michael Lacey, editor of the liberal and aggressive *New Times* weekly. "People come out here, they create their own histories, they create their own reputations. It's not based on who your family is. Sure, Phoenix is pretty conservative, politically and morally. But entrepreneurially, things are still up for grabs here."

There is trouble in entrepreneurial paradise, however. Intoxicated by the boom, Phoenix never got around to effectively planning its growth or managing its resources. Consequently, air pollution is bad enough in winter that Valley motorists have to use EPA-mandated oxygenated gasoline—and on most mornings, a phlegmatic yellow-brown cloud hangs over the Valley like an inverted bowl.

Phoenix has never effectively controlled development on most of the metropolitan area's numerous mountains and buttes. Pretentious houses encrust the slopes of landmarks such as Camelback Mountain, and developers still gouge roadways across ridgelines and into canyons for eventual subdivisions.

Water demand is outstripping the capacity of the Salt and Verde watersheds to supply it, so the metropolitan area is now counting on the Central Arizona Project, which channels water from the Colorado River uphill to Phoenix and Tucson. But even this may not be enough to ensure either city's survival: the Colorado River, already dammed and diverted and drained to within an inch of its life, may not have enough water in it to meet CAP projections. The experts are divided.

Contemporary Phoenix, however, is behaving very much like a city with a future. Having pumped new life into its downtown, civic leaders seem to have gained a confidence and an optimism they previously lacked. Perhaps they can solve the other problems, as well.

The Nelson Fine Arts Center at Arizona State University in Tempe.

■ DOWNTOWN PHOENIX *map pages 188–189*

The one-square-block **Heritage and Science Park** encompasses three important Phoenix institutions, all connected by a tree-lined walkway that runs from Monroe Street south to Washington Street.

Heritage Square contains more than a half-dozen restored homes from the turn of the 19th century, some of which house museums and are open for tours. *Monroe and Seventh Streets; 602-262-5071.*

The **Phoenix Museum of History** shows what life was like in early Phoenix. Some examples: the local "jail" was a rock with a chain attached; oyster parlors were a major fad; and townsfolk left clothes hanging in trees at the edge of town so Native Americans entering Phoenix could comply with an ordinance requiring all people to be fully dressed while in town. *105 North Fifth Street; 602-253-2734.*

Best of all, especially if you're traveling with kids, is the adjacent **Arizona Science Center,** a massive complex that includes a planetarium and an Iwerks theater. Exhibits change regularly, but one constant is an air-traffic control center that lets you see (for better or worse) what's going on at Sky Harbor International Airport. *600 East Washington Street; 602-716-2000.*

The **Orpheum Theatre,** an ornate Spanish Baroque Revival–style confection that debuted in 1929, has gone through as many incarnations as its downtown Phoenix location: over the years it has served as a vaudeville house, movie theater (screening English- and Spanish-language films in different decades), and even, occasionally, a venue for plays. The completion of a $14 million restoration, begun in 1988 and financed by a combination of municipal bonds and private donations, was marked by a January 1997 production of *Hello Dolly!,* starring Carol Channing. *203 West Adams Street; 602-534-5600.*

Bank One Ballpark, a retractable-roof stadium with air conditioning, became home to Major League Baseball's Arizona Diamondbacks in 1998. Between the Phoenix Suns basketball and the Phoenix Coyotes hockey teams, and the Diamondbacks, downtown Phoenix is guaranteed more than 160 days of sporting events each year. However, when nothing is happening, visitors can take hour-and-a-half guided tours of BOB, as it's affectionately known. Highlights include the private pool area near third base, the National Baseball Hall of Fame, and the field seeded with DeAnza grass, a hybrid especially developed for the stadium to withstand both sun and air-conditioning. *401 East Jefferson Street at Seventh Street; 602-462-6799.*

Mae West motored over to the Orpheum Theatre in 1933 to promote the premiere of her movie I'm No Angel. *(Famous line: "When I'm good, I'm very good, but when I'm bad, I'm better.")*

The **Burton Barr Central Library**—designed by Will Bruder, who was also responsible for the Scottsdale Museum of Contemporary Art—is an architectural delight, worth visiting even if you don't need reading material. The futuristic copper structure was inspired by Monument Valley, and the top-floor reading room's skylights are designed to create a once-a-year illusion: visit at noon on June 21— the summer solstice—and it will appear that the place has burst into flames. *1221 North Central Avenue; 602-262-4636.*

The **Heard Museum** contains more than 35,000 Native American artifacts and artworks, ranging from prehistoric to contemporary, with the focus on the Southwest. Opened in 1929 in the Spanish Colonial–style home of Dwight and Mae Heard, the museum has evolved over the years into one of the best places in the country to learn about Indian history and art. You'll see lots of traditional crafts here, but you'll also find exhibits that counter stereotypes of Indian art. In addition, historical displays on controversial topics, such as the transport of Indian

children to boarding schools, help give a well-rounded picture of the relationship of Native Americans to white culture. There's an excellent sculpture garden, and on the weekends, Native American artisans and craftspeople offer frequent demonstrations. The World Championship Hoop Dance Competition is held here in early February, and the Guild Indian Fair and Market in early March. *2301 North Central Avenue; 602-252-8840.*

The **Phoenix Art Museum** is the Southwest's largest art museum, with more than 17,000 pieces in its collection of American, European, Asian, Latin American, and contemporary art. The paintings of the American West include Maxfield Parrish's richly hued *Arizona* (1950), along with works by Bierstadt, Remington, and other genre notables. The permanent holdings aren't especially impressive, but the visiting shows often are; if a major exhibition is coming to Arizona, the odds are good it will appear here. The museum's Cowboy Artists of America sale takes place in October. *1625 North Central Avenue; 602-257-1222.*

(above) The interactive exhibits at the popular Arizona Science Center intrigue children and adults. (opposite) The 1895 Rosson House is one of the restored houses in Heritage Square.

Spring training baseball at Scottsdale Stadium.

Spring Training

For the most concentrated dose of Cactus League fever, take a hotel room in March in Scottsdale, Phoenix's upscale neighbor. Preferably, find a hotel (like the Day's Inn) that also houses the players of one of the nine or so major league teams that base their training operations in the Phoenix area. But then again, that isn't really necessary; you're pretty close to most of the action just being in Scottsdale.

Within a few blocks of the major hotels on Scottsdale Road is modern Scottsdale Stadium, where the San Francisco Giants play their games. A 20-minute drive will pass at least two other ball parks, one of which is sure to have a game. The Oakland Athletics and the Milwaukee Brewers play in Phoenix (at Phoenix Municipal Stadium and Maryvale Baseball Park, respectively), and the Anaheim Angels are close by at Tempe Diablo Stadium.

Several other baseball stadiums lie within 45 minutes of Scottsdale. The town of Mesa is home to the Chicago Cubs, the Seattle Mariners play at a Peoria park that is also home to the San Diego Padres, and a new stadium in the town of Surprise hosts the two newest additions to the Cactus League: the Kansas City Royals and the Texas Rangers. A two-hour drive down I-10 brings you to Tucson, where the Colorado Rockies hold forth at Hi Corbett Field, and the Arizona Diamondbacks and Chicago

White Sox share Tucson Electric Park. It's a good idea to order your tickets before you even go to Arizona; spring baseball has become awfully fashionable. The Mesa Convention and Visitors Bureau (800-283-6372; www.mesacvb.com) has all the contact information and schedules.

In addition to the regularly scheduled major league games, you should consider other, potentially more intimate baseball experiences. Call the team offices to learn when the "B" games are scheduled; usually these are played in the mornings, at smaller facilities that allow real contact with the younger players. (As a rule, you won't find too many front-line players at these games.) You can also search out training fields where teams teach technique and hold minor-league scrimmages—try Indian School Road in Scottsdale, or near Tempe Diablo Stadium.

After the game, or for dinner, try the **Pink Pony** (3831 North Scottsdale Road; 480-945-6697), once the traditional stomping ground of real baseball people but now more of a hot spot for visitors and fans. The steaks are good and the bar is hopping. Not too far away is **Don and Charlie's** (7501 East Camelback Road; 480-990-0900), which is "home" to Cubs and Giants and their fans. The waitresses are often wives or girlfriends of players, and they can talk baseball knowledgeably. Back in Phoenix, there is good food and lots of baseball life at **Avanti** (2728 East Thomas Road; 602-956-0900). Be sure to make reservations at these places, as they're crowded during the spring.

When you come, expect the weather to be good and hot. Bring your swimsuit, sun block, and extra-dark shades. Plan on renting a car (a pink Cadillac convertible is the automobile of choice), because the Valley of the Sun is laid out like Los Angeles and public transportation is inconvenient.

—Gene Seltzer

■ **PAPAGO PARK AREA** *map pages 188–189*

Papago Park, which straddles east-central Phoenix and Tempe and abuts Scottsdale, encompasses several key attractions. (The Hohokam Indians, who built canals and villages in this area, were long known as the Papago—thus the name.) The highlight, the **Desert Botanical Garden,** is discussed in the "Deserts" chapter.

The **Phoenix Zoo,** next door to the botanical garden, is home to more than a thousand animals in habitats that closely resemble their natural settings. Environments include a tropical rainforest, grasslands, mountains, temperate woodlands, and, of course, the desert. *455 North Galvin Parkway; 602-273-1341.*

The **Pueblo Grande Museum and Archaeological Park** provides a stark contrast between Phoenix past and Phoenix present, with its Hohokam ruins sandwiched between several freeways near Sky Harbor International Airport; some of the artifacts showcased in the adjacent museum were unearthed when a new runway was being built. A 2.5-mile path leads around remains of a Hohokam village, including a platform mound and ball court. *4619 East Washington Street; 602-495-0900 or 877-706-4408.*

The **Hall of Flame Firefighting Museum** showcases more than 100 pieces of fire equipment dating from as far back as 1726. Exhibits include three operating alarm rooms, one of which was used by the Phoenix fire department in the 1950s. Tours are self-guided, but the retired firefighters who volunteer here are happy to elaborate on the displays. *6101 East Van Buren Street; 602-275-3473.*

The **Arizona Historical Society Museum** covers the entire state's past with sophisticated displays, but the standout sections are those about World War II—largely responsible for Phoenix's modern development. Arizona was the site of the two largest flight training centers in the country and hosted 23 prisoner of war camps, one of which gained notoriety for having the largest mass POW escape in the United States. *1300 North College Avenue; 480-929-0292.*

■ VALLEY OF THE SUN

About 22 satellite communities orbit around Phoenix—the exact number is slightly vague because towns are always changing incorporation status. Some towns feel like suburbs, but others have distinct personalities—and histories—of their own. The little town of Guadalupe, for example, squeezed between Tempe and Phoenix's South Mountain Park, is a Yaqui Indian settlement, founded in 1904 as a refugee camp. The Yaquis, indigenous to Mexico, were around that time being conscripted into forced labor by Mexican President Porfirio Diaz, and thousands gained sanctuary in Arizona. Another sanctuary at the opposite corner of the valley is Sun City, manufactured in 1965 as one of the first retirement villages in the nation. Sun City's statutes still prohibit home ownership by anyone younger than 55, and 80 percent of its registered voters are Republican. It has its own professional symphony orchestra. Mesa, 15 miles east of Phoenix, is Arizona's third-largest city and its fastest-growing one; it was founded by Mormons, and is a place where people raise families.

Shane James inspects T. Rex at the Mesa Southwest Museum.

THE GREATER PHOENIX SHOP-A-THON

Shopping in the Valley of the Sun has been raised to Olympic competition level, with Scottsdale the winner in almost every category. A short scorecard:

SCOTTSDALE

Art galleries and tony boutiques are concentrated in Old Town and downtown, and upscale malls of every size and configuration can be found all around the city. One standout is the posh **Scottsdale Fashion Square** (Scottsdale Road and Camelback Road; 480-941-2140), where Nordstrom, Neiman Marcus, and 200 high-end specialty shops help fill nearly 2 million square feet of indoor space. Also impressive is **Kierland Commons** (Scottsdale Road at Greenway Parkway; 480-348-1577), an outdoor village–style complex fairly new to the scene but already thriving.

PHOENIX

The gift shop at the Heard Museum is the best reason for the retail-bound to head downtown. A not-so-close second is the **Arizona Center** (Van Buren Street between Third and Fifth Streets; 602-271-4000), more of an outdoor entertainment complex than mall, but with small shops and carts that are good for souvenirs, especially those bearing Phoenix sports-team logos. At central Phoenix's **Biltmore Fashion Park** (Camelback Road and 24th Street; 602-955-8400), upscale emporiums like Saks and Gucci mingle with middle-of-the-roaders such as Macy's and Pottery Barn.

TEMPE

Mill Avenue, from University Drive near the Arizona State University campus to Rio Salado Parkway, is less quirky than it used to be, but it's still young and hip. **Arizona Mills** (I-10 and U.S. 60; 480-491-9700) is home to discount outlets like Last Call Neiman Marcus and Marshall's, and oversized retailers such as Virgin Megastore and Oshman's Supersports USA. An IMAX theater and a branch of Steven Spielberg's high-tech GameWorks play center make it extremely kid-friendly.

GLENDALE

About a 20-minute drive west of downtown Phoenix, Glendale is the Valley's antiques mecca, with more than 90 stores devoted to remembrances of things past. **Old Towne Glendale,** on Glendale Avenue between 57th Avenue and 58th Drive, has the largest concentration of shops, but the converted bungalows in the historic **Catlin Court district,** a few blocks to the north, are well worth a treasure hunt.

Frank Lloyd Wright built his winter home, Taliesin West, in Scottsdale, designing the structure to blend in with its desert surroundings.

■ SCOTTSDALE *map pages 188–189*

Scottsdale, with a population of 214,090 and growing, represents wealth, resorts, and art galleries. It's also one of the most progressive communities in the state with regard to preserving its natural beauty. Founded as a farm village in 1888 by Winfield Scott, an army chaplain, it was for the following 60 years determinedly bucolic. A 1913 headline in the *Arizona Gazette*—with classic Arizona booster-ism—described it as a "lovely oasis where olives and fruit vie with cotton and alfalfa in paying tribute to soil of great richness."

The boosters eventually attracted enough attention to the lovely oasis that agri-culture shrank into eclipse. Frank Lloyd Wright came in 1937 to build his winter home, Taliesin West, at the foot of the McDowell Mountains. A stream of artists followed the famous architect. Dude ranches sprang up, eventually to be replaced by world-class resorts. Eleanor Roosevelt, among others, came to shop. By the late 1960s, Scottsdale had international fame as a winter resort and art center.

Students of urban development appreciate Scottsdale for other reasons. Because land in Arizona historically was cheap and seemingly unlimited, towns and cities typically oozed into the horizons along spines of strip-zoned commercial development. Garish signs and billboards lined the strips, bleating for attention and generating visual cacophony. Scottsdale was the first Arizona city to attack this blight, enacting a restrictive sign ordinance in 1969. Drive today along Scottsdale Road, the town's most important artery, and there is relative visual tranquility compared with most of the other main streets in the state.

Scottsdale used to promote itself as "The West's Most Western Town." Today, the only remnants of the frontier are the very expensive Western paintings in the galleries clustered along **Fifth Avenue.** Other types of art are represented in Scottsdale too. The **Scottsdale Center for the Arts** (7380 East Second Street; 480-994-2787) has changing exhibits in its lobby gallery as well as an impressive performing arts series in its 800-seat theater. Right next door in a former movie theater sits the **Scottsdale Museum of Contemporary Art** (7380 East Second Street; 480-994-2787), which mounts some of the Valley's most interesting, cutting-edge shows.

Civic Center Mall hosts numerous events among its grassy knolls, shade trees, fountains, and flower gardens—particularly in late winter and early spring, when temperatures are near perfect. There is a Festival of the Arts in March, a renowned Culinary Festival in April, and free outdoor concerts every Sunday afternoon until the weather gets unbearably hot. *Scottsdale Road; 480-994-2787.*

Set in the foothills of the McDowell Mountains in northeast Scottsdale is **Taliesin West,** founded in 1937 as the winter home of Frank Lloyd Wright and his school of architecture. The low-slung Taliesin West buildings—built of stone and redwood beams—exemplify Wright's philosophy that structures should fit into their natural settings and "grow from the inside out." Associates and students at Taliesin West continue to follow in Wright's footsteps. The gift shop aside, the grounds may only be visited on guided tours, which are conducted year-round. *12621 Frank Lloyd Wright Boulevard, at Cactus Road; 480-860-8810.*

Farther north in Scottsdale, in the El Pedregal complex near the Boulders Resort, is a smaller branch of the **Heard Museum.** This outpost doesn't have the scope of the one in downtown Phoenix, but often puts on excellent original shows. *34505 North Scottsdale Road, Suite 22; 480-488-9817.*

A welcome sign in Old Scottsdale points visitors to the town's Chamber of Commerce.

■ TEMPE *map pages 188–189*

Tempe's highlights are its great downtown and **Arizona State University**—the state's largest university, with more than 45,000 students on its main campus. Tempe started life as a ferry landing on the Salt River in 1871. Its original name was Hayden's Ferry, but a later visitor thought the landscape, punctuated with hulking gray-red buttes and groves of mesquite, reminded him of the Vale of Tempe in Greece.

Tempe's future character was ordained in 1885, when the Territorial Legislature voted to build the state's normal school, or teachers college, in the town. That future, however, was a very long time in gestation. Tucson and graduates of its University of Arizona lobbied successfully for decades to keep their little rival in Tempe both poor and obscure. Finally in 1958, while the legislature still cowered, a statewide referendum resulted in a change of name to Arizona State University (ASU). Academic respectability and parity with the old university to the south were inevitable, given the Valley's political muscle, but this still took another 20 years to achieve.

Thanks to the university, Tempe has a more animated night life and more entertainment options than all the other Valley towns except Scottsdale. ASU hosts one of college football's major bowl games, the Fiesta Bowl, and the school's **University Art Museum** is known for its collection of American, Latin American, contemporary, print, and craft art. *Nelson Fine Arts Center, Mill Avenue and 10th Street; 480-965-2787.*

Tempe's compact downtown also has more life in it than all of the other satellites combined (again, excepting Scottsdale)—the result of a rare urban renewal success story. On **Mill Avenue,** the city widened the main street sidewalks, planted a forest of ficus trees, and restored three blocks of handsome turn-of-the-19th-century commercial buildings.

Even more dramatically, in the late 1990s, the city transformed the Salt River and its flood plain—which cuts off downtown on the north—into the 220-acre **Tempe Town Lake.** Retail and restaurant development along its shores has proceeded slower than the planners anticipated, but the 5-mile linear **Tempe Beach Park** became instantly popular with bikers, joggers, and water-sports enthusiasts: From the kiosk (480-517-4050) on West Rio Salado Parkway you can rent canoes, kayaks, and electric boats.

■ OUTDOOR PLACES AND PURSUITS *map pages 188–189*

Phoenix's several mountain ranges are not as high as those surrounding Tucson, but they are worth exploring. Other outdoor pursuits include tubing and golfing.

■ PIESTEWA PEAK (SQUAW PEAK)

Squaw Peak was renamed in 2003 to honor Army Pfc. Lori Piestewa, a casualty of the Iraq War and the first Native American female to be killed in combat. The summit trail, which rises 1,200 feet in 1.2 miles, is a hikers' highway, especially in winter. At the top, you find yourself on the edge of a wilderness preserve that stretches for several miles within the city. *Nine miles north of downtown. Take the Squaw Peak Drive turnoff north from Lincoln Drive near 20th Street.*

■ CAMELBACK MOUNTAIN

At 2,704 feet, Camelback Mountain is the area's highest peak. The summit trail from Echo Canyon climbs 1,260 feet in just over a mile. Along it are large boulders, palo verde trees, and saguaro cactus. *Accessible via Echo Canyon, off McDonald Drive east of Tatum Boulevard on the eastern edge of Phoenix.*

■ SOUTH MOUNTAIN PARK PRESERVE

At 16,400 acres, the world's largest municipal park, this desert preserve has the Valley's best selection of trails. They range from an easy 1-mile loop to the very rugged 14.3-mile round-trip National Trail, and several take you past petroglyphs. *10409 South Central Avenue (about 2 miles past Baseline); 602-534-6324.*

■ TUBING THE SALT RIVER

A traditional spring pastime (if there's been enough winter snow in the mountains) is "tubing" the Salt—floating down the gentle Salt River east of Phoenix in an inner tube. Boating and jet skiing are also popular on the chain of lakes created by the dams on the Salt; Roosevelt Lake, 50 miles east of Phoenix, is the largest.

■ GOLFING

There are more than 200 courses in the Valley, from municipal links to championship layouts. It can cost a fortune to play golf here during winter, and courses are often crowded. Summertime brings bargain green fees and wide-open play. *Course information: Arizona Golf Association; 602-944-3035.*

T U C S O N

There is something special, even mystical, in the desert light of Tucson. Lynn Taber-Borcherdt, an artist who moved here from Chicago, says, "In the early works here, I began painting sharp, over-exaggerated shadows. You would know what time of day it was in the painting by the shadows. Then I started noticing that sometimes when the sun was setting, and I would be on the other side of a cholla, I could see it glowing. So then I moved into making the objects in the painting glow, or almost pulsate, with light. Now my new thing is to let different colors of light bathe my paintings—the amber of twilight, the blue-green cast of moonlight on the mountainside. I'm fascinated with luminosity and iridescence. If I hadn't come to Tucson, none of this would have found its way into my work. My paintings in Chicago were dark, dark, dark, dark, dark."

Taber-Borcherdt's observation reaffirms an old Tucson aphorism: you get paid in sunshine. It's true enough in economic terms—Tucson is a low-wage city, but there are always plenty of people willing to stick around and take the low-wage jobs, supplementing their paychecks, in a sense, with the psychological rewards of living in a place with a (mostly) benign climate and astounding natural beauty. But the light—constantly changing, toying with the forms and textures of the mountain slopes—is a source of inspiration all by itself.

Nature has not created many more spectacular natural settings for a city. Metropolitan Tucson's 890,000-odd people sprawl across a desert basin defined by four mountain ranges, each lying in a cardinal direction from the city's midpoint and each exuding a distinctive character. The Santa Catalinas on the north (the highest, Mount Lemmon, rises 9,157 feet) are heroic and craggy, a late Beethoven sonata of gneiss and granite. The Rincons, to the east, appear smooth and rounded, as if they had been buffed. The twin peaks of the Santa Ritas, to the south, often wear caps of snow; the summit of Mount Wrightson towers to 9,453 feet. The small Tucson Mountains close off the western horizon like randomly sized sawteeth. While Phoenix's much smaller mountains seem to poke up in the middle of the urban area, like geological afterthoughts, Tucson is contained by its mountains.

The city, sorry to report, has not lived up to its stage setting. Strip-zoned arteries 6, 8, or 10 miles long, choked with billboards and speculative shopping centers, carry rivers of traffic between the mountains. There is little distinguished public architecture. In writing about his hometown for the *Arizona Republic,* Kenneth LeFave admitted, "At first glance, Tucson is one of the ugliest cities on Earth. . . . Tucson from the highway looks like a truck stop."

Tucson's character, however, is not illustrated in its architecture. Its story is more complex than that.

■ BOOBY PRIZE PAYS OFF

The seminal event in Tucson's history as an American town was a rainstorm a few hundred miles away. This was in 1885, and Tucson had dispatched its delegate, C. C. Stephens, to the Territorial Legislature in Prescott with instructions to bring home some political pork. His stagecoach got stuck in the mud, and by the time he arrived, the legislature had parceled out the coveted insane asylum to Phoenix and the teachers college to Tempe, leaving only the university for Tucson. In the crude frontier town this was so widely regarded as the booby prize that when Stephens came home to explain it at a public meeting, he was pelted with eggs, rotten vegetables, and a dead cat.

Sonoran-style adobe buildings still lined Tucson's Stone Avenue in the 1880s.

Tucson in 1900.
Tucson today.

The University of Arizona opened for business in 1891 with one building, 36 students, and six professors. Its curricula tilted heavily in the direction of mining and agriculture, the two sciences that had immediate application in 19th-century Arizona. At this point there was still no high school in the territory, so the professors had to teach prerequisites as well as college courses. With such a modest beginning, it was a decade or two before Tucson began to feel the influence of its frontier university and forgave poor C. C. Stephens.

The University of Arizona today has almost 35,000 students, a massive research establishment, and a major intercollegiate sports juggernaut: The Wildcats basketball team is often in the NCAA's Final Four playoffs, and won the national championship in 1997. The university shapes the city's character as pervasively as the mountains have shaped its geography. Compared with Phoenix, Tucson is more liberal, more cosmopolitan, more intellectual, more conceited—and less wealthy. The university is the city's largest employer, and the spine of its economy. When Tucson is mentioned in the national news, it is usually because of the university. The process of dendrochronology—tree-ring dating—was developed on its campus, as was the newer science of garbology—the study of contemporary human cultures by analyzing what they throw away. The university's facilities have attracted everything from a scrap of the Shroud of Turin (for testing) to a postseason college football game, the Copper Bowl.

■ EMBRACING THE DESERT

Tucson also distances itself from Phoenix by its attitude toward the Sonoran Desert. Phoenix repudiates the desert; Tucson embraces it. There is relatively little agriculture in Tucson's history, no irrigation, and no river comparable to the Salt. Tucson's "rivers" are its network of arroyos, dry most days out of the year, but periodically tearing through town on muddy, rain-swollen rampages. Even when dry, however, these arroyos nourish what biologists call a xeroriparian habitat, a word marrying Greek and Latin roots for "dry" and "riverbank." These are linear forests of mesquite and palo verde trees and bird habitats, and they extend tendrils of the lushest imaginable desert through the urban landscape. Reminded so frequently of the desert they live in, Tucsonans tend to be more respectful of it.

Grass lawns—a preposterous waste of water in this climate—still grow in the older, central part of the city, but in many newer subdivisions grass isn't even allowed. Most Tucsonans, in fact, have learned to *hate* grass.

The truth is, Tucson will never be much like Phoenix, because its people have always been more individualistic, more contentious, unwilling to agree on any single vision for the city. It seems as though most Tucsonans have not, for the most part, moved here in order to build a great city, but to be left alone and pursue personal dreams. They fight incessantly, but mostly they fight *against* things, such as freeways and rezonings of virgin desert land, rather than *for* things. There are more environmentalists per square mile in Tucson than anywhere else in Arizona, yet there was little support for quality-of-life urban projects for many years.

"I think people have moved here to get away from things: cold weather, families, commitments," the Arizona Theatre Company's former director, Gary Gisselman, once said. He tried to schedule plays that would encourage people to think about community, but there is no evidence so far that this has borne fruit.

But is this metropolis of 850,000 determined individualists an unproductive place? Decidedly not. The sanctuary movement to defy the U.S. government and protect Central American refugees from deportation was born in Tucson. Biosphere 2, a controversial experiment in which eight "bionauts" spent two years in a sealed ecosystem, is just outside of town. And despite all odds, in November 1999, Tucson voters approved $350 million in future taxes to be set aside for Rio Nuevo, a multifaceted plan to revitalize downtown. The ambitious project originally included, among other things, reclaiming the Santa Cruz River, restoring its connection with "A" Mountain (formerly Shtook-Shone, site of Tucson's first Native American settlement and the source of the city's name), renovating historic buildings, constructing roadways, and embarking on several new projects: a new Sonoran Sea Aquarium, an International Visitors and Trade Center, a new home for the Arizona Historical Society Museum and for the Flandrau Science Center and Planetarium, a Presidio Historic Park, and a new convention hotel.

Significant private-sector investment was crucial to the plan, and by 2003, the recession had made things a bit iffy; the aquarium, for example, had already been scrapped. But archaeological digs in preparation for the project have unearthed fascinating data, including the fact that Tucson's first dwellers might have arrived 4,000 years ago—making the city the longest continuously occupied settlement in North America. And, if nothing else, there's been more focus on renewing downtown.

■ DOWNTOWN TUCSON *map page 209*

The **Barrio Histórico,** 13 square blocks just south of downtown on Main, Meyer, and Convent Avenues, has some wonderful Sonoran adobe row houses and the city's most prominent museum, which is packaged with nearby structures as the **Tucson Museum of Art and Historic Block.**

The collections in the main building of the **Tucson Museum of Art** focus on modern art, but they're not the museum's strong point. More interesting are the Western paintings and sculpture in the 1867 adobe Edward Nye Fish House; the pre-Columbian, Spanish Colonial, and Latin American folk art in a similar building, the Palice Pavilion; the Arts and Crafts furnishings of the 1907 mission revival–style J. Knox Corbett House; and La Casa Cordova, a Mexican-style adobe house with two small rooms that interpret life in the 1850–1880 era. *140 North Main Avenue (between Alameda Street and Washington Avenue); 520-624-2333.*

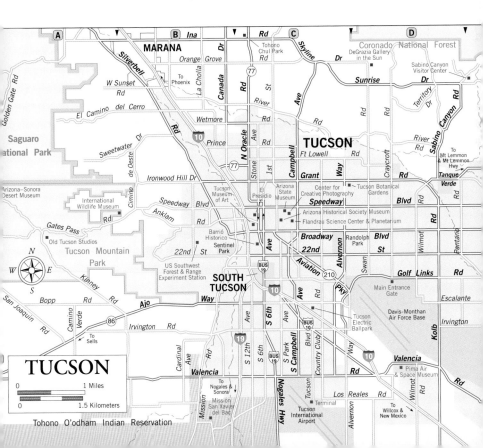

THE AMBIENCE THAT PHOENIX LACKS

"Downtown," began a senior official in the city administration, "it's a place for ex-hippie entrepreneurs to occasionally go broke. Perhaps some have tried chemical substances and think that because they have nostalgia for certain items, so do others. Your average downtown store changes owners and merchandise maybe every five years. The rationale is certainly not economic, but maybe—as far as some of the store owners are concerned—therapeutic. Ultimately, after the last ex-hippie, say, goes broke, the city may try a major renovation, with potted plants on the sidewalks and stores that sell more things that people want. But the record in the Southwest suggests that even when this type of thing is done right, the nearest mall still beats it to shit." Whatever the truth of such comments, this downtown helped give Tucson the ambience that Phoenix lacked.

—Robert D. Kaplan, *An Empire Wilderness,* 1998

El Presidio, one block north of downtown, illustrates in the space of one block the transformation of Tucson from a Mexican to an American village. The Spanish army built El Presidio del San Augustin del Tucson in 1776, and enclosed the fortress in 1783 with an adobe wall—a section of which is still visible on the second floor of the **Pima County Courthouse,** built in 1927. The Spanish Colonial Revival courthouse stands on the edge of El Presidio Park, the district's central plaza. *Bordered by Franklin and Pennington Streets and Main and Church Avenues.*

■ **CENTRAL TUCSON** *map page 209*

Of the many attractions at the University of Arizona open to the public, one of the best is the **Arizona Historical Society Museum,** headquarters for the state's historical society. The library has an excellent collection of old photographs, and interesting lectures take place on many evenings in high season. *949 East Second Street at Park Avenue; 520-628-5774.*

The collections of the fine **Arizona State Museum** occupy two buildings: the original 1893 south building, focusing on fossils and dendrochronology, and the 1990s north building, with multimedia exhibits on native Arizonans and northern Mexican cultures. *Near Park Avenue at University Boulevard; 520-621-6302.*

Ansel Adams conceived the **Center for Creative Photography,** which holds his work and that of other art photographers. *1030 North Olive Road, south of Speedway Boulevard; 520-621-7968.*

Flandrau Science Center and Planetarium is a great place to learn about astronomy. In the evening, weather permitting, you can take pictures through a 16-inch telescope. *Cherry Avenue and University Boulevard; 520-621-7827.*

Because of cactus competition from the Arizona–Sonora Desert Museum and Saguaro National Park, the **Tucson Botanical Gardens** receive less attention than they would if they were anywhere else in the world, but they provide a center-city oasis. Among the gardens are one designed to attract birds and one that dates from the 1930s. *2150 North Alvernon Way, south of Grant Road; 520-326-9686.*

■ AROUND TUCSON

■ FOOTHILLS

The two-lane **Mount Lemmon Highway** travels through the spectacular Santa Catalina Mountains on the city's northern edge (see page 60). Closer to Tucson, **Sabino Canyon's** 4.2-mile Phone Line Trail offers fine views (see page 84).

The University of Arizona's Center for Creative Photography.

■ NORTHWEST

A lush 48-acre desert preserve, **Tohono Chul Park** features demonstration gardens, a greenhouse, a small art gallery, two excellent gift shops, and a tearoom/restaurant that is especially popular for Sunday brunch. *7366 North Paseo del Norte, one block west of Ina Road; 520-742-6455.*

■ WEST SIDE

Arizona–Sonora Desert Museum (Tucson Mountain Park, 2021 North Kinney Road; 520-883-2702), a zoo, arboretum, and natural-history museum, exhibits Sonoran animals and plants in their natural settings (see page 34).

Saguaro National Park (off I-10 east and West of Tucson; 520- 733-5100) is the Sonoran Desert's most fascinating and famous cactus forest (see page 34).

It's touristy and kid-oriented these days, but **Old Tucson Studios** was built in 1939 for the motion picture *Arizona*—starring William Holden, Rita Hayworth, and Glenn Ford—and was used as a movie location through the 1980s. Most of the old sets burned down in a mid-1990s fire and financial woes have made the site's future uncertain, but it's still fun to come for the production shows, simulated shoot-outs, and film clips of classic westerns. *Tucson Mountain Park, 201 South Kinney Road; 520-883-0100.*

■ EAST SIDE

The **Pima Air and Space Museum** has one of the world's largest private collections of historic aircraft, displayed in 75 outdoor acres and five huge indoor hangars. Among the 250 aircraft are an SR-71 Blackbird—the fastest jet ever built—and the surprisingly modest Air Force One plane used by Presidents John F. Kennedy and Lyndon B. Johnson. Tours of Davis-Monthan Air Force base also leave from here. *6000 East Valencia Road, off I-10; 520-574-0462.*

Among the world's largest dry caverns, **Colossal Cave** is so vast that parts of it still haven't been explored. Guided tours mix scientific facts with romantic legends—such as the one about the gold reputed to be hidden here from a stagecoach robbery. The beautiful surrounding desert and the historic visitors center, built by the Civilian Conservation Corps between 1934 and 1938, add to the appeal. *Twenty miles east of Tucson. Take Broadway Boulevard or East 22nd Street to Old Spanish Trail, then turn right to Colossal Cave Road; or take I-10 to Exit 279 (Vail-Wentworth) and follow signs; 520-647-7275.*

■ SOUTH OF TOWN

Arguably the most important historic site in Tucson, **Mission San Xavier del Bac** is a monument to Spanish baroque architecture. Built by Franciscan missionaries in the late 1700s, with elegant arches and domes covered in a skin of gleaming white stucco, the adobe-brick structure has twin bell towers (the top of one was left unfinished), a central dome, and an ornately carved stone portal. Inside the mission's mesquite doors lies a treasure trove of late Mexican baroque art. In the 1990s, a large restoration project was undertaken by members of the same team that restored the Sistine Chapel in Rome; they trained many of the church's parishioners to participate. As a result, interior frescoes and carved wooden figures have a new luster. *Follow I-10 east to I-19 south, and then take Exit 92 to the Mission; 520-294-2624.*

At the **Titan II Missile Museum,** you can take an hour-long guided tour (involving many steps) to view a disarmed ICBM—the only one of the country's 54 Titan II missiles that wasn't destroyed by mid-1987 as a result of a treaty with the Soviet Union—in its underground silo. You won't find many Cold War relics more fascinating than this one. *Twenty miles southeast of Tucson, off I-19, Duval Mine Road Exit (head west); 520-625-7736.*

■ NORTH OF TOWN

Biosphere 2 Center has managed to stay in the news since the early 1990s, when four men and four women were locked into a 3-acre airtight structure that looks like a giant terrarium. The plan was to research an ecosystem's ability to recycle air, water, and nutrients in order to sustain plant and animal life. It was controversial, and not only because members of the opposite sex were sealed off from the rest of the world together: in addition, many of the members and the project's backer had belonged to a New Mexico cult; their scientific credentials were dubious; and one of the experiment's objectives was to learn how to live on Mars if necessary.

Columbia University took over the facility as a western campus in 1995, lending it legitimacy. Guided tours focus on the scientific experiments conducted there, with a little bit of gossip thrown in. But the Biosphere tradition of controversy continues: in late 2002, citing lack of funds, Columbia announced its intention to terminate its 10-year contract with Biosphere. Lawsuits are now in process. *32540 South Biosphere Road, Oracle, 5 miles northeast of the junction of Route 79 and Route 77; 800-828-2462.*

(following pages) Saguaros frame the beautiful facade of the Mission San Xavier del Bac.

ARIZONA TOWNS

Phoenix and Tucson grab much of the spotlight in Arizona, but the state reveals its varied personality more fully in its many small towns: desert towns, mountain towns, Native American towns, Hispanic towns, mining towns, company towns, farm towns, cow towns, border towns, retirement towns, tourist towns, and ghost towns. What follows is not an all-inclusive, objective tour, but an idiosyncratic stroll through some of the more engaging ones.

■ SOUTHEASTERN ARIZONA *map page 13*

■ BISBEE

"Bisbee—the city of foul odors and sickening smells," sniped the *Tucson Citizen* at the turn of the 19th century. Brewery Gulch, one of its main streets, was an open sewer, "covered with a slime several inches deep and about four feet wide." Gambling and prostitution were endemic, and beds in the rooming houses were booked in shifts. The classical image of the early Bisbee copper miner is that of a man who spent eight hours underground in the mine, the next eight hours boozing and wenching, and the next eight hours sleeping it off. Certainly not everyone's lifestyle conformed to this scenario, but enough did to solidify Bisbee's status as the quintessential Western mining town.

Serious copper mining began in 1880 in these hills and gulches 6 miles north of the Mexican border. By 1900, Bisbee was the largest, most prosperous settlement in Arizona Territory, crude yet remarkably cosmopolitan. The mines attracted immigrants from Germany, Serbia, Italy, Ireland, Mexico, and even Russia. Each group clustered in its own "town" or neighborhood—the Germans making wine, the Serbs raising goats (their neighborhood was called "Goat Grove"), the Irish raising hell. Underground, in the mines, these people depended on each other for their lives, so they got along well. Aboveground, Bisbee was tense with ethnic rivalries. "You never went to the show by yourself; you always took someone with you," recalled Les Williams, a retired miner. "Each 'town' had its own gang. We stole burros from each other, we'd play baseball with each other, then we'd fight after the games."

No longer a mining town, eclectic Bisbee has reinvented itself.

One group, though, was excluded from Bisbee's ethnic stew: an unwritten law held that no "Chinaman" could stay in town overnight. The prejudice was anchored in economics: in early Bisbee, some widows of men killed in mine accidents eked out a living by taking in laundry, and the citizenry feared competition from the Chinese.

The mining era ended in Bisbee in 1975. It had been the town's sole industry, and the economic shock waves were enormous, with houses tumbling onto the market for as little as $800. The low prices attracted a wave of artists, bohemians, and assorted dropouts, and kicked off Bisbee's "hippie era," as older townspeople disdainfully called it, which lasted about a decade. Eventually one of the "hippies" turned 30, opened a restaurant, became mayor, and then opened up a B&B.

Today the town—located on U.S. 80, 94 miles southeast of Tucson—still has some bohemians, many serious artists, wonderful Italianate architecture, no industry (despite persistent rumors that the mines will reopen), and a delightfully seductive spirit. Bisbee is Aspen turned inside out, kicked into a time warp and trapped in a happy reverse universe devoid of traffic lights, designer labels, and pretentious boutiques. Here, you can walk the narrow, decaying streets and hear someone practicing Bach fugues on a piano in a questionable key, or browse galleries displaying Tarahumara artifacts or locally made contemporary pottery. More than any other town in Arizona, Bisbee is a place in which to reinvent oneself; the presence of more than 6,000 people doing just that makes it the most fascinating small town in Arizona.

Bisbee hosts an impressive number of annual events. The Bisbee Arts Commission's Annual Art Auction lures a sizable crowd each Mother's Day, and Brewery Gulch Days, held on Labor Day weekend, include events and contests related to mining. You can also learn about the town's mining past on a tour of the underground **Copper Queen Mine** or the enormous **Lavender Open Pit Mine** (see pages 154–155).

One last piece of advice about visiting Bisbee: bring a camera. The colors, textures, and historic buildings of the town are a photographer's dream.

■ TOMBSTONE

No newspaper ever wore a more memorable masthead than the famous *Tombstone Epitaph*. In its silver-boom prime of the early 1880s, Tombstone was the West's most notoriously violent town. Though its history has been embellished by popular historians and Hollywood, it was undeniably a place in which men lived fast and

Architecturally, the Cochise County Courthouse exuded order and dignity—qualities hard to find anywhere else in Tombstone.

died in trivial quarrels. Killings were so common that the *Epitaph* ran the accounts under a standing headline, "Death's Doings." Lawlessness was abundant enough that in 1882 it even attracted the notice of President Chester A. Arthur, who threatened to send in the army. In the finest tradition of Arizona boosterism, the *Epitaph* responded with an editorial ridiculing Arthur and insisting, "We were never in a more peaceable community than Tombstone and law and order is absolute." In the three months preceding that editorial, the paper had chronicled eight killings.

It was a uniquely colorful town, a mélange of adventurers, drunks, whores, rustlers, wealthy sophisticates, and honest working stiffs. The silver mines were generating enough money that Tombstone built ambitious show halls and imported vaudeville and serious theater. At one point 110 establishments held liquor licenses; according to historian John Myers, Tombstone also offered "the best food between New Orleans and San Francisco."

COWBOY WEDDING

There's two things a cowboy's afraid of: Bein' stranded afoot and a decent woman. I went to a cowboy wedding recently where the bridegroom had found him a decent woman. This was not yer normal walk-down-the-aisle, kiss-the-bride kind of wedding. This was the merger of two Arizona ranching families, complete with rings made out of barbwire, a fiddle playin' "Here Comes the Bride," and mosquitoes.
. . . The bridesmaids all looked beautiful in their long dresses. The groomsmen, however, presented a different picture. Putting a suit on some of those cowboys was like puttin' croutons on a cow pie.... These fellers looked like they were still hangin' in the closet—paralyzed.

Part of their condition could be attributed to the forty-eight-hour bachelor party that preceded the knot tyin'! The groom was maneuvered around on the wedding day like a NASA moonwalker. . . .

It rained a little but no one cared. The bride was lovely. She stood out like a penguin in an asphalt parking lot. The priest asked Dad, "Who gives this woman in matrimony?" He replied, "Her mother and I and the Valley Bank." When it came time for the kiss to seal the vows, the bride and groom spit out their chew and laid to it.

At the bride's request, we played "Walkin' the Dog" as the wedding party marched out. It was fitting, I guess, 'cause Billy's ol' dog, Bronc, caught the bouquet.

—Baxter Black, *Horseshoes, Cowsocks, and Duckfeet,* 2002

The cowboy poet and NPR commentator Baxter Black lives in Cochise County, where he "runs a few cows."

But Tombstone has secured enduring fame not for its culture or cuisine, but for flying lead. The shootout at the O.K. Corral in 1881 remains the most notorious gunfight of all time.

The shootout's complicated prologue was essentially a struggle for political spoils in the newly created Cochise County. On one side were Sheriff Johnny Behan and the Clanton clan, ranchers who moonlighted as cattle rustlers and harbored stagecoach robbers. The (relatively) good guys were U.S. Marshal Wyatt Earp, his brothers Virgil and Morgan, and the infamous alcoholic gunfighter "Doc" Holliday. On the afternoon of October 26, the Earps and Holliday strode

Helldorado Days in Tombstone includes reenactments of the shoot-out at the O.K. Corral.

purposefully into the vacant lot at Fremont and Third Streets, where five young members of the Clanton gang were rumored to be looking for a fight. According to later testimony by Ike Clanton, Wyatt Earp shoved his pistol into Clanton's belly and growled, "You son of a bitch, you can have a fight." Clanton turned white and fled, pistols and shotguns began blazing, and in about 30 seconds— Wyatt Earp's estimate—three of the Clanton men lay dying and Virgil and Morgan Earp had been seriously wounded.

The story doesn't end there, and the aftermath tells much about the nature of life and justice in frontier Tombstone. The Earps and Holliday faced a hearing on murder charges, and were cleared. Two months later, a midnight marksman tried to take out Virgil Earp, but succeeded only in crippling his left arm for life. Three months after that, an assassin did kill Morgan Earp. Wyatt, operating well outside the law on the trail of vengeance, gunned down three of the men he suspected of killing his brother, and then left Cochise County for good.

Seventy miles southeast of Tucson on U.S. 80, Tombstone these days is a tourist town, making a living off its historic infamy. The restored **Crystal Palace Saloon**

The Hotel Nobles in Tombstone, ca. 1888.

(Fifth and Allen Streets; 520-457-3611), among others, is open for business, as is the disheveled **Bird Cage Theater** (Sixth and Allen Streets; 520-457-3421). Though no shows are held here now, Enrico Caruso, Sarah Bernhardt, and Lillian Russell all performed at the Bird Cage, which was a major venue. Just northwest of town, the **Boot Hill Graveyard** (Route 80; 520-457-3944) sells tombstone-shaped souvenirs. Helldorado Days every October includes a parade, gunfight reenactments, and, in several recent years, visits by Edward Earp, a descendant of Wyatt. **Allen Street,** once lined with bars, casinos, and cathouses, has been beautifully restored. (The street has served as a set for Japanese crews filming samurai Westerns.) The original Cochise County Courthouse—built in 1882 and now called **Tombstone Courthouse State Park** (Toughnut and Third Streets; 520-457-3311)—is Arizona's most sophisticated piece of Victorian neoclassical architecture, an anomaly to ponder while listening to the reenacted gunfights echoing in the street two blocks away.

◾ TUBAC

This unincorporated village in the lee of the Santa Rita Mountains is the oldest non-Indian settlement in Arizona and a place redolent with history. Several times in its first 150 years of existence it was a locus of the conflict between Europeans and Native Americans.

Tubac was established as a *visita,* or chapel served by an itinerant priest, in about 1726—that, at any rate, is the date of the first recorded baptisms by one Fr. Agustín de Campos. The next generation was a time of increasing tension in the upper Pima Indian lands (the *Pimería Alta*), with not only more Jesuit missionaries but also Spanish silver miners flooding in. The European attitude was summed up in the term *gente de razón*—"people of reason"—which the Spanish used in census documents to describe themselves, as opposed to the unenlightened (even if freshly baptized) native *bárbaros.* In 1751, the Pimas revolted, killing two priests and more than 100 ranchers and miners, and burning churches—including the one at Tubac. The following year the Spanish established the presidio of Tubac, their first permanent military presence in Arizona.

The 50 soldiers stationed with their families at Tubac succeeded in quieting the Pimas, but the Apaches proved to be the presidio's doom. In 1774 Tubac's commander, Juan Bautista de Anza, made his famous expedition to open a route to California and established the settlement that would become San Francisco. Two years later the Tubac garrison was moved to Tucson, where it could more effectively protect the route. Thus disarmed, Tubac was repeatedly raided, abandoned, and resettled. The journalist J. Ross Browne, who passed through Tubac in 1864, described it in the most pathetic terms: ". . . harassed on both sides by Apaches and Mexicans and without hope of future protection, the inhabitants of Tubac for the last time have abandoned the town, and thus it has remained ever since, a melancholy spectacle of ruin and desolation."

Eventually Tubac did rise again, as the grasslands of the surrounding Santa Cruz Valley seemed ideal for ranching. Then in 1948, a nationally known artist named Dale Nichols established an art school here, and though it lasted but a year, it placed Tubac on the map as an art center.

Charming, slow-paced, and unpretentious, Tubac attracts visitors to its annual festivals, such as the Tubac Festival of the Arts in February, Tubac Art Walk in the spring, and Anza Days in the fall. The town, about 45 miles south of Tucson, has about 100 boutiques and galleries—prices for art are substantially lower in Tubac than in Scottsdale and Sedona—and the excellent **Tubac Presidio State Historic Park** (1 Burruel Street; 520-398-2252). Exhibits here include the town's old schoolhouse, along with older Spanish artifacts. The park is especially lively on Sunday afternoons from October through March, when historic reenactments take place.

The 4.5-mile-long road between the old Tubac presidio and San José de Tumacácori National Historic Park (see page 262) has been designated part of the **Juan Bautista de Anza National Historic Trail,** which will eventually cover de Anza's entire route from the Mexican border to San Francisco. The Tubac section provides a gentle walk along the banks of the Santa Cruz River and, in three spots, across it.

■ CENTRAL ARIZONA

■ PRESCOTT

"Norman Rockwell America," the *Los Angeles Times* once called Prescott. "For those of us who grew up in bland, instant suburbs, Prescott is a glimpse of a childhood we might have chosen instead, had anyone thought to ask," pined the *Tucson Citizen.*

Prescott (say PRESS-kit), a city of 34,000 people, is indeed a picturesque place, and its collection of prim Victorian homes—more of them, by far, than anywhere else in Arizona—inevitably triggers wistful lines from visiting writers. Add a near-perfect mile-high climate with four distinct seasons, none of them harsh, and Prescott seems like everyone's choice for an ideal place to live. Unfortunately, the secret is out, and a rush of new residents and developments in the 1990s erased some of the community's small-town charm. Weekend traffic jams have become commonplace as people head for Bucky's Casino on the Yavapai Reservation near the center of town, or the Hassayampa Golf Course, or the new Westcor mall, or one of the special events that take place in courthouse square almost every weekend between Memorial Day and Labor Day.

Prescott was founded as a consequence of the Civil War. President Lincoln had designated Arizona a territory in 1863 and dispatched his appointed governor, John G. Goodwin, to set up a government. En route Goodwin heard that there was a nucleus of Confederate sympathizers at Tucson, the presumptive capital. The gubernatorial party went instead to Fort Whipple, an army post in northern Arizona, and in 1864 founded the capital of Prescott on politically virgin ground.

Prescott lost its status as capital to Tucson just three years later (eventually the political hub migrated yet again to Phoenix), but nearby gold mining and ranching delivered a boom to the town anyway. It became as legendary for drinking as Tombstone was for gunfighting; by the early 1900s about 40 saloons lined Montezuma Street, still known today as "Whiskey Row." In his book *Roadside History of Arizona,* Marshall Trimble swears that the "macho custom of thirsty cowboys in off the range was to start their binge, or 'whizzer' as they called it, at the Kentucky Bar and take a drink in every bar all the way to the Depot House, thirty-nine saloons away." Forty drinks! There remain a few token historic bars on Whiskey Row, and on Saturday nights they sound boisterous enough to convince passersby that at least a sliver of the tradition endures.

Despite its current growing pains, Prescott remains bucolic compared with Phoenix or Tucson. Industry is small and nonpolluting. There's relatively little crime. The people are friendly. It's not exactly Norman Rockwell America anymore, but it might be as close as you get in the 21st century.

About 100 miles north of Phoenix along U.S. 89, Prescott is home to the excellent **Sharlot Hall Museum** (415 West Gurley Street; 928-445-3122), which sprawls through several historic buildings and details the history of Prescott and Arizona Territory. Smaller but also worth seeing are two museums nearby. The

Palace Bar, Prescott, Arizona

A colorized postcard of the Palace Bar on Whiskey Row in Prescott, ca. 1880.

Smoki Museum (147 North Arizona Avenue; 928-445-1230) is as striking for its pueblo-style architecture as for its collection of Native American artifacts. The **Phippen Art Museum** (4701 North U.S. 89; 928-778-1385), in the Granite Dells just north of town, was founded by the first president of the Cowboy Artists of America and focuses on works by Western artists. The surrounding **Prescott National Forest** is laced with delightful mountain hiking trails; ask for a map at the U.S. Forest Service office in town (344 South Cortez Street; 928-771-4700).

Prescott has an inordinate number of festivals and annual events for a town its size. Among them: the Bluegrass Festival (June); Territorial Days, which include a crafts fair, entertainment, and tours of historic homes (June); and Frontier Days and the World's Oldest Rodeo (July). Horse racing season at Prescott Downs is from late May to late August.

■ WICKENBURG

Geographically speaking, it's much closer to Phoenix, but physically and spiritually Wickenburg bears a far greater resemblance to Tucson—or at least to Tucson as it might have looked a half-century ago, when its population was around 5,500. Both Tucson and Wickenburg share an elevation of roughly 2,000 feet, as well as spectacular high-desert surroundings. Moreover, Wickenburg, which was incorporated in 1863, is the oldest town north of Tucson. Wickenburg also has the Hassayampa River, which runs largely underground through town and is linked to a colorful legend. In the late 19th century, when Wickenburg residents tended to exaggerate the town's wealth, the word "Hassayamper" came to refer to someone who played fast and loose with the facts. Those who drank from the Hassayampa River, it was said, would never utter a word of truth again.

Not all of Wickenburg's wealth was hyped, however. The Vulture Mine, founded by a Prussian prospector named Henry Wickenburg, produced about $30 million worth of gold and silver, making it the most profitable mine in Arizona in the 1880s. After the area's mineral resources were exhausted, Wickenburg mined a nascent interest in things Western and became the self-proclaimed Dude Ranch Capital of the World in the 1930s. Only three of these all-inclusive horse resorts—now more politely called guest ranches—remain, but the town still maintains many traditions from its dude-ranch prime.

Dude ranch riders cruise through the saguaro cactus along the Volcano Trail in Wickenburg.

Wickenburg is about 60 miles northwest of Phoenix on U.S. 60. Most people come here to relax and soak up some sun and local color at one of the guest ranches on the town's outskirts, but forays into the historic center are well rewarded. At the **Desert Caballeros Western Museum** (21 North Frontier Street; 928-684-2272), a small institution with a surprisingly large scope, Remingtons, Russells, and other Western-art classics share space with antique saddles, spurs, and sundry historic artifacts. The special exhibits, such as one dedicated to the bola tie, invented in Wickenburg, are always top-rate too.

One of the few places in town where Wickenburg's underground water source surfaces is at the Nature Conservancy's **Hassayampa River Preserve** (49614 U.S. 60; 928-684-2772), 3 miles southeast of town near Mile Marker 114. The moisture attracts many species of birds, as well as other local wildlife. In days past, local wildlife of the human variety got some rather unusual treatment: from 1863 to 1890, outlaws were chained to a large mesquite tree instead of being locked up. You can still see the **Jail Tree,** now more than two centuries old, at Tegner Street and Wickenburg Way, right next to the Circle K mini-mart.

■ SEDONA

"There are only two places in the world I want to live," the German-born surrealist painter Max Ernst told his friends: "Paris and Sedona." Ernst, who emigrated to Arizona in the 1940s, built a house in the lee of the red rocks of Sedona; he was one of many thousands who have been enchanted by the place.

Another typical Sedona story is that of the New York stockbroker who flew in on a visit in 1973, fell instantly in love with the rocks, and bought a house the next day. Impulsive? "No," he said. "Impulsive would be the same day." The jazz drummer Louis Bellson, who once appeared at the Jazz on the Rocks festival, looked up at the great red buttes towering from 500 to 2,000 feet over the town and spoke for his wife, the legendary Pearl Bailey, who was ill at home. "If Pearly was here," Bellson said, "She would say, 'God lives here.' "

Maybe God does: the landscape certainly is supernal.

Bell Rock, Courthouse Butte, Capitol Butte, Bear Mountain—these erosion-sculpted rocks, which change color and character almost hourly, seem almost alive. In a gray, woolly fog they seem to float, eerily, like velvet ghosts. Under a mid-morning sun they might reflect a pale and cool violet, but as the day burns on they shift into reds and oranges. After sunset, when the fire colors have burned out, the

The sculptor and rancher Marguerite Brunswig Staude commissioned Sedona's Chapel of the Holy Cross in 1953; she called it "a spiritual fortress so charged with God that it spurs man's spirit godward!"

rocks turn the color of rust (which is what, on the surface, they are) against a violet sky, and all their crevasses and canyons blacken into impenetrable, ominous mystery. It would make a perfect stage set for a production of Wagner's *Götterdämmerung* (Twilight of the Gods) in a production staged by the gods themselves.

The town of Sedona has a short but intriguing history. It was founded in 1902 by a young Missouri couple, Carl and Sedona Schnebly. Beginning in the 1960s it became an art colony, and in the 1970s it exploded with retirees. In the early 1980s Page Bryant, a psychic, claimed to have divined four metaphysical vortices in the red rocks around it (some people claim there are as many as a dozen of these energy centers), and Sedona also became a New Age mecca. In 1987 the Harmonic Convergence drew at least 5,000 people to town, a few of whom willingly paid

$75 for tickets to sit on Bell Rock at the moment that it was supposed to depart for the galaxy of Andromeda. For the most part, however, the New Age crowd in Sedona has proven to be quiet, unobtrusive, and simply searching for ways to heal the Earth and its inhabitants.

The New Agers and artists who are left, that is. The price of real estate rose so much in the 1990s that few of them can afford to live here anymore. Tourism has become Sedona's prime industry, and room rates have kept up with real estate rates, making Sedona the most expensive place to stay in Arizona outside Scottsdale. That hasn't kept visitors from coming in droves, and creating a commensurate increase in traffic—especially in Uptown Sedona, a strip largely filled with Jeep-tour operators and souvenir shops. All in all, Sedona (population 10,200) is becoming more and more like a miniature Santa Fe (though without the New Mexico city's rich history), banking on its beauty and its spiritualism.

Located 120 miles north of Phoenix, via I-17 and Route 179, Sedona, like Santa Fe, has become a prime destination for culture vultures. In addition to its many art galleries—more than 50 of them—it has a major performing arts venue, the spectacular 50-acre **Sedona Cultural Park** (250 Cultural Park Place in West Sedona; 928-282-0747). With an outdoor amphitheater in an 80-foot-deep natural bowl flanked by forest and red rocks, the park has become the summer venue for several performing-arts organizations, including the Phoenix Symphony. Art galleries, crystal shops, and clothing boutiques abound at shopping enclaves such as Tlaquepaque, Hillside, Hozho, Sinagua, and Sacagawea.

The red rocks must be explored at close hand, of course, and the best way is on foot; excellent trail maps are available at the U.S. Forest Service Sedona District office. On the west side of town, **Red Rock State Park** (4050 Red Rock Loop Road; 928-282-6907), offers several easy hikes; 7 miles to the north, along Oak Creek, **Slide Rock State Park** (U.S. 89A; 928-282-3034) is a great place to cool off after a trek—if you can find a parking spot. Jeep tours of the red rocks are readily available, and hot-air balloon, helicopter, and small-plane concessions let you view the landscape from every imaginable angle.

Among the annual festivals held here are the Sedona Chamber Music Festival (late May) and Jazz on the Rocks (September). Jazz aficionados who think their music is naturally a creature of the night, properly played only in smoky nightclubs, invariably are converted by the latter festival, an extended lawn party that attracts major stars.

■ JEROME

Indians were mining Mingus Mountain for its copper when the Spanish arrived in the area more than 300 years ago, but Jerome, the first American town here, was not founded until 1876. For the next 60 years it was assaulted by floods, fires, and epidemics, but the wealth buried under Mingus Mountain kept the town booming. At its peak, 15,000 people lived here, and the mountain—honeycombed with more than 100 miles of mine shafts—endured continuous blasting. Finally, the tormented mountain responded. After a season of abnormally wet weather, a piece of it collapsed in a colossal mudslide that swept away hundreds of structures. A quaint fraction of Jerome, 300 buildings, still hugs the mountainside. Today, Jerome has fewer than 500 citizens, but they are a colorful lot.

Jerome lies between Prescott and Flagstaff on U.S. 89A. Outside town stands the former home of mining magnate James S. Douglas, now converted into the

Jerome has become a magnet for artists and art galleries.

Jerome State Historic Park (Douglas Road, U.S. 89A; 520-634-5381), which has an excellent museum. The town's other historic homes are a jumble of cottages and Victorian structures clinging to the steep slopes of Cleopatra Hill—many of them abandoned and deteriorating, others restored and well kept. The freewheeling spirit of Jerome's old mining days prevails, and tourists now visit the former jailhouse, the mine museum, a brothel-turned-restaurant, and an array of funky shops, art galleries, and cafés.

■ FLAGSTAFF

Except for the winter and spring winds, which can be ferocious, this town of 61,000, 148 miles north of Phoenix on I-17, enjoys the best location in the state. It curls around the southern base of 12,643-foot Humphreys Peak, the highest point in Arizona. In winter, people flock to Flagstaff to ski; in summer the perspiring hordes swarm up from Phoenix and Tucson to escape the heat. So many geological and prehistoric attractions cluster around Flagstaff that one suspects the town was founded as a tourist magnet (it wasn't). The ruins of Walnut Canyon and Wupatki lie, respectively, 11 and 25 miles away. Oak Creek Canyon creases into the plateau 10 miles south; the Grand Canyon is 80 miles north. Sunset Crater, looking like the mother volcano to a brood of baby cones, is 15 miles out of town.

Flagstaff will regret this spectacular setting only if a new or reactivated volcano someday appears on its horizon. It could happen; Sunset Crater last erupted in A.D. 1065—just a few moments ago in geologic time.

Like so many other Arizona settlements, Flagstaff hasn't made the best of its lovely physical setting. The main commercial arteries through town, Milton Road and Santa Fe Avenue (the old Route 66), are jammed with signs and billboards clamoring for attention, and cheap motels and fast-food joints line many of the surrounding streets. The refurbished downtown is charming and strollable, though; and away from the tourists passing through town en route to the Grand Canyon, "Flag's" green, forested neighborhoods and cool, pine-scented air make it a wonderfully enticing place.

Flagstaff's first permanent resident was a rancher and prospector named Thomas F. McMillan, who homesteaded a ranch in 1876. When the railroad arrived in 1881, both the cattle and timber industries boomed. Tourists and astronomers followed. In 1894, Percival Lowell and his wife founded and personally supervised

The Museum Club in Flagstaff keeps the spirit of Route 66 alive.

construction of the hat-shaped **Lowell Observatory** on a mesa just west of town. Lowell planned to map Mars; he theorized that its recently discovered patchwork of lines was a canal system to carry water from its polar ice caps to the arid red deserts. Lowell died in 1916 unable to prove that the Martian lines were canals, but he correctly predicted the existence of Pluto by observing the minute wobble of Uranus. In 1930, Clyde W. Tombaugh discovered Pluto—then defined as a planet but now thought by some astronomers to be an asteroid—with the Lowell scope. Activities at the observatory include nighttime viewing programs, and there are interactive science exhibits. *1400 West Mars Hill Road; 928-774-3358.*

Timothy and Michael Riordan, two lumber baron brothers, also played a major role in Flagstaff's history. Their timber wealth provided them entrance into other local industries, such as cattle, banking, and politics. Meanwhile, their marriages to Carolyn and Elizabeth Metz, two sisters from Cincinnati, linked them to one of the town's other prominent families: the Metzes were cousins of the Babbitt brothers, pioneer traders and ranchers. Several Babbitt-originated businesses still remain in Flagstaff, and descendant Bruce Babbitt was an Arizona governor and Secretary of the Interior under Bill Clinton.

Riordan Mansion State Park contains the Riordans' most interesting legacy: two attached (and mirror-image) log-and-volcanic stone mansions designed by Charles Whittlesey, who also created Grand Canyon's El Tovar Lodge. This 13,000-square-foot, 40-room compound, which was completed in 1904, hosted Theodore Roosevelt, Zane Grey, Henry Ford, and other prominent guests and is considered Arizona's finest example of Arts and Crafts architecture. Surrounding the mansion, which you can view on guided tours, is the campus of Northern Arizona University. *409 Riordan Ranch Road; 928-779-4395.*

A high priority of any Flagstaff visit should be a trip to the ancient Indian ruins at **Walnut Canyon National Monument** and **Wupatki National Monument.** The **Museum of Northern Arizona** is also a worthy stop. Its exhibitions cover the natural history and human settlement of the Colorado Plateau, and its excellent Native American marketplaces operate from July through September. For more about the monuments, see the "Ancient Ruins" section of the "The First Arizonans" chapter. For more about the museum, see that chapter's museums sidebar.

The **Arizona Snowbowl** on the San Francisco Peaks offers Arizona's highest-elevation skiing, with runs dropping from 11,200 feet. For more about the mountain, see the "Mountains" chapter.

■ ROUTE 66

Constructed in the 1920s to replace the earlier cobble of dusty thoroughfares between Chicago and California, Route 66 became John Steinbeck's "Mother Road" during the Depression, when Dust Bowl refugees drove it to flee to the West Coast. In the 1950s, the highway was associated with freedom, fast cars, and drive-ins, and in the 1960s a TV series was devoted to it. Bypassed by the interstates and no longer the quickest way to get from here to anywhere, Route 66 has nevertheless maintained its allure. Today its run-down remnants are this country's most nostalgia-tinged slivers of macadam.

In Arizona, Route 66 was inextricably linked with tourism. It was the highway to the Grand Canyon and the Petrified Forest. Old Route 66 markers have been revived in Flagstaff, and classic neon signs and kitschy buildings like the Museum Club still cast a nostalgic glow, but the small towns directly to Flagstaff's east and west yield an even better feel for the era of roadsters, malt shops, and Burma Shave rhymes.

(above) A 1940s billboard touts the Arizona attractions accessible off the fabled Route 66. (following pages) You can still get your kitsch on Route 66.

■ HOLBROOK

Once a rough-and-tumble cattle town, Holbrook, population 5,000, is notable these days for its wigwam motel court, one of the few remaining in the country. You might be able to resist spending the night in a tipi—they're small, dark, and pointy, as might be expected—but at least take a look at the **Wigwam Motel** (811 West Hopi Drive; 928-524-3048), which opened for business in the 1940s.

Holbrook is a jumping-off point for **Petrified Forest National Park** (see page 32), which explains the towering fiberglass dinosaurs that front rows of shops selling petrified wood and Route 66 souvenirs. But kitsch isn't the only reason to stop in Holbrook: the town is close enough to the state border to be influenced by New Mexican cooking, which means you can get hot chile-laden enchiladas—as opposed to the blander Arizonan-Mexican variety—in several casual cafés, including **Romo's Café** (121 West Hopi Drive; 928-524-2153). And the historic 1898 **Navajo County Courthouse** (100 East Avenue Street; 928-524-6558) contains a much-graffitied jail cell. The town's visitors center is located here.

Dinosaurs by I-40 greet visitors to Holbrook, the gateway town for Petrified Forest National Park.

■ **WINSLOW**

Started as a railroad town in the 1880s, and still a passenger stop on Amtrak, Winslow saw a revival 100 years later with the reopening of **La Posada Hotel,** the town's most interesting sight and its premier place to stay. Designed by Mary Colter—the architect for the Fred Harvey Company and best known for Desert View, Hopi House, Phantom Ranch, and other Grand Canyon buildings—La Posada, completed in 1930, was fashioned to look like a hacienda belonging to a family of wealthy Spanish colonial cattle ranchers. (Winslow was settled by Basque ranchers.) Colter considered La Posada her masterpiece, in part because, as was not the case with her other big commissions, she had complete control over the hotel's entire look and ambience, from the architecture to the maid's uniforms. *303 East Second Street; 928-289-4366.*

After a visit to La Posada, there's not much else to do in Winslow (population 9,450) besides look at the mural in the small **Standin' on the Corner Park.** Talk about art imitating life—or, to be more precise, art imitating life imitating art. So many visitors inquired about the fictional "corner in Winslow, Arizona," in the Eagles song "Take It Easy" that the town's leaders finally picked an intersection and built a park, which was dedicated in 1999. The highlight here, John Pugh's trompe l'oeil mural of a girl ("my Lord") in a flatbed Ford reflected in a storefront window, might also herald Winslow's future. In the last few years, artists have started snapping up the once-cheap downtown lofts. Winslow will never be as charming as Bisbee—it's too flat, for one thing—but it's likely to start showing some evidence of this new influx of energy and talent in the next decade or two. *Second and North Kinsley Streets.*

The small **Old Trails Museum** displays some Route 66 memorabilia and artifacts from the town's railway days. Many of these mementos are from La Posada. *212 North Kinsley Avenue; 928-289-5861.*

At **Homolovi Ruins State Park,** 3 miles northeast of Winslow, the remains of 300 ancestral Puebloan dwellings sit on a bleak, windswept plain. Hiking trails lead through the ruins, which include prehistoric pit houses and a variety of petroglyphs. *Route 87 off I-40, Exit 257; 928-289-4106.*

About 20 miles west of Winslow is **Meteor Crater,** the world's largest meteorite-formed crater—570 feet deep and wide enough to fit 20 football fields. Eerily lunar, the crater was used by NASA astronauts to simulate moonwalks. You can't descend into it, but you can walk around its rim. *I-40, Exit 233; 928-289-2362.*

■ WILLIAMS

Poor Williams. The population (about 3,000) of this pretty town nestled in the Kaibab National Forest is roughly the same as it was during the area's 1890s logging and railroading heyday—though there aren't nearly as many bars, brothels, opium dens, and other entertainment options as there were back then.

Williams's lack of growth is partly attributable to the evolution of transportation in 20th-century America. The Atchison, Topeka & Santa Fe Railroad's Grand Canyon spur from Williams was a major boon when it debuted in 1901, but rail travel waned as bus, car, and even plane visits to the canyon became increasingly popular. In 1927, the high point of the train's popularity, 70,382 people rode the rails to the canyon. But this was also the first year that the number of automobile passengers exceeded the number of rail passengers. Forty-one years later, only three lonely souls boarded the Williams–Grand Canyon train for its final run. And though Williams was the last of the Route 66 towns to be bypassed by an interstate—the stretch of I-40 near Williams was completed in 1984, despite the town's best efforts to prevent it—by then most of the Grand Canyon tourists were driving via Flagstaff.

But things have been looking up for Williams lately. In 1989, Max and Thelma Biegert, who made much of their fortune in aviation, invested $15 million to get several historic steam trains running again. Whether it was ecoconsciousness, nostalgia, parking problems at the canyon, or a combination of all these factors, the reincarnated Grand Canyon Railway has proved a huge success, with ridership reaching 179,000 passengers in 2002. A modern version of the 1908 Fray Marcos railway hotel opened in 1995 at the retooled depot, which has helped keep visitors from tootling away from Williams without spending any time—or money—in town.

Williams bills itself as the "Gateway to the Grand Canyon," and much of the town is devoted to getting tourists to the abyss. But the Mother Road is an economic mother lode, too. *Route 66 Magazine* is published in Williams, and the **Route 66 Magazine & Gift Shop** (401 West Railroad Avenue; 928-635-4322) sells everything from replicas of vintage gasoline pump globes to Burma Shave soap sets. An earlier heritage is celebrated too: Bill Williams, for whom the town was named, was one of the frontier fur trappers known as "mountain men." During the annual Rendezvous Days, held on Memorial Day weekend, their springtime regrouping is reenacted.

The London Bridge in Lake Havasu City.

■ DESERT TOWNS ON THE COLORADO RIVER

■ LAKE HAVASU CITY

On its face, it appeared a truly absurd scene: a gaggle of sun-baked British tourists aboard an imitation sternwheeler named the *Dixie Belle*, sailing past a fake British village under the real London Bridge on a man-made lake in the Mojave Desert.

The one American aboard wondered aloud whether any of the Britons found this just a touch silly. Three replies:

Julia Smyth: "A lot of people felt upset when London Bridge left London. It'd be the same if someone took your Golden Gate, wouldn't it? But all of us who've seen it here have found it quite lovely."

George Griffith: "It's wonderful; it's as if you've taken us back in time. When we go into a shop in England now we're bombarded with such horrible music. Here it's very quiet and pleasant."

Peter Penrose: "It's fantastic what you Americans can do. Where you don't have any history, you just make it."

In Penrose's few words is the story of Lake Havasu and the small, young city of 42,000 people on its eastern shore. Until 1938, the year Parker Dam was completed downstream, there was no lake here—just the ruddy Colorado slinking its way through the parched Mojave Desert. The town dribbled into existence a couple of decades later, and its famous attraction, the London Bridge, went up in 1971. When the bridge arrived as a kit of 33,000 tons of Dartmoor and Aberdeen granite stones, there was nothing for it to span, so a channel was dredged at the edge of the lake, thereby manufacturing an island.

The town and the bridge were the brainchildren of California magnate Robert McCulloch, who moved his factory to Lake Havasu in 1964. According to local legend, McCulloch and his partner, C. V. Wood Jr., were watching *The Tonight Show* one evening when host Johnny Carson noted that the obsolete London Bridge, built in 1824, was for sale. McCulloch turned to Wood and said, "Let's buy it." They did, for $2.4 million.

McCulloch's purchase drew international ridicule at the time—Britons in particular were incensed—but it turned out to be a remarkably canny purchase. It became the second biggest tourist draw in Arizona (after the Grand Canyon) and brought a constellation of supporting attractions, from an English heraldry shop to speedboat regattas. McCulloch died in 1977, and 10 years later his chainsaw factory, which at its peak had employed 1,800, moved to Tucson. Without tourism, Lake Havasu City would have vanished as quickly as a puddle in the Mojave Desert. McCulloch's flight of whimsy, the London Bridge, saved the town from the flight of McCulloch's factory.

Fishing enthusiasts face a dilemma when visiting here. The best months for fishing the lake's bass, crappie, catfish, and bluegill are from May through September, but these are truly hot times in the Mojave Desert. Lake Havasu City's average May daily high is 95.3 degrees Fahrenheit; in July it's 108.6 degrees, and in September 102.5 degrees. Early mornings on the lake are reasonably cool, of course, but what does one do the rest of the day?

The rest of the year Lake Havasu, on Route 95, 206 miles west of Phoenix, is very pleasant for anyone not frustrated by the uninterested fish. Winter boating is a popular pastime (January's average high is 67.3 degrees), and the major local festival, London Bridge Days, is held in October. The London Bridge itself is more than a curio (or Arizona's heaviest antique, as it has been dubbed). Look closely for the many pockmarks on its stones; these are compliments of Nazi fighters strafing the bridge during World War II.

■ YUMA

Poor Yuma. Possibly no small city on the continent has suffered such consistently bad press for so long a time. J. Ross Browne wrote in 1864, "Everything dries: wagons dry; men dry; chickens dry; there is no juice left in anything living or dead by the close of summer. . . . Chickens hatched at this season, old Fort Yumers say, come out of the shell ready cooked; bacon is eaten with a spoon; and butter must stand for an hour in the sun before the flies become dry enough for use. . . ."

Two decades later, Charles H. Phelps penned a travelogue in verse that must surely rank among the nastiest poems ever published about a town. An excerpt:

> Through all ages baleful moons
> Glared upon thy whited dunes;
> And malignant, wrathful suns
> Fiercely drank thy streamless runs. . . .

The abuse continues today, with hapless Yuma still strafed by missiles of hostile wit lobbed afar. Bob Boze Bell, Phoenix's satirical cartoonist, once drew a two-page spread in the *New Times* weekly, proposing fresh civic slogans to the Chamber of Commerce: "Join the Yuman race—out of town" Or: "You don't live in Yuma, Yumarinate." The Chamber has responded, gamely enough, with brochures that begin by asking: "Where's Your Sense of Yuma?"

Culture in territorial Yuma: the Philharmonic Band, 1895.

Pearl Hart (with guitar) was one of Yuma Territorial Prison's celebrated inmates; she did hard time from 1899 to 1902 for robbing a mail stage.

Yuma came into existence because of the California gold rush. To reach California and its promise of wealth, prospectors somehow had to cross the Colorado River—a much more formidable barrier than it is today, with five states now sucking water out of it. A U.S. Army report in 1846 estimated that the river was 600 feet wide at its narrowest. By 1850, both Indian and Anglo entrepreneurs were operating ferry services, and, as happened at so many other points of commingling, friction ensued. The army established Fort Yuma on the California side of the river (although it was under the Arizona command) and subdued the eponymous Yuma tribe. The wagon traffic increased, and a civilian settlement, originally christened Colorado City, began to grow across the river from the fort.

It is not difficult to understand why Yuma has had public-relations woes. In territorial days it was the hottest and driest place Anglos had yet attempted to settle in Arizona—and with San Diego 170 miles off over one treeless horizon and Tucson 220 miles in the opposite direction, it was easily the most remote as well.

In 1876, Yuma won its second industry, the Territorial Prison, which was essentially carved into a bluff overlooking the river. Nowadays, **Yuma Territorial Prison State Historic Park** is a captivating attraction and an illustration of how the Sonoran Desert itself functioned as punishment. Inmates from around the country were shipped here, and they termed it, without humor or affection, the "Hell Hole." Think about it: 9- by 8-foot cells, with two tiers of three bunks each, one bucket for a latrine (emptied once a day), and 120-degree summer temperatures. By the time the facility closed in 1909, more than 3,000 convicts had slowly simmered through their sentences there, and only 26 of them—fewer than one per year—had successfully escaped. *1 Prison Hill Road; 520-783-4471.*

Modern Yuma, a city of about 77,500 people, has managed to make an asset of this improbable climate. About 60,000 snowbirds, mostly from the Pacific Northwest and Canada, descend on the area every winter. Questioned by *Arizona Highways* about why they chose Yuma over Phoenix or Tucson, most cited the small-city friendliness and relaxed pace. The extreme rarity of freezes in this very low desert basin makes it an ideal location for citrus farming. In fact, if Arizona had huddled all its agriculture along the Colorado River instead of trying to force the central deserts to bloom, the state would not have as serious a water problem as it does today.

Yuma's role as a military post and river port—made obsolete when the railroad arrived in 1877—is commemorated at **Yuma Crossing State Historic Park** (201 North Fourth Avenue; 520-329-0471). Several companies also offer boat trips up the Colorado River to visit prehistoric petroglyph sites and the Imperial and Cibola National Wildlife Refuges.

■ VISITING MEXICO

"Sonora is where civilization ends and *carne asada* begins," wrote the Mexican philosopher José Vasconcelos. Sonora is the Mexican state adjoining Arizona. Carne asada (literally "roasted beef," although it is normally grilled) is one of its great attractions—along with sensational seafood, unspoiled beaches, folk-baroque Spanish missions, and, once away from the border, warm and hospitable people.

Tourists to southern Arizona often visit **Nogales,** the industrial Mexican border city 60 miles south of Tucson. Generally they travel nowhere else in Sonora. This is a mistake. Nogales ("Walnut trees" in translation), neither historic nor quaint, is a teeming chemical reaction between an affluent nation and the edge of the Third World. The tragedy is that the *norteamericano* who becomes acquainted with Mexico through Nogales (or any other border city) not only will misunderstand the country but may also leave with unwarranted prejudices.

A few years ago, shopping in Nogales meant trying to negotiate the best price for a black-velvet painting of Jesus or Elvis. In the last few years, though, many shops have gone upscale, offering impressive Mexican folk art, crafts, and imports. Their sheer variety is almost entertainment enough; in one small store shoppers may find leather duffel bags, fake Toltec icons, margarita glasses, statues of St. Francis of Assisi, and double basses. (Bargain prices, for the most part, are history.) Most of the tourist shops are along the first three blocks of Calle Obregón, up to its intersection with Calle Aguirre. Obregón continues south for about 5 miles, however, with shops mainly serving Mexican clientele. These are interesting, too.

A different experience awaits the visitor in Sonora's interior. There is little developed tourism in the state, so visitors see Mexican society as it really is—the unrestrained passion of the crowd at a semi-pro *beisbol* game; the old itinerant tool sharpener who plods through the residential streets of Hermosillo, the capital, playing melodies on his panpipes. Sonorans are outgoing and curious about foreigners, and it's easy to strike up conversations in the streets if you speak some Spanish—few Sonorans, other than those who work in the tourist shops and hotels, have studied English.

Rocky Point and **Guaymas,** two shrimping towns on the Gulf of California, offer superb seafood in unpretentious restaurants at prices that are at most half what one would pay on the coasts of California or Texas. Rocky Point (Puerto Peñasco), the closest beach to Phoenix and Tucson, has become very popular with

The Great Cathedral of Alamos in Sonora, Mexico, was built in the 1780s and is a splendid example of Spanish colonial architecture.

Americans. Americanized beachside resorts and campgrounds are easy to reach and draw big crowds on winter weekends. (And don't even think about going to Rocky Point during spring break, when it's overtaken by partying college students.) **San Carlos,** adjacent to Guaymas, also has excellent restaurants and seaside resorts, as well as great diving and sport fishing. However, it is mostly a colony of U.S. expatriates and weekend condo dwellers, and exudes little of the character of a Mexican town.

Far off any beaten track is the quiet village of **Tubutama,** which though it contains no hotels or even restaurants, is worth visiting just to see the folk-baroque mission church of San Pedro y San Pablo de Tubutama, built in 1788. The church's facade is an architectural carnival of spirals, quatrefoils, sculpted seashells, flowers, and even a pair of angels with the bodies of children and the faces of old men, floating heavenward and carrying what appear to be chickens. The effect is simultaneously naive and ambitious—the church radiates a sensation of perfect innocence and purity.

Alamos is a seductively beautiful Spanish colonial town that grew out of the wealth generated by the nearby Sierra Madre silver mines in the 1700s. Scores of

restored mansions line its narrow, tunnel-like streets, their rhythmic Romanesque colonnades forming a kind of visual music that serenades the stroller. The central plaza and courtyards of the mansions are awash in bougainvillea, jasmine, and the poplar trees (*alamos*) that gave the town its name. Most of the mansions have been lovingly restored by Americans, a few as hotels and restaurants. Alamos is no more typical of Sonora today than is Nogales, its cultural opposite, but it is lovely.

The silver city of Alamos in Sonora, Mexico.

U.S. citizens need no passport or visa for visits to Mexican border towns unless the stay exceeds 72 hours. Visits to the interior, if you're driving, require a visa and *turista* permit for the car, an "automotive importation" fee, and a blizzard of bureaucracy.

Should one even try driving? There are other difficulties. First, most U.S. auto insurance companies do not insure policyholders driving into the interior of Mexico; supplemental insurance must be bought from a company specializing in it (see the Yellow Pages in Tucson or Nogales). Major U.S. auto rental companies do not allow their cars to be taken into Mexico, although a handful of local firms do. Supplies of unleaded (*"sin plomo"*) gasoline are no longer a problem, although road maintenance definitely is. As for the issue of road safety, it depends on the individual's level of comfort in coping with unfamiliar situations. Mexican traffic may appear anarchic to *norteamericanos,* but at least everything happens in slow motion.

For those not wanting to drive in Sonora, there are excellent organized bus tours run by the **Southwestern Mission Research Center** (520-628-1269) and **La Ruta de Sonora Ecotourism Association** (520-792-4693). Both of these Tucson-based nonprofit organizations conduct excursions that visit the historic mission churches at San Ignacio, Tubutama, Oquitoa, Pitiquito, and Caborca. The missions are wonderful, and these small towns, all but untouched by tourism, represent the real Mexico.

BACK ROADS ITINERARIES

I ease my car off the deserted forest road by the Mogollon Rim and onto a carpet of straw-colored pine needles. This is very close to the place, as best as I can tell, where the Tonto Apaches introduced themselves to Gen. George Crook, the U.S. Army's premier Indian fighter, one autumn afternoon in 1871. General Crook and his men were blazing a trail and gaping at the scenery, just as tourists do today, when suddenly the crisp alpine air was clotted with arrows. The troops scrambled for cover. Most of the Apaches melted back into the woods, but two of the Indians found themselves trapped right on the rim, a sheer escarpment overlooking another forest—2,000 feet below.

The soldiers closed in. The Apaches leaped over the edge, apparently choosing suicide over capture. Crook's men stared in horrified amazement. But when they peered over the rim to look for the corpses, what they saw were two very live Apaches spidering down the nearly vertical wall. Crook fired, and an arm of one of the fugitives went limp, blood spurting from an artery. His pace never slowed.

I peer over the rim myself and try to imagine doing that with one arm—and suddenly I feel very much as Crook did. Because of encounters like this, he eventually developed a profound respect for the people he had been sent to Arizona to subdue. They understood this beautiful but treacherous land in ways that the incoming wave of white settlers never would. If I had not made the effort to get to the Mogollon Rim—and it took three attempts, because the gravel road is often blocked by snow—I never would have fully understood this chasmic difference between our culture and theirs. This is one of the compelling reasons for leaving Arizona's cities and freeways behind, and taking the back roads. There is no better way to get to know the state than to walk it.

This chapter outlines eight drives, all rich in scenery, history, and surprises—such as the world-class bookstore on a desert ranch 40 miles from the nearest big city. All start from one of Arizona's three main urban areas: Phoenix, Tucson, or Flagstaff. Some are easy day trips; some will take two, three, or four days. Most of the roads on the suggested routes are paved, and all are accessible to two-wheel-drive passenger cars except in heavy rain or snow.

Snowfall on the red rocks near Sedona as seen from Schnebly Hill Road.

One's sense of adventure may occasionally be called upon, however. The last time I drove U.S. 191 from Alpine to Clifton, I encountered exactly three other cars in 95 miles. It's a great scenic highway, but not a great place for your fuel injection to take early retirement. In summer or winter, *always* carry emergency drinking water while driving in Arizona.

■ ANCIENT ARIZONA TRAIL *map page 254*

This trip begins and ends in Flagstaff. As outlined here, it would cover about 575 miles and take four full days, passing by a wealth of prehistoric ruins, petroglyphs, and improbable land forms. Most of the drive is on the Navajo Reservation, offering opportunities to engage a distinct contemporary culture as well. *Best times: From April through October.*

■ DAY 1

From Flagstaff, drive 7 miles east on I-40 to **Walnut Canyon National Monument,** a V-shaped furrow 385 feet deep, lined with Sinagua ruins halfway down the canyon walls. This is a perfect place to contemplate the question of whether Arizona's prehistoric cultures, in the throes of a population boom after A.D. 1100, faced the threat of war over limited resources. Walnut Canyon's settlements certainly *look* defensive; why else would they have been built in such preposterous locations? Tantalizingly, an archaeologist has found one "foreign" arrowhead in the rib cage of a Sinagua woman buried here—but just one.

The next stop is **Petrified Forest National Park,** 105 miles east on I-40. Petrified Forest's ruins aren't worth a long visit, but near the Puerco Ruin is one of the most prolific and astounding collections of ancestral Puebloan petroglyphs in existence. The Park Service doesn't point it out, so most visitors miss it. Walk south from the ruin to the edge of the mesa it's on and look among the rocks just below.

After Petrified Forest, turn north into the Navajo Reservation and visit the **Hubbell Trading Post,** in business since 1876 and now a National Historic Site. The days when you could buy an inexpensive Navajo rug are now as remote as the era of nickel Cokes, but the weaving is as imaginative as ever. The prehistoric and geologic wonders of **Canyon de Chelly,** another 36 miles north on U.S. 191, are described in more detail in the "Canyons" and "The First Arizonans" chapters. Stay overnight, preferably in the historic Thunderbird Lodge.

■ Day 2

Take the 18-mile South Rim Drive to Canyon de Chelly's Spider Rock Overlook early in the morning, then take either a half-day or full-day tour of the canyon floor and its ancestral Puebloan ruins with a (required) Navajo guide. Anyone who hasn't done this hasn't experienced even a fraction of the wonders of this canyon. Guides may be hired at the visitors center, or at Thunderbird Lodge (which arranges trips in six-wheel military surplus vehicles).

In late afternoon, hike the 2.5-mile round-trip trail to White House Ruin, the one trail on which visitors are allowed without guides. In the evening, drive 81 miles to Kayenta, where you will need reservations (there are few motels). The next morning, you'll visit the largest and most astonishing ancestral Puebloan ruins in Arizona.

■ Day 3

The two ruins of **Navajo National Monument** are **Betatakin** and **Keet Seel,** both built in deep sheltering alcoves in the walls of Tsegi Canyon. Betatakin is a three-hour hike in and out, led by a park ranger and limited to 60 people a day (first come, first served). Keet Seel is a 16-mile round-trip best taken on horseback; the hike is a death march through soft, wet sand. The Park Service opens Betatakin and Keet Seel only from Memorial Day through Labor Day.

Reservations for Keet Seel are essential and must be made one to two months in advance; call the Navajo National Monument at 928-672-2366. If you take only the half-day Betatakin tour, return to Kayenta in the afternoon, then take U.S. 163 19 miles north to **Monument Valley.** The 17-mile dirt road through the Navajo Tribal Park is rough but manageable. Plan to be on the mesa at the park entrance for sunset.

■ Day 4

Head west on U.S. 160, and then south on U.S. 89 to **Wupatki National Monument** and **Sunset Crater.** Skip the northernmost ruins, Lomaki and the Citadel, and go to the Wupatki ruin (behind the visitors center) and Wukoki. These ruins are labeled as Sinaguan, but their architecture has ancestral Puebloan written all over it. At the end of the Ancient Arizona Trail, you now know enough archaeology to be suspicious.

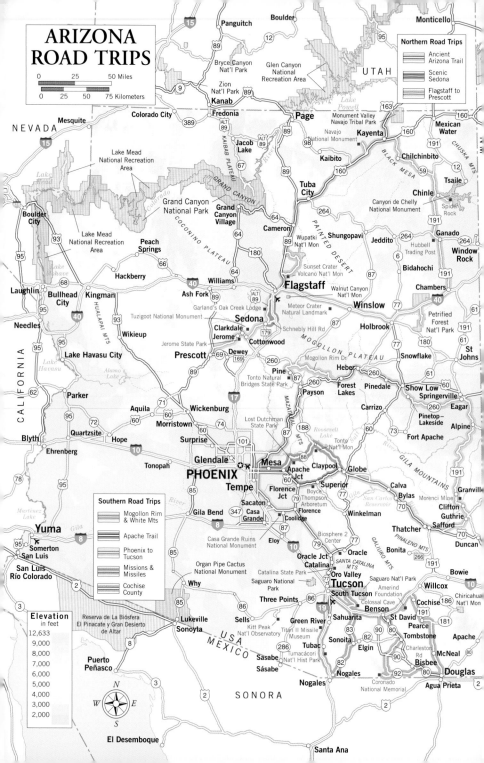

■ SCENIC SEDONA TRAIL *map page 254*

Many folks staying in Flagstaff visit Sedona, 28 miles to the south. There are two scenic ways to go, and a day trip offers an opportunity to experience both. *Best times: From March through November.*

From the beginning of I-17 in Flagstaff, drive south 19 miles to Schnebly Hill Road, and then take this little-traveled 15-mile graded dirt road into Sedona. Your reward will be a spectacular view into the mouth of Oak Creek Canyon from 1,800 feet overhead. The mountain road "demands a driver's attention," as *Arizona Highways* author James E. Cook has written, but it normally isn't dangerous.

After a day among Sedona's galleries and red rocks, take U.S. 89A back to Flagstaff. For about 15 glorious miles, the road winds alongside the creek on Oak Creek Canyon's floor. En route, gape at the polychromatic sandstone and limestone strata on the canyon walls, and the erosion-sculpted gargoyles on the ridges. One special recommendation: although it's almost impossible to get an overnight reservation at **Garland's Oak Creek Lodge** (U.S. 89A, 8 miles north of Sedona; 928-282-3343)—regulars book rooms a year in advance—dinner reservations are easily obtainable. You'll be seated with strangers (who generally prove engaging) and enjoy some of the best food between Phoenix and Denver.

■ FLAGSTAFF TO PRESCOTT, SCENIC ROUTE *map page 254*

This drive begins in Flagstaff and ends in Prescott, a distance of just 90 miles over the prescribed highways. With all the attractions and mountain switchbacks en route, however, it makes for a long one-day trip, though the actual driving time is just three hours. *Best times: From March through November.*

Take U.S. 89A 28 miles through Oak Creek Canyon to Sedona. Continue on U.S. 89A to **Tuzigoot National Monument,** a fascinating Sinagua pueblo ruin on a hill cresting 100 feet over the Verde River Valley. Like Walnut Canyon, this defensive citadel implies a distinct fear of invasion. Continue south on U.S. 89A to Jerome and Mingus Mountain. **Jerome** is a retired Victorian mining town now blossoming with boutiques and art galleries, most of which are funkier and cheaper than Sedona's. Continuing on over 7,743-foot Mingus Mountain, U.S. 89A offers rim-of-the-world views. Around the junction of U.S. 89A and U.S. 89, 5 miles north of Prescott, are the Granite Dells, a garden of Precambrian boulders weathered into improbable shapes. There's no state or national park at the Dells, but they're worth an exploratory stop.

■ MOGOLLON RIM/WHITE MOUNTAIN SCENIC DRIVE
map page 254

Most visitors to Arizona, if they encounter the Mogollon Rim at all, see it from below: as a vast green wall, planed flat on the top, butting against the sky 90 miles northeast of Phoenix. Seeing it for the first time, a wide-eyed U.S. Army Capt. John C. Bourke wrote in 1891 that "it is a strange upheaval, a strange freak of nature, a mountain canted up on one side."

Various chambers of commerce in this area would like the world to believe that the **Coronado Trail,** also known as U.S. 191, traces the route taken by Francisco Vásquez de Coronado in 1540. Perhaps it does, but a surer bet is that you'll sight elk, deer, raccoons, wild turkeys, and even black bears right from your car. And brief side excursions on gravel logging roads will transport you to pristine streams and canyons that aren't seen by more than a few dozen people a year. This 582-mile round-trip from Phoenix will take two full days. *Best times: From April through October.*

■ DAY 1

Leaving Phoenix, head north on Route 87 to Tonto Natural Bridge State Park. The 90-mile drive, which climbs gradually from the low Sonoran Desert to the 5,500-foot elevations of Tonto National Forest, skirts beautiful mountain scenery. After a wet winter, the roadside parade of wildflowers in March and April is spectacular. **Tonto Natural Bridge,** a 400-foot limestone arch spanning a 150-foot-deep canyon, deserves a visit. From the natural bridge, continue up Route 87 to the top of the rim. Just beyond milepost 281 is the Mogollon Rim Road (Forest Road 300) to the right. It's 42 miles of well-graded, lightly traveled gravel road with vertiginous views over the rim, just to your right.

Stop often to take in the scenery, but keep an eye out for logging trucks rumbling around blind curves and beware of wind gusts that may whip you while you are peering over the rim. At day's end, stay either in Pinetop-Lakeside or Springerville. The former has more interesting choices in accommodations; the latter is 56 miles on down the road, which will slice an hour's driving time off the next day's rather long route.

On a hot summer day, the alpine setting of the Mogollon Rim offers a welcome respite from the desert heat and urban crowds.

■ DAY 2

From Springerville, head south on U.S. 191 to Clifton. This 123-mile drive will demand four to five hours even without stops, and you should stop frequently to enjoy the astounding mountain scenery and wildlife. Check weather forecasts before departing; a sign just south of Alpine warns that the road isn't maintained on "nights, weekends, or during storms." Another reports that the next services are 90 miles away.

The highest paved road in Arizona, U.S. 191 crests at 9,092 feet at Hannagan Meadow. Between Hannagan Meadow and Clifton, U.S. 191 resembles a 60-mile-long corkscrew mashed into the Ponderosa pine forest and lathered with asphalt. Its hairpin turns are as tight as Scrooge's Christmas budget; the 15- and 20-mph warnings are, for once, realistic. Several automotive magazines have cited it as one of the best serious-driving roads in America. Decide whether you intend to enjoy serious (i.e., quick) driving or the scenery; you cannot do both. Either way, watch out for wildlife crossing the highway. Excursions a few miles off U.S. 191 to the **Blue River** and the **Black River** are particularly rewarding, though the state highway map offers little help in navigating these dirt and gravel roads. Stop at an **Apache-Sitgreaves National Forest** office in Springerville or Alpine and buy a detailed forest map. Rangers are happy to direct visitors to the prettiest scenery and offer advice on road conditions.

Twelve miles north of Clifton, the highway exits the national forest and begins weaving down toward the desert. Six miles later is the **Morenci Mine,** the world's second-largest open-pit copper mine. Reactions of passersby range from awe at the astounding scale of the operation to revulsion at the scarring of the now lifeless land. One mile farther, off the east side of the road, is an oddly poignant sight: a hillside cemetery, not moist and green and shady, but choked with prickly pear and cholla cacti. The graves, dating from 1900 to the 1930s, are marked with hand-made wrought-iron memorials and lead-pipe crosses, works of folk art. They form a silent monument to the harshness and bleakness of these early miners' lives. Until 1937, Clifton's copper was all extracted from underground mines.

From Clifton, take U.S. 70 west to Globe, then U.S. 60 to the **Boyce Thompson Arboretum.** Three miles west of Superior, the arboretum has a fine nature trail through a virtual desert forest; many desert plants here are also for sale. From the arboretum, continue on toward Phoenix. *520-689-2723.*

■ APACHE TRAIL *map page 254*

This one-day, 164-mile loop through the Sonoran Desert east of Phoenix today has nothing to do with Apaches—it doesn't even quite reach the San Carlos Indian Reservation. During the Apache wars, however, U.S. Army troops and Indian scouts combed the desert and mountains around here, trying to track down bands of Apache guerrillas. The loop passes the dramatic **Superstition Mountains,** three of the lakes devised by damming the Salt River in the early 1900s, a **Salado Indian ruin,** and the **Boyce Thompson Arboretum.** Despite the short distance, it could take a long day. *Best times: From October through April.*

From Phoenix, take U.S. 60 (the Superstition Freeway) east and then Route 88 to **Lost Dutchman State Park,** at the base of the Superstitions. The park's loop drive provides a gateway for day hikes into the mountains. Walk the **Siphon Draw Trail** at least a couple of miles; the awesome brute thrust of the craggy walls at your side will make you feel altogether insignificant.

Past Tortilla Flat, the highway deteriorates into a gravel road on its way toward Roosevelt Dam. Theodore Roosevelt, who came to dedicate the dam in 1911, called this road "one of the most spectacular, best-worth-seeing sights of the world." Roosevelt's eponymous structure, claimed to be the world's largest masonry arch dam, isn't a disappointing sight either, and the road provides a striking view of it. Roosevelt Lake, an improbable sprawl of water 17 miles long, is well stocked with fish and, on weekends, Phoenix party animals. Five miles southeast of the dam, still on Route 88, stop at **Tonto National Monument,** the lone ruin of the prehistoric Salado people open to the public. The Salado furrow archaeologists' brows; researchers can't agree on who these people were or where they came from. The main cliffside pueblo, with 16 remaining rooms, was inhabited from about A.D. 1250 to 1450. Drop by the Boyce Thompson Arboretum (described in the preceding drive) en route back to Phoenix.

■ PHOENIX TO TUCSON: SCENERY AND SCIENCE
map page 254

The 110-mile commute between Arizona's two large cities normally takes just under two hours on I-10, but nobody enjoys the desolate drive. Take this slightly longer route (132 miles), and you'll experience less traffic, more scenery, several bits of history, and the controversial Biosphere 2. *Best times: From October through April.*

From Phoenix, take U.S. 60 east to Apache Junction, and then Route 79 south to Florence. This little desert town, home to several state and federal prisons, doesn't draw many tourists, or, for that matter, voluntary residents—a large percentage of the town's population of 14,540 is behind bars. But Florence has several interesting Territorial adobe buildings, including one, the **Clark House,** with Italianate detailing. (Unfortunately, the building is nearly in ruins.) More extravagant is the second **Pinal County Courthouse** (Pinal and 11th Streets), built in 1891 and topped by a French Second Empire cupola.

For the grisly minded, there's the **Pinal County Historical Society Museum,** the only Arizona museum to devote a room to execution paraphernalia. On display here are the actual nooses used in 25 hangings at the Arizona State Prison between 1920 and 1930—complete with mug shots of the men (and one woman) whose necks they embraced. Built in 1891, it still serves as a three-dimensional billboard advertising a grand future that never materialized for Florence. *715 South Main Street; 520-868-4382.*

A 9-mile side trip from Florence is **Casa Grande Ruins National Monument,** the one remaining high-rise left from the prehistoric Hohokam civilization. Archaeologists theorize that this four-story mud building was used as a solar observatory to mark summer and winter solstices, and perhaps as housing for a Hohokam priesthood or managerial elite. It also seems likely, though, that they also needed to keep watch on some external threat.

Forty-two miles south of Florence on Route 79, turn left on Route 77 for a visit to **Biosphere 2.** The sealed, 3-acre terrarium, which sustained eight Biospherians for two years of experimental captivity, is 5 miles east of the highway junction. For this privately funded $150 million project, four men and four women were locked into the near-airtight terrarium with 3,800 species of plants and animals. The immediate objective was to see if the eight humans could sustain themselves for two years with only the food and oxygen generated inside the container; the long-range goal turned out to be the colonization of Mars. A theme-park air prevails— the Biospherians' former quarters are open to public tours, and William Shatner of *Star Trek* narrates the introductory film—but science seems to be going on as well.

Return to Route 79 and drive 27 miles south to Tucson. If enough daylight is left, stop at **Catalina State Park,** which offers a wonderful hiking trail—Romero Canyon—probing the north face of the Santa Catalina Mountains.

Spring flowers line hiking trails in Lost Dutchman State Park.

■ MISSIONS AND MISSILES *map page 254*

Visitors staying in Tucson routinely make the swift 60-mile drive down I-17 to the Mexican border city of Nogales. Here's how to make a very full day of it, and see much more than the tourist shops of Calle Obregón. *Best times: Any time of year.*

The not-quite-twin bell towers of **Mission San Xavier del Bac** pop into view to the west off I-17 soon after you leave Tucson. (The east tower was never crowned with a dome; the least exotic but most likely explanation is that the remote parish simply ran out of money.) The church is the most elaborate Spanish mission in what is now the United States, and is not to be missed.

Twelve miles south of San Xavier on I-17 is the **Titan Missile Museum,** an actual (though now disarmed) ICBM resting in its underground silo. Once, it was programmed to target a Soviet city; the museum will not say which one. In a reversal of cold war tensions, Russian visitors now tour it alongside Americans.

Another few minutes' drive south on I-17 will bring you to the Spanish presidio of **Tubac,** now jammed with art galleries and boutiques. Practically next door is

Wine grapes flourish in the acidic terra rossa soil of southern Arizona. Above is a selection of Sonoita wines.

Arizona's other Spanish mission, **San José de Tumacácori,** now a national historical park. South along the access road from Tumacácori is the retail store of the Santa Cruz Chili & Spice Co., the most seductively aromatic room in Arizona.

Nogales, in the Mexican state of Sonora, is the obvious stop for lunch. Tourists generally gravitate toward one of three restaurants: La Roca on Calle Elias, and El Cid and El Greco, both on Calle Obregón. All three serve seafood, steaks, and Mexican food; El Greco is at once the least expensive and the most pleasant. All three are only a few blocks across the border; park in one of the pay lots on the U.S. side and walk—parking on the Mexican side is a bear.

The best route back to Tucson is not the same quick zip up I-17, but a leisurely 80- to 100-mile meander through what is becoming known as Arizona's wine country. From Nogales, drive north on Route 82. These beautiful rolling grasslands, punctuated by groves of billowing oak trees wherever a depression collects extra rain, used to be prime rangeland. The recent discovery that the soil underneath is of the helpfully acidic *terra rossa* variety is now encouraging a boomlet in grape cultivation and winemaking. Southeastern Arizona has several wineries: tasting and tours are available at **Callaghan Vineyards, The Village of Elgin Winery,** and **Sonoita Vineyards,** all near the tiny village of **Elgin;** and **Dark Mountain Brewery and Winery,** on the I-10 frontage road west of the Sonoita exit. Arizona wine is not a match for California's, either in consistency or value; only Callaghan is given serious attention outside of Arizona. But the state has come a long way in the last two decades. Return to Tucson via Route 83 and I-10, after no more than modest indulgence in some Arizona wines.

■ COCHISE COUNTY *map page 254*

Cochise County's 6,400 square miles bristle with history and break hearts with scenery. Birders worldwide know about Cochise County; the San Pedro riparian forest alone supports more than 350 species of migratory or breeding birds. The original county seat was Tombstone, the old West's most notorious town; the present county seat is Bisbee, modern Arizona's most entertaining town. On a lonely ranch out here is the Southwest's most engaging bookstore. Although the Cochise County line lies only 30 miles east of Tucson, a basic introduction to its scenery and civilization will cover some 425 miles in three days. *Best times: any.*

■ DAY 1

Don't take any of the obvious connections from Tucson to I-10. Drive east on Broadway to Old Spanish Trail and meander southeast: this is the scenic route, and it's worth the few extra minutes. The **Old Spanish Trail** winds past **Saguaro National Park, Colossal Cave,** and a private castle crowning a ridge half a mile southeast of the cave. At I-10, drive 23 miles east and take the U.S. 80 exit to **Tombstone.**

From Tombstone, veer southwest to **Coronado National Memorial,** a Huachuca Mountain preserve that probably was never even approached by Coronado, but perhaps appreciated in the distance as he and his band slogged along the San Pedro River 10 miles to the east. Take the snaking drive up the paved Memorial Road to 6,575-foot **Montezuma Pass,** and you can see the obvious route the Spanish explorers would have taken through the valley below. In summer, you also will see squadrons of hummingbirds assaulting the plentiful flowers of the mountain yucca here, and possibly even the elusive coati—a raccoon relative that moves with the grace of a cat.

Spend the night in Sierra Vista if you prefer predictable chain-motel comfort, or in **Bisbee** if you're open to steep, crumbling streets, bed-and-breakfasts in old rooming houses, and unsolicited entertainment. The last time I was just about to drift off to sleep in Bisbee, someone in Brewery Gulch began serenading the moon on a tenor sax. Bisbee is built on the sides of two intersecting gulches, so the wail echoed all over town. No matter, this was Bisbee, and nobody had anything important to do the next day anyway.

■ Day 2

Rise early and drive to the **Chiricahua National Monument,** the most dramatically sculpted mountain range in the state. Plan to spend half the day on one or more of the monument's many hiking trails. En route to or from the Chiricahuas, stop in the border town of **Douglas** to see a drop-dead architectural masterpiece: the lobby of the 1907 **Gadsden Hotel,** an opulent, two-story marble neo-Renaissance wonderland. The architect was Henry Trost, who had fallen under the spell of Louis Sullivan in Chicago a dozen years earlier. Don't be discouraged by the building's plain exterior; go inside. If you want to spend the night, rooms are inexpensive, though hardly as stunning as the lobby. Otherwise, return to Bisbee.

■ Day 3

Take U.S. 191 north for a sneak visit to the **Willcox Playa,** that strange Pleistocene-era dry lake bed—which may become a vast, few-inches-deep wet lake with the rains of late summer. The playa is no state or national park; there are no posted instructions for going there. Look for the railroad tracks 3.5 miles south of I-10, turn left and follow the dirt road paralleling the tracks to the edge of the playa.

En route back to Tucson, stop first in Dragoon at the **Amerind Foundation.** Dragoon is just an unincorporated clump of ranches, but Amerind, founded in 1937 by a Connecticut businessman who became mesmerized by the remnants of prehistoric Arizona, is one of the Southwest's best archaeology museums.

This 30-year-old sign marks the entrance to the Singing Wind Bookshop.

Fifteen miles west off I-10, even more improbably, is the **Singing Wind Bookshop,** which has enjoyed acclaim in the *Los Angeles Times,* the *Wall Street Journal,* and even the *Congressional Record.* It's the dream of rancher Winn Bundy, who has more than 100,000 titles for sale, along with a wealth of free literary wisdom, in two rooms of her ranch house. The shop's emphasis is on books of the Southwest, but anything else that happens to interest Bundy or her fanatically loyal customers is here also. Take the Ocotillo exit at Benson, drive 2.3 miles north, look for the "Singing Wind Ranch" mailbox ventilated with bullet holes, turn right, and let yourself through the gate. For any pilgrimage through Arizona and the Southwest, this place is both the beginning and end.

PRACTICAL INFORMATION

■ AREA CODES AND TIME ZONE

There are three area codes for the greater metropolitan Phoenix area: 602 for the city of Phoenix; 623 for west side communities; and 480 for east side communities. For Tucson and most of southern Arizona, use 520. The area code for the rest of the state is 928.

Arizona is in the Mountain time zone. However, the state does not observe Daylight Savings Time (except on the Navajo Reservation, which straddles several states), so for half the year Arizona is effectively in the Pacific Time zone. This causes endless confusion to people who telephone Arizonans, though not to locals, who (Navajos aside) never have to change their clocks.

■ METRIC CONVERSIONS

1 foot = .305 meters   1 mile = 1.6 kilometers   1 pound = .45 kilograms
Centigrade = Fahrenheit temperature minus 32, divided by 1.8

■ CLIMATE

Ideally, a prolonged visit to Arizona will be in the fall or spring; these seasons offer temperate weather in the deserts and high country at the same time. Cost-conscious travelers may want to schedule their visits in the following seasonal windows, which usually include both tolerable weather and off-season hotel/motel rates:

Flagstaff and the high country: April, May, and November.
Phoenix: April, and from October to December.
Tucson: April, and from October to December.

If economy is not the most important consideration, visit the high country from May through October and the deserts from November through March.

One important accessory, in summer and winter alike, is sunblock with a protection factor no lower than 15. This is not only to prevent sunburn: Southern Arizona has the world's second-highest rate of melanoma, a deadly skin cancer, and cumulative exposure to the sun is the prime cause. As enticing as a well-bronzed body may seem, Arizona doctors speak as one in this recommendation: forget sunbathing.

TEMPS (F°)	AVG. JAN.	AVG. MARCH	AVG. JULY	AVG. SEPT.	AVG. NOV.	RECORD HIGH	LOW
Phoenix	65°	75°	105°	98°	75°	122°	16°
Tucson	64°	72°	98°	94°	73°	117°	16°
Flagstaff	42°	49°	82°	74°	51°	97°	-30°

PRECIPITATION (inches)	AVG. JAN.	AVG. MARCH	AVG. JULY	AVG. SEPT.	AVG. NOV.	ANNUAL AVG.
Phoenix	.75"	.80"	.74"	.60"	.57"	7.3"
Tucson	.86"	.71"	2.54"	1.34"	.59"	11.6"
Flagstaff	2.21"	2.30"	2.45"	1.54"	1.75"	21.0"

■ GETTING THERE AND AROUND

■ BY AIR

Phoenix Sky Harbor International Airport (PHX) receives daily flights from most major U.S. cities, in addition to international flights, including nonstops from Mexico, Canada, and a few European cities. *3400 Sky Harbor Boulevard (3 miles east of downtown Phoenix); 602-273-3321, www.phxskyharbor.com.*

Tucson International Airport (TUS) is the state's secondary hub for domestic flights, with some international service. *7005 South Plumer Avenue (10 miles south of central Tucson); 520-573-8000, www.tucsonairport.org.*

Flagstaff-Pulliam Airport (FLG) serves the city of Flagstaff and northern Arizona. *5200 South Pulliam Drive (4 miles south of Flagstaff, exit 337 off I-17); 928-556-1234.*

■ BY CAR

The major east-west thoroughfare through southern Arizona is I-10, which runs from New Mexico through Tucson and Phoenix, ending up in Los Angeles; I-8, which originates near San Diego, merges with I-10 south of Phoenix. In northern Arizona, I-40 is the major east-west route. The north-south route cobbles together several highways: I-19 leads from the Mexican border at Nogales to I-10 in Tucson, which merges with I-17 north in Phoenix; I-17 ends in Flagstaff, where you can pick up Route 89 north to Utah. This north-south route has a couple of dubious distinctions: It includes two interstates (I-19 and I-17) that begin and end in Arizona; and it confuses drivers in Tucson and Phoenix, where signs direct you "west" and "east" rather than "north" and "south." However, it's also wonderfully scenic along U.S. 89, which traverses the Painted Desert for a long stretch.

Speed limits on the interstates are 75 mph in rural areas and 55 mph in the cities. Radar enforcement is ubiquitous, but detectors are legal and in common use. With long distances to cover between settlements, Arizonans tend to drive fast. State law requires the use of seat belts.

The state highway map, published by *Arizona Highways,* is available at tourist information centers in every town, as well as at many bookstores. For extensive travel on the Navajo and Hopi reservations, a very detailed map called "Indian Country" is published by the Automobile Club of Southern California.

■ BY TRAIN

Amtrak serves northern and southern Arizona. In the north, it roughly covers the same route as I-40, with Flagstaff as its main terminus. In the south, its main stop is Tucson. There is no train service to Greater Phoenix. *800-872-7245; www.amtrak.com.*

■ BY BUS

Both Phoenix and Tucson have extensive municipal bus services, but in these sprawling, low-density cities, mass transit simply is not practical for most users. Taxis are expensive because there are long distances to cover. For the visitor arriving by air, frankly, a rental car is the only realistic choice.

Greyhound provides service to Phoenix, Tucson, and other cities. *800-231-2222; www.greyhound.com.*

■ RESTAURANTS

The first meal I ate in Arizona was a Papaburger at the A&W in Benson—not an auspicious introduction to the state's cuisine. But back then, in the early 1970s, Arizona dining wasn't terrifically distinguished. Every small town like Benson, I quickly learned, would have one good Mexican restaurant and one bad Chinese restaurant, plus the usual assortment of fast feeders and everyday cafes. Phoenix and Tucson both had many good Mexican restaurants and many bad Chinese restaurants. "Continental" menus groaning with hoary standards like Veal Oscar were what passed for fine dining. As a major tourist destination, Arizona seemed to deserve better.

In the intervening decades, however, it has gotten better, much better, echoing the revolution in culinary adventure all across the land. Places such as Rox Sand in Phoenix and Cafe Terra Cotta in Tucson have earned national acclaim for their New Southwestern cooking, and they deserve it. "Continental" is as dead as the A&W in Benson, and scores of excellent ethnic restaurants, from Catalonian to Cuban, provide a parade of intriguing tastes. But I still don't know of a good Chinese place.

Mexican food is Arizona's specialty and the culinary passion of every native. There's both good and bad news on this front. Good: the variety and sophistication of Mexican cooking in Arizona has improved greatly in the last decade. Bad: the Center for Science in the Public Interest issued a report in the 1990s accusing Mexican food of being outrageously high in fat and cholesterol.

Arizonans rightly were outraged. The best response, which came from the owner of Tucson's El Charro: "They should get a life."

Maybe they should just get a chimichanga—a tortilla filled with stewed spiced beef and deep-fried until golden. Mmmm.

Phoenix Magazine and the *Arizona Republic* have reliable reviews of restaurants throughout the Valley of the Sun. In Tucson, *The Arizona Daily Star* and *Tucson Weekly* offer comprehensive restaurant listings.

■ EATING IN ARIZONA

"Oh! If we could only live as the Mexicans live, how easy it would be!" pined Martha Summerhayes, a young Army bride who came to Arizona in 1874. "For they had their fire built between some stones piled up in their yard, a piece of sheet iron laid over the top: this was the cooking-stove . . . a kettle of frijoles [beans] was put over to boil. These were boiled slowly for some hours, then lard and salt were added, and they simmered down until they were deliciously fit to eat, and had a thick red gravy. . . ."

Summerhayes went on to rhapsodize about several other staples of the Mexican table in Arizona Territory, including chile colorado and chile verde (red and green chile beef stew, respectively), tortillas, and carne seca (sun-dried beef simmered with onions and peppers). Recipes for these dishes have endured virtually unchanged for more than a century, and Arizonans, both newcomers and natives, rhapsodize still. Mexican food is Arizona's culinary religion.

This is only proper. In fact, it should be in the state constitution. It perpetuates our historic roots. For gringos, it cracks open a door, at least, into Mexican culture. And of course it tastes wonderful. Forgive me if I turn moist-eyed and mystical, but there is something about Mexican cuisine that seems akin to the essence of life. Its forms are those of nature's geometry: the circle (tortilla), the cylinder (flauta), the arch (taco). Its flavors are likewise elemental: habañero chiles evoke pure fire; a very fresh guacamole laced with lime and cilantro captures both the color and mood of springtime. Mexican food also can reflect the complexity of nature; it isn't merely hot. Huachinango a la Veracruzana is a perfect example. This is red snapper filet sautéed with onion, garlic, tomatoes, green olives, capers, and—if the chef is really cookin'—nutmeg. All these flavors form rival factions of piquancy that circle each other warily, struggle briefly for power on the taste buds, and finally embrace and trip down the tube dancing and singing in tight-woven harmonies. Snapper can be a dull fish, but not when prepared in a Veracruz pan. Huachinango a la Veracruzana remains relatively rare on Mexican restaurant menus in Arizona. Most kitchens still cling to the frontier; this is a conservative region.

The traditional Mexican restaurant meal here invariably begins with a basket of deep-fried tortilla chips (usually complimentary) and an accompanying salsa of chopped or puréed tomato, jalapeño chile, onion, and cilantro. Depending on how the restaurant perceives its clientele, this salsa may range from annoyingly mild to incendiary. The entrées typically consist of a wide choice of "combination plates" mixing tacos, enchiladas, tamales, flautas, burros, and chiles rellenos, accompanied by rice, beans, and warm flour tortillas. Dessert is likely to be flan, a

Chiles make decorative garlands, but they're more than a garnish in the cuisine of Arizona.

CHILE SCORCH SCALE

Chiles enhance taste, are intriguing to look at, and can scorch the unsuspecting. How is chile heat measured? In 1911 a Mr. Scoville gave us a guide to chile heat by testing a range of chiles on some non-chile eaters (how they later fared is unrecorded). Some common chiles and their heat levels are recorded below.

CHILE	SCOVILLE HEAT UNITS	RATING
Mild Bell	0	0
R-Naky, Mexi-Bell	100–500	1
NuMex Big Jim	500–1000	2
Pasilla, Española	1000–1500	3
Sandia, Cascabel	1500–2500	4
Jalapeño, Mirasol	2500–5000	5
Serrano	5000–15,000	6
Cayenne, Tabasco de Arbol	15,000–30,000	7
Aji, Piquin	30,000–50,000	8
Santaka, Chiltepin	50,000–100,000	9
Habanero, Bahamian	100,000–300,000	10

creamy cinnamon-flavored custard. Nobody pretends that this is a heart-smart diet, but some restaurants at least have begun to substitute vegetable oils, which are lower in saturated fat, for the traditional lard. This has a slightly deleterious effect on the flavors of some dishes, but it seems like a sensible trade-off.

There are some other pleasing trends developing in Mexican dining around the state. One is the gradual appearance of regional cuisines other than the beefy ranch-style Sonoran that has prevailed since—well, since Arizona was part of Sonora. Mexican food is a far larger universe than most *norteamericanos* ever imagine, and this should come as no surprise: Mexico comprises tropics, deserts, and more than 5,000 miles of seacoasts; and Aztecs, Mayas, Pimas, Spaniards, French, and Americans have all exerted their influence in different regions. Thus a *pan de cazon,* which is kind of a shark-and-bean sandwich from the Yucatán peninsula, has no family ties to birria, a savory goat pot roast from Guadalajara. Both, along with other regional specialties, gradually are becoming more widely available in Arizona. So is Sonoran coastal cooking, in which spicy shrimp replace shredded beef in tacos and enchiladas.

Finally, there are several new shoots and permutations of Mexican cuisine that fall under no single culinary label, although "nouvelle Southwestern" covers some of it. This cooking weds Mexican and Native American ingredients to the latest French techniques, often to smashing effect but occasionally to bizarre ends. I have tried Anaheim chiles stuffed with lobster and brie and fried with beer batter, which were stunning, and Mexican sea bass swimming in blueberry sauce, a very unstable marriage of ingredients. Generally, the new cuisine is much more expensive than the old.

Innovation and a wide variety of non-Mexican ethnic dining came fairly late to Arizona, for at least a couple of reasons. Our two principal cities were not large until recently, and except for Mexican-Americans, they had no concentrated ethnic enclaves. The influence of the frontier may have had a lingering effect, too: a mean land demands a mean cuisine. Emblematic of territorial Arizona was cowboy stew, or, as more colorfully labeled in Louise DeWald's *Arizona Highways Heritage Cookbook,* "Son-of-a-Bitch Stew." Ingredients: all the meat and most of the internal organs of a freshly butchered calf, slowly boiled for five hours. Warns the classic recipe, "Never add spices or vegetables to a Son-of-a-Bitch; spoils the true flavor of the ingredients."

By the late 1970s the last remnants of the s.o.b. culinary philosophy finally were swept aside by new waves of immigrants and an increasingly alert tourist industry. The maturation process has been astoundingly rapid: today you can eat as well in Arizona as in California—and a lot less expensively. There is not yet a distinctive "Arizona cuisine" except for traditional Sonoran, but this simply reflects the character of our land: a young, volatile, attractive haven for a great stew of immigrants. A London-born Indian who along with his three brothers has built a successful trio of Punjabi restaurants in Flagstaff, Tempe, and Tucson explained it simply: "Arizona looked like an interesting change for us."

■ LODGING

The good news: Arizona has a huge range of lodgings. The bad news: You generally won't find all types in a single city or region. The exception to this rule is Tucson, which has everything from cheap No-Tell motels and inexpensive B&Bs to historic hotels, guest ranches, upscale resorts, and destination spas. The configurations are endless: B&Bs in the center of town or out in the desert, resorts that once were guest ranches, and even chain motels with history (the Best Western Ghost Ranch Inn, with a logo designed by Georgia O'Keeffe). The Valley of the Sun specializes in expensive resorts with every imaginable amenity; these tend to be concentrated in Scottsdale, though there are several in Phoenix, which is also home to some upscale high-rise hotels. Chain motels proliferate in the Valley, but it's hard to find inexpensive ones in prime tourist areas. Because of zoning restrictions, there are few B&Bs, and guest ranches here have long since gone the way of the buffalo.

In central Arizona, the largest concentration of lodgings is in Sedona, which has a few resorts, an abundance of very pricey B&Bs, a number of overpriced chain motels, and some good rustic lodges along Oak Creek Canyon. The lodging pickings are pretty slim in northern Arizona, although Flagstaff has some interesting B&Bs and Grand Canyon National Park offers several historic hotels; otherwise chains are the name of the game.

That's especially true of the northern Indian reservations (here the exception is the historic Goulding's Lodge near Monument Valley). Other pockets of lodging interest around the state include Prescott and Bisbee, both home to appealing Victorian-era hotels and B&Bs; Route 66, which retains several classic neon-fronted motels; and Southeast Arizona and Wickenburg, which, between them, host most of the state's remaining guest ranches.

The super-deluxe Rancho de los Caballeros in Wickenburg.

■ Reservation Services

Arizona Association of Bed & Breakfast Inns. This statewide organization has quality controls for its members and does regular inspections. *800-284-2589; www.arizona-bed-breakfast.com.*

Arizona Dude Ranch Association. The association's Web site links to all the guest ranches in the state and has a useful comparison chart. *www.azdra.com.*

■ Hotel and Motel Chains

AmeriSuites. *800-833-1516; www.amerisuites.com.*

Baymont Inns & Suites. *877-299-6668; www.baymontinns.com.*

Best Western. *800-528-1234; www.bestwestern.com.*

Comfort Inn. *800-228-5150; www.comfortinn.com.*

Days Inn. *800-325-2525; www.daysinn.com.*

Doubletree. *800-222-8733; www.doubletree.com.*

Econo Lodge. *800-553-2666; www.econolodge.com.*

Embassy Suites. *800-362-2779; www.embassysuites.com.*

Four Seasons Hotels and Resorts. *800-819-5053; www.fourseasons.com.*

Hampton Inn. *800-426-7866; www.hampton-inn.com.*

Hilton Hotels. *800-445-8667; www.hilton.com.*

Holiday Inn. *800-465-4329; www.6c.com.*

Hyatt Hotels. *800-233-1234; www.hyatt.com.*

La Quinta Motor Inns. *800-531-5900; www.laquinta.com.*

Marriott Hotels. *800-228-9290; www.marriott.com.*

Motel 6. *800-466-8356; www.motel6.com.*

Omni Hotels. *800-843-6664; www.omnihotels.com.*

Quality Inns. *800-228-5151; www.choicehotels.com.*

Radisson. *800-333-3333; www.radisson.com.*

Ramada Inns. *800-272-6232; www.ramada.com.*

Sheraton. *800-325-3535; www.sheraton.com.*

Super 8 Motels. *800-800-8000; www.super8.com.*

Travelodge. *800-255-3050; www.travelodge.com.*

Westin Hotels. *800-228-3000; www.westin.com.*

Wyndham Hotels. *800-996-3426; www.wyndham.com.*

■ CAMPING IN ARIZONA

With its varied terrain, vast undeveloped areas open to the public for recreation—a whopping 80 percent of the country's sixth-largest state—and abundance of sunshine, Arizona is a mecca for outdoor enthusiasts. You can camp in and near deserts, canyons, forests, lakes, and rivers, and you can camp somewhere in Arizona at any time of the year: The lowland deserts are temperate in winter, the upland forests and canyons in summer. In addition, many areas of the state, especially those in the high desert, are temperate enough to keep the campgrounds open year-round.

Most areas have developed campgrounds with such amenities as electricity, toilets, and hot showers; primitive camping is available in the national forests and on several of the Indian reservations.

Arizona Public Lands Information Center. *602-417-9300; www.az.blm.gov/camping.htm.*

Arizona State Parks. *602-542-4174; www.pr.state.az.us.*

Grand Canyon National Park (Backcountry Information Center). *928-638-7875; www.nps.gov/grca/pphtml/camping.html.*

KOA Campgrounds, Arizona. *800-562-6823; www.koa.com/where/az.*

National Park Service. *602-640-5250; www.nps.gov/parks.*

National Recreation Reservation Service. *877-444-6777; www.reserveusa.com.*

U.S. Forest Service. *602-225-5200; www.fs.fed.us.*

■ ARIZONA PUBLICATIONS

Arizona's most famous publication, *Arizona Highways,* has a circulation of more than 300,000, about 80 percent of it out of state, and a nonpareil reputation for spectacular photography. The magazine was founded in 1925 as a newsletter published by the Arizona Highway Department and sold for 10 cents per copy. It chronicled highway construction and administrative humdrum within the department, and its purpose was to promote road building in the young state. The modern concept of *Arizona Highways* began in 1938 with the editorship of Raymond Carlson, which lasted three decades. Carlson introduced four-color photography, which was rare at the time, and rhapsodic prose. Today the photography is better than ever, the writing more journalistic than promotional. But its mission remains the same: to promote tourism in Arizona. It does so with great success.

The state's largest newspaper and its most comprehensive for news about Arizona and the nation, the Phoenix-based *Arizona Republic*, is available everywhere. Tucson's *Arizona Daily Star*, the city's largest-circulation newspaper, can be found all around southern Arizona; its evening competitor, the *Tucson Citizen*, is distributed mainly in the Tucson area. Neither Tucson paper is particularly adept at anything beyond local coverage; the *Star* tends to be more liberal, the *Citizen* more conservative.

Other publications of use to the visitor include *Tucson Guide* and *Valley Guide*, both quarterly magazines with features and entertainment suggestions; *Phoenix* magazine, which has some excellent writing and provocative features; *Tucson Lifestyle*, which is relentlessly upscale; the *Phoenix New Times*, which often wins awards for its news-breaking journalism; and the opinionated but less hard-hitting *Tucson Weekly*. The latter two, available free in street boxes and stores, offer the best guides to dining and entertainment.

■ **ONLINE EDITIONS**

Arizona Daily Star. *www.azstarnet.com.*

Arizona Daily Sun. Flagstaff's newspaper, and the best source of non-Indian news in northern Arizona. *www.azdailysun.com.*

Arizona Highways. The magazine's site lists the excellent photo workshops offered by the staff. *www.arizonahighways.com.*

Arizona Republic. *www.arizonarepublic.com.*

Navajo Times. Excellent Navajo Nation resource. *www.thenavajotimes.com.*

Phoenix New Times. *www.phoenixnewtimes.com.*

Tucson Citizen. *www.tucsoncitizen.com.*

Tucson Weekly. *www.tucsonweekly.com.*

Yuma Daily Sun. One newspaper that almost always lives up to its name—because the sun shines nearly every day here. *www.yumasun.com.*

■ OFFICIAL TOURIST INFORMATION

Arizona Office of Tourism. *602-364-3700 or 866-298-3795; www.arizonaguide.com.*

Bisbee. *520-432-5421; www.bisbeearizona.com.*

Flagstaff. *928-774-9541; www.flagstaffarizona.org.*

Holbrook. *928-524-6558; www.ci.holbrook.az.us.*

Jerome. *928-634-2900; www.jeromechamber.com.*

Lake Havasu. *928-855-4115; www.golakehavasu.com.*

Phoenix. *602-254-6500; www.visitphoenix.com.*

Prescott. *928-445-2000; www.prescott.org.*

Sedona–Oak Creek. *928-282-7722; www.visitsedona.com.*

Tombstone. *520-457-9317; www.tombstone.org.*

Tubac. *520-398-2704; www.tubacaz.com.*

Tucson Convention & Visitors Bureau. *520-624-1817; www.visittucson.org.*

Wickenburg. *928-684-5479 or 928-684-0977; www.outwickenburgway.com.*

Williams. *928-635-1418; www.williamschamber.com.*

Winslow. *928-289-2434; www.winslowarizona.org.*

Yuma. *928-783-0071; www.visityuma.com.*

■ USEFUL WEB SITES

Arizona Game & Fish Department. *www.gf.state.az.us.*

Arizona Golf Association. *www.azgolf.org.*

Arizona Historical Society. Links to the many affiliated museums, exhibits, and research facilities. *www.ahs.state.az.us.*

Arizona Humanities Council. Info about cultural and historical events, lectures, exhibits, and book festivals. *www.azhumanities.org.*

Arizona Trail Association. Reports about what will eventually be a 790-mile trail traversing the state from Mexico to Utah. *www.aztrail.org.*

Central Arizona Museum Association. A guide to more than 60 museums in Central Arizona, some of them fairly offbeat. *www.azcama.com.*

Mountain Bike Association of Arizona. Extensive information on trails and group rides, and links to other statewide sites for fat-tire enthusiasts. *www.mbaa.net.*

Nature Conservancy, Arizona. Information about the many Arizona preserves that fall under the aegis of the national conservation organization. *www.nature.org/arizona.*

Sierra Club. The Web site of the national environmental organization's Grand Canyon Chapter focuses on statewide political issues and lists local outings and hikes. *arizona.sierraclub.org.*

Southeastern Arizona Bird Observatory. Includes birding activities, organized trips, hot spots, and calendar of events. *www.sabo.org.*

Tasting Arizona. Arizona's food network, with links to the state's wineries and a calendar of food-related events. *www.tastingarizona.com.*

Welcome to Hopi/Kuwawata. Hopi tribe's site has tourist information, explanations of customs and ceremonies, and history. *www.hopi.nsn.us.*

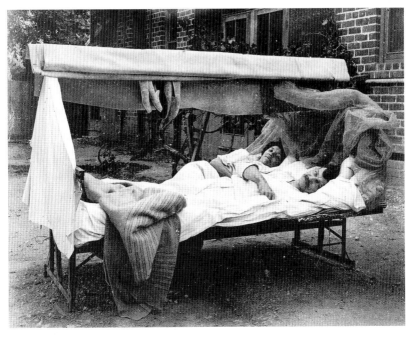

Summer sleeping in central Arizona before air-conditioning.

Cactus League baseball.

■ FESTIVALS AND EVENTS

■ JANUARY
Fiesta Bowl, Tempe. Nationally televised New Year's Day college football game. *480-350-0900.*

Phoenix Open. The PGA's best golfers tee off at the Tournament Players Club. *602-870-4431.*

■ FEBRUARY
Festival of the Arts, Tubac. Oldest arts and crafts fair in Arizona, focusing mostly on the visual arts. *520-398-2704.*

Jaycees' Parada del Sol Rodeo, Scottsdale. Rodeo, parade, and daredevil ride by the Hashknife Pony Express. *480-990-3179.*

Jaycees' Silver Spur, Yuma. Rodeo and parade. *928-344-5451.*

La Fiesta de los Vaqueros, Tucson. Rodeo and parade. *520-741-2233.*

■ **MARCH**

Heard Museum Indian Fair & Market, Phoenix. More than 300 of the nation's top Native American artists perform and sell artwork. *602-252-8840.*

Spring Festival of the Arts, Tempe. More than 600 artists, crafters, and food vendors. *480-967-4877.*

■ **APRIL**

Culinary Festival, Scottsdale. One of the nation's best food events. *480-945-7193.*

International Mariachi Conference, Tucson. North America's largest festival of mariachi performances and workshops. Always a sellout; obtain tickets in advance. *520-884-9920.*

■ **MAY**

Northern Arizona Heritage Program, Flagstaff. The Museum of Northern Arizona celebrates the Zuni, Hopi, Pai, and Navajo cultures with dancing, artwork, and exhibits one weekend each month from May to July. *928-774-5211.*

Paseo de Casas, Jerome. Tour of homes ranging from Victorians on Company Hill to renovated miners' shacks. *928-634-2900 or 928-634-5477.*

Route 66 Fun Run, Seligman/Topock. Road rally on the longest remaining stretch of historic Route 66. *928-753-5001.*

■ **JUNE**

Bluegrass Festival, Prescott. Big crowds turn out for this frolicking music festival, held annually at Courthouse Square. *928-445-2000.*

Old West Days & Bucket of Blood Races, Holbrook. Arts and crafts, car show, foot and bike races, Native American song and dance. *928-524-6558.*

Territorial Days, Prescott. Rodeo, golf tournament, 10k run, dancing, carnival. *928-445-2000.*

■ July

Frontier Days, Prescott. One of the oldest professional rodeos. *928-445-3103.*

White Mountain Native American Art Festival, Pinetop/Lakeside. Performances by many of the Southwest's finest Native American artists, demonstrations, children's activities. *928-367-4290.*

■ August

Arizona Cowboy Poets Gathering, Prescott. Singing, songwriting, and cowboy yodeling, as well as traditional and contemporary cowboy poetry. *928-445-3122 or 877-928-4253.*

Payson Annual Rodeo. Many of the country's top cowboys compete in calf- and steer-roping contests. *928-474-4515 or 800-672-9766.*

Southwest Wings Birding Festival, Bisbee. Field trips, displays, lectures, bat stalks, owl prowls. *520-378-0233 or 800-946-4777.*

■ September

Brewery Gulch Days, Bisbee. Mining contests, dancing, parade. *520-432-5578 or 520-432-5421.*

Chamber Music Festival, Grand Canyon. Evening concert series feature classical and jazz. *928-638-9215 or 800-997-8285.*

Coconino County Fair, Flagstaff. Pig races, lumberjack show, magicians, carnival, horse show tournament. Labor Day Weekend. *928-774-5130.*

Fiesta Del Tlaquepaque, Sedona. Includes mariachi bands, piñatas, folklorico dance performances, and flamenco guitarists. *928-282-4838.*

Jazz on the Rocks, Sedona. The state's top jazz festival, with a full day of outdoor performances. Sells out fast; request tickets months in advance. *928-282-1985.*

Music in the Garden, Phoenix. Concert series held at the Desert Botanical Garden. *480-941-1225.*

Navajo Nation Celebration and Rodeo, Window Rock. One of the largest American Indian fairs and rodeos in the country. Intertribal powwow, concerts, parade, traditional singing, arts and crafts. *928-871-6703 or 928-871-6478.*

Old-Time Fiddlers' Contest, Payson. Storytellers, food, crafts, fiddle-makers. *928-474-4515 or 928-474-3398.*

Verde River Days, Cottonwood. Sand-castle building, rubber duck race, live music, canoe rides, nature walks, geological and archaeological tours. *928-634-7593.*

■ OCTOBER

Andy Devine Days, Kingman. Rodeo and parade. *928-753-6106.*

Arizona State Fair, Phoenix. Rides, concerts, Native American and cowboy dancing, 4-H Club events, cotton candy and carnival atmosphere—a classic American state fair. *602-268-3247 or 800-343-3247.*

Helldorado Days, Tombstone. Shootouts, 1880s fashion show, rodeo, parade, and other entertainment. *520-457-9137.*

London Bridge Days, Lake Havasu. Boat regattas, a parade, and other good old-fashioned fun in the shadow of the original London Bridge. *928-855-5655 or 800-242-8278.*

Rex Allen Days, Willcox. Rodeo, fair, and music concert. *520-384-2272 or 800-200-2272.*

■ DECEMBER

Cowboy Christmas, Wickenburg. Cowboy poetry, live music, crafts, and breakfast. *928-684-5479.*

Fall Festival of the Arts, Tempe. Downtown streets shut down for a three-day fair of music, food, and local arts. *480-967-4877.*

RECOMMENDED READING

■ MODERN DESCRIPTION AND TRAVEL

Cook, James, Sam Negri, and Marshall Trimble. *Travel Arizona: The Back Roads.* Phoenix: Arizona Highways, 1999. One of the best of the lavishly illustrated *Arizona Highways* books, which cover the state. Others include *Tucson to Tombstone: A Guide to Southeastern Arizona; Arizona Hiking: Urban Trails, Easy Paths and Overnight Treks;* and *Arizona's 144 Best Campgrounds.*

Kosik, Fran. *Native Roads: The Complete Motoring Guide to the Navajo and Hopi Nations.* Tucson: Treasure Chest, 1999. A useful guide that goes road marker by road marker, combining history with practical advice about visiting reservations.

■ ESSAY COLLECTIONS

Abbey, Edward. *Desert Solitaire: A Season in Wilderness.* New York: Ballantine Books, 1991. Originally published in 1971, this is the earliest and most treasured of Abbey's collections: passionate, combative, keenly focused, and achingly beautiful in its use of the English language. Much of the book describes Arches National Monument in Utah.

Banham, Reyner. *Scenes in America Deserta.* Cambridge, Massachusetts: MIT Press, 1989. The late Banham, an architectural historian, shaped these 1982 essays around human beings' impact on the Mojave and Sonoran Deserts. They are not academic, but sharp-eyed, passionate, and occasionally eccentric.

Bowden, Charles. *Blue Desert.* Tucson: University of Arizona Press, 1992. As is true of his friend Abbey, the earliest of Bowden's collections is also the best. These prickly essays cover an astonishing range, but the constant thread is decline and death—of animals, humans, and ways of life.

Kingsolver, Barbara. *High Tide in Tucson: Essays from Now and Never.* New York: HarperPerennial, 1996. Better known for her sometimes glib fiction, Kingsolver is thoughtful and meditative in this format.

Shelton, Richard. *Going Back to Bisbee.* Tucson: University of Arizona Press, 1992. Shelton has lived in southern Arizona since 1958, and this gracefully written and entertaining book is a memoir of his encounters with the region's natural history, critters, and people.

Shoumatoff, Alex. *Legends of the American Desert: Sojourns in the Greater Southwest.* New York: HarperPerennial, 1997. These essays, derived from Shoumatoff's frequent visits to the Southwest in search of the exotic, are always acutely observed and fresh.

Wilbur-Cruce, Eva Antonia. *A Beautiful, Cruel Country.* Tucson: University of Arizona Press, 1987. A woman who grew up on a ranch near the Mexican border in the first two decades of this century has transformed that experience into a personal history graced with lovely and softly lyrical prose.

■ NATURAL HISTORY

Alcock, John. *Sonoran Desert Spring.* Tucson: University of Arizona Press, 1994. A biologist writes both authoritatively and lyrically about the life of the Sonoran Desert. A highly readable and informative personal journal. His later book, *Sonoran Desert Summer,* is a wonderful follow-up to the earlier volume.

Hartmann, William K. *Desert Heart: Chronicles of the Sonoran Desert.* St. Paul, Minnesota: Motorbooks International, 1991. This superb book centers on the volcanic Sierra Pinacate, which sprawls, black and malevolent, across the Arizona-Sonora border. But it manages to elucidate much of the natural and cultural history of the entire Sonoran Desert—from Hohokam to modern *narcotraficantes.*

Pyne, Stephen J. *How the Canyon Became Grand: A Short History.* New York: Viking Press, 1998. An intelligent foray into exploring the forces that have made the canyon into a celebrated showpiece of America's wild places; a well-crafted read by the Arizona-based environmental historian.

Van Dyke, John C. *The Desert.* Salt Lake City: Peregrine Smith Books, 1987. The classic 1901 work on the Southwest deserts, written by a New Jersey art historian and librarian who for three years explored this land, in his words, "as a lover."

Whitney, Stephen. *A Field Guide to the Grand Canyon.* New York: Quill, 1982. The perfect companion for the amateur canyon naturalist, with exhaustive information and illustrations covering its geology and biology.

■ DETECTIVE FICTION

Hillerman, Tony. *The Blessing Way.* New York: HarperCollins, 1990. Originally published in 1970, this is first in a hugely popular series of mysteries set on the Navajo reservation. Navajo detectives Joe Leaphorn and Jim Chee are engaging characters, the details of Navajo culture are assiduously researched, and these books provide a good introduction to the psychological and literal landscape of Arizona's Indian Country.

Jance, J. A. *Skeleton Canyon.* New York: HarperCollins, 1998. The fifth in the author's excellent Joanna Brady series, and one of the most interesting. Here the Bisbee-based sheriff has to confront Anglo-Hispanic relationships in Cochise County in the course of solving the obligatory murder.

■ HISTORY

Bourke, John G. *On the Border With Crook.* Lincoln: University of Nebraska Press, 1971. An indispensable account of 1870s Arizona, written by an aide to Gen. George Crook, most successful commander of the Apache campaigns. Bourke's high respect for the Apaches is revealing, and he insightfully observes that "The moment [the Indian] concludes to live at peace with the whites, that moment all his troubles begin." The most essential book on the Apache wars and life in Arizona Territory.

Byrkit, James. *Forging the Copper Collar: Arizona's Labor-Management War of 1901–1921.* Tucson: University of Arizona Press, 1982. Its title does this superb book no favor. It is no dry and arcane navigation of an obscure historical narrows, but a dramatic story of Arizona's painful political puberty. Byrkit is both a careful historian and a fine, bold writer.

Howard, Kathleen L. and Diana F. Pardue. *Inventing the Southwest: The Fred Harvey Company and Native American Art.* Flagstaff: Northland Publishing, 1996. Done in conjunction with the Heard Museum and based on an exhibition there, this lavishly illustrated book details the story of how the Fred Harvey Company not only directed tourism trends in the Southwest, but also dictated the focus of a great deal of the region's Native American art.

Wickenburg's Kay El Bar Ranch, started in 1909 and still in operation, is on the National Register of Historic Places.

Luckingham, Bradford. *Phoenix: The History of a Southwestern Metropolis.* Tucson: University of Arizona Press, 1989. A comprehensive history of the city.

Officer, James E. *Hispanic Arizona, 1536–1856.* Tucson: University of Arizona Press, 1987. Definitive and fascinating.

Pfefferkorn, Ignaz. *Sonora: A Description of the Province.* Tucson: University of Arizona Press, 1989. A book about Sonora, not Arizona, but the two were culturally and politically one during Padre Pfefferkorn's ramblings between 1756 and 1767. His curious and observant eye records details as fine as the Piman bowstrings: ". . . made by twisting the intestines of various animals, and about as thick as the quill of a raven's feather."

Poling-Kempes, Lesley. *The Harvey Girls: Women Who Opened the West.* New York: Marlowe & Company, 1991. Waitressing for the Fred Harvey Company took guts in late 19th and early 20th century, when the Santa Fe Railway line was just opening the West to tourism. The story of the women who stayed on and helped build the West makes fascinating reading.

Sonnichsen, Leland. *Tucson: The Life and Times of an American City.* Norman: University of Oklahoma Press, 1982. Informal, but the best among the several available Tucson histories.

Southwestern Mission Research Center. *Tucson: A Short History* (Anthology). Tucson: Southwestern Mission Research Center, 1986. Engaging writing by six experts; more depth than one would expect in 150 pages.

Summerhayes, Martha. *Vanished Arizona.* Lincoln: University of Nebraska Press, 1979. The fascinating memoir of a cultivated Massachusetts woman who came to Arizona as an Army bride in 1874.

Trumble, Marshall. *Arizona: A Cavalcade of History.* Tucson: Treasure Chest Publications, 1989. Bursting with anecdotes, this history is written in a tone that occasionally crosses the line from informal to cloyingly folksy.

Watkin, Ronald J. *High Crimes and Misdemeanors.* New York: William Morrow & Co., 1990 (out of print). For political junkies, this is the only thorough and relatively objective chronicle of Gov. Evan Mecham's chaotic 1987–88 administration and impeachment—a story with more drama and strange characters than most works of fiction.

■ NATIVE AMERICANS

Fontana, Bernard. *Of Earth and Little Rain.* Tucson: University of Arizona Press, 1989. An intimate and affectionate portrait of the Tohono O'odham people of southern Arizona, written by a field historian who has lived at the reservation's edge for 25 years.

Iverson, Peter. *The Navajo Nation.* Albuquerque: University of New Mexico Press, 1983. A history of the Navajo people, with emphasis on the last 50 years.

Waters, Frank. *Book of the Hopi.* New York: Penguin Books, 1977. Waters lived among the Hopis people, and he writes about their religion and ceremonies with insight.

Yetman, David. *Where the Desert Meets the Sea.* Tucson: Pepper Publishing, 1987. A jewel-like book, sparkling with warmth, insight, and gentle humor, about the scarcely known Seri Indians of the Sonoran coast.

■ Arts and Architecture

Berke, Arnold. *Mary Colter: Architect of the Southwest.* New York: Princeton Architectural Press, 2002. Still not the definitive Colter biography, but an excellent illustrated survey of the work of the woman who helped redesign the look of the nation's national parks with her ground-breaking Grand Canyon buildings.

Griffith, James S. *Southern Arizona Folk Arts.* Tucson: University of Arizona Press, 1988. Griffith is the walking encyclopedia on the folk arts of Native American, Hispanic, and Anglo Arizonans; this book offers a well-researched introduction to many different traditions.

Murray, John A. *Cinema Southwest: An Illustrated Guide to the Movies and Their Locations.* Flagstaff: Northland Publishing, 2000. Did you know that much of *Oklahoma!* was shot in Arizona? If you've ever wanted to know where classic Westerns from *The Searchers* to *Thelma and Louise* were filmed, this is your book.

Page, Susanne and Jake Page. *Field Guide to Southwest Indian Arts and Crafts.* New York: Random House, 1998. Essential for even casual buyers of Native American wares, offering both historical context and practical information, such as how to spot fakes.

INDEX

COMPASS AMERICAN GUIDES

Alaska	Las Vegas	Pennsylvania
American Southwest	Maine	San Francisco
Arizona	Manhattan	Santa Fe
Boston	Massachusetts	South Carolina
Chicago	Michigan	South Dakota
Coastal California	Minnesota	Tennessee
Colorado	Montana	Texas
Connecticut & Rhode Island	Nevada	Utah
Florida	New Hampshire	Vermont
Georgia	New Mexico	Virginia
Gulf South	New Orleans	Wine Country
Hawaii	North Carolina	Wisconsin
Idaho	Oregon	Wyoming
Kentucky	Pacific Northwest	

Compass American Guides are available at special discounts for bulk purchases for sales promotions or premiums. Special editions, including personalized covers, excerpts of existing guides, and corporate imprints, can be created in large quantities for special needs. For more information, contact your local bookseller or write to Special Markets, Fodor's Travel Publications, 1745 Broadway, New York, NY 10019. Inquiries from Canada should be directed to your local Canadian bookseller or sent to Random House of Canada, Ltd., Marketing Department, 2775 Matheson Boulevard East, Mississauga, Ontario L4W 4P7. Inquiries from the United Kingdom should be sent to Fodor's Travel Publications, 20 Vauxhall Bridge Road, London, England SW1V 2SA.

COMPASS AMERICAN GUIDES

Critics, booksellers, and travelers all agree: you're lost without a Compass.

"This splendid series provides exactly the sort of historical and cultural detail about North American destinations that curious-minded travelers need." —*Washington Post*

"This is a series that constantly stuns us...no guide with photos this good should have writing this good. But it does." —*New York Daily News*

"Of the many guidebooks on the market, few are as visually stimulating, as thoroughly researched, or as lively written as the Compass American Guide series." —*Chicago Tribune*

"Good to read ahead of time, then take along so you don't miss anything." —*San Diego Magazine*

"Magnificent photography. First rate."—*Money*

"Written by longtime residents of each destination...these handsome and literate guides are strong on history and culture, and illustrated with gorgeous photos." —*San Francisco Chronicle*

"The color photographs sparkle, the archival illustrations illuminate windows to the past, and the writing is usually of the utmost caliber." —*Michigan Tribune*

"Class acts, worth reading and shelving for keeps even if you're not a traveler. " —*New Orleans Times-Picayune*

Beautiful photographs and literate writing are the hallmarks of the Compass guides." —*Nashville Tennessean*

"History, geography, and wanderlust converge in these well-conceived books." —*Raleigh News & Observer*

"Oh, my goodness! What a gorgeous series this is."—*Booklist*

ACKNOWLEDGMENTS

Compass American Guides would like to thank Rachel Elson for copyediting the manuscript, Ellen Klages for proofreading it, Joan Stout for indexing it, and Kristin Moehlmann and Chris Culwell for their editorial contributions.

All photographs in this book are by Kerrick James unless otherwise noted below. Compass American Guides would like to thank the following individuals and institutions for the use of their photographs or illustrations:

DESERTS
Page 25, Desert Botanical Garden

MOUNTAINS
Page 48, Southeastern Arizona Bird Observatory (Sheri Williamson)
Page 56, Kitt Peak National Observatory

CANYONS
Page 84, Grand Canyon National Park

THE FIRST ARIZONANS
Page 96, George H.H. Huey

MODERN INDIANS
Page 110–111, George H.H. Huey
Page 114, Arizona Historical Society
Page 124, Eduardo Fuss

HISPANIC ARIZONA
Page 127, Arizona Historical Society
Page 132, Arizona Historical Society
Page 134, Arizona Historical Society

MAKING ARIZONA
Page 141, Arizona Historical Society
Page 144, Arizona Historical Society

■ ABOUT THE AUTHORS

Lawrence W. Cheek

Lawrence W. Cheek worked for the *Tucson Citizen* for 14 years as a reporter, music and architecture critic, essayist, and Saturday editor. He then edited Tucson's *City Magazine,* a free-ranging monthly that comprised investigative reporting, politics, popular culture, and the arts. His work frequently appears in *Arizona Highways* magazine, which also has published three of his books: *Scenic Sedona, Photographing Arizona* and *A.D. 1250: Ancient People of the Southwest.* In addition, Mr. Cheek is the author of Compass American Guides' *Santa Fe.*

Edie Jarolim, the revisor of this edition of *Compass Arizona,* was a senior editor at Fodor's in New York before moving to Tucson in 1992. She was the restaurant critic for *Tucson Monthly* magazine during its short but interesting life, and is a regular contributor to *Tucson Guide Quarterly, Tucson Home,* and *Arizona Living* magazines. Her articles about the Southwest and Mexico have appeared in numerous national publications, including *Art & Antiques, America West Airlines Magazine, National Geographic Traveler,* the *New York Times Book Review,* and the *Wall Street Journal,* and she is the author of three guidebooks.

■ ABOUT THE PHOTOGRAPHER

Kerrick James and sons

Kerrick James claims his photography is enriched both by his lifelong love of geology and mineralogy and by his admiration for American writers such as Edward Abbey and Mark Twain. A scholarship to study mining engineering in New Mexico introduced him to the Southwest, and today his territory is the American West, northern Mexico, and Hawaii. His work appears in travel magazines, school texts, and guidebooks. He lives in Arizona with his wife, Theresa, and their two sons, Shane and Royce.